THE
HOT SWAMP

R. M. BALLANTYNE

1st WORLD
LIBRARY
Literary Society

The Hot Swamp

R. M. Ballantyne

© 1st World Library, 2007
PO Box 2211
Fairfield, IA 52556
www.1stworldlibrary.com
First Edition

LCCN: 2007934203

Softcover ISBN: 978-1-4218-9675-5
Hardcover ISBN: 978-1-4218-9775-2
eBook ISBN: 978-1-4218-9575-8

Purchase *"The Hot Swamp"*
as a traditional bound book at:
www.1stWorldLibrary.com/purchase.asp?ISBN=978-1-4218-9675-5

1st World Library is a literary, educational organization
dedicated to:

- Creating a free internet library of downloadable ebooks

- Hosting writing competitions and offering book publishing
scholarships.

Interested in more 1st World Library books? contact:
literacy@1stworldlibrary.com
Check us out at: www.1stworldlibrary.com

1st World Library Literary Society

Giving Back to the World

"If you want to work on the core problem, it's early school literacy."

- James Barksdale, former CEO of Netscape

"No skill is more crucial to the future of a child, or to a democratic and prosperous society, than literacy."

- Los Angeles Times

"Literacy... means far more than learning how to read and write... The aim is to transmit... knowledge and promote social participation."

- UNESCO

"Literacy is not a luxury, it is a right and a responsibility. If our world is to meet the challenges of the twenty-first century we must harness the energy and creativity of all our citizens."

- President Bill Clinton

"Parents should be encouraged to read to their children, and teachers should be equipped with all available techniques for teaching literacy, so the varying needs and capacities of individual kids can be taken into account."

- Hugh Mackay

CHAPTER ONE

A ROMANCE OF OLD ALBION

OPENS WITH LEAVE-TAKING

Nearly two thousand seven hundred years ago—or some-where about eight hundred years BuCu—there dwelt a Phoenician sea-captain in one of the eastern sea-ports of Greece—known at that period, or soon after, as Hellas.

This captain was solid, square, bronzed, bluff, and resolute, as all sea-captains are—or ought to be—whether ancient or modern. He owned, as well as commanded, one of those curious vessels with one mast and a mighty square-sail, fifty oars or so, double-banked, a dragon's tail in the stern and a horse's head at the prow, in which the Phoenicians of old and other mariners were wont to drive an extensive and lucrative trade in the Mediterranean; sometimes pushing their adventurous keels beyond the Pillars of Hercules, visiting the distant Cassiterides or Tin Isles, and Albion, and even penetrating northward into the Baltic, in search of tin, amber, gold, and what not.

One morning this captain, whose name was Arkal, sauntered up from the harbour to his hut, which stood on a conspicuous eminence overlooking the bay. His hands were not thrust into his pockets, because he had no pockets to put them into—the simple tunic of the period being destitute of such appendages. Indeed, the coarse linen tunic referred to constituted the chief part of his costume, the only other portions being a pair of rude shoes on his feet, a red fez or tarbouche on his bushy brown locks, and yards of something wound round his lower limbs to protect them from thorns on shore, as well as from the rasping of cordage and cargo at sea.

At the door of his hut stood his pretty little Greek wife, with a solid, square, bluff, and resolute, but not yet bronzed, baby in her arms.

"Well, Penelope, I'm off," said the captain. At least he used words to that effect, as he enveloped wife and baby in a huge embrace.

Of course he spoke in a dialect of ancient Greek, of which we render a free translation.

The leave-taking was of the briefest, for just then a loud halloo from his mate, or second in command, apprised the captain that all was ready to set sail. But neither Penelope nor her husband were anxious souls or addicted to the melting mood. The square baby was rather more given to such conditions. In emulation of the mate it set up a sudden howl which sent its father away laughing to the harbour.

"No sign of the young men," remarked the mate, as his superior came within hail.

"It is ever the way with these half-fledged boys who think themselves men while their faces are yet hairless," growled the captain, casting a glance at his unfailing chronometer, the rising sun. "They have no more regard for the movements of that ball of fire than if it was set in the sky merely to shine

R. M. Ballantyne

and keep them warm, and had no reference whatever to time. If this youth from Albion does not appear soon, I shall set sail without him, prince though he be, and leave him to try his hand at swimming to the Cassiterides. His comrade and friend, Dromas, assured me they would not keep us waiting; but he is no better than the rest of them—a shouting, singing, smooth-faced, six-foot set they are, who think they inherit the combined wisdom of all their grandfathers but none of their weaknesses; reckless fear-nothings, fit only for war and the Olympic games!"

"Nevertheless, we could not do well without them," returned the mate, glancing significantly at the ship's crew, a large proportion of which was composed of these same stalwart fear-nothings of whom his leader spoke so contemptuously; "at least they would make a fine show at these games, and our ventures at sea would not prosper so well if we had not such to help us."

"True, true, and I would not speak slightingly of them, but they do try one's patience; here is the wind failing, and we all ready to hoist sail," returned the captain with another growl, a glance at the sky, and a frown at his vessel, everything about which betokened readiness for instant departure. The crew—partly composed of slaves—were seated at the oars; the fighting men and seamen were all on board arranging their shields round the vessel's sides, and the great sail was cast loose ready to hoist as soon as the mouth of the harbour should be cleared.

Just then a band of young men issued from the town, and the captain's good humour was restored as they hurried towards him. They seemed to be much excited, and talked in loud tones as they advanced, their manners and costumes indicating that they belonged to the upper ranks of society.

One of the band, a fair youth, towered, like Saul, head and shoulders above his fellows. Another, of dark complexion, handsome features, and elegant, active frame, hurried forward to salute the captain.

"I fear we have kept you waiting," he said with a pleasant expression that disarmed reproof.

"I will not deny that, Dromas," answered the captain, "but you have not detained me long. Nevertheless, I was on the point of sailing without your friend, for the winds and waves respect no one."

"But you are neither a wind nor a wave," remarked the youth.

"True, but I am the humble friend of both," retorted the captain, "and am bound to accommodate myself to them. I suppose this is the prince you spoke of," he added, turning to the towering youth already referred to, with the air of a man who had as little—or as much—regard for a prince as a peasant.

"Yes, Captain Arkal, this is Prince Bladud. Let me present him to you."

As the prince and the seaman joined hands the latter looked up from an altitude of five feet six and squared his broad shoulders with the air of a man ready to defy all creation, and anxious rather than otherwise to do so. The prince, on the other hand, looked down from an eminence of six feet seven, and bent his head with a modest grace and a genial smile that indicated a desire to be on good terms, if possible, with the world at large.

Although almost equal as to physical strength, the inequality of the two men in height rendered their experience in those rude warlike times very dissimilar, for, whereas the sailor was often compelled to give proof of his strength to tall unbelievers, the prince very seldom had occasion to do so. Hence, partly, their difference in manner, the one being somewhat pugnacious and the other conciliatory, while both were in reality good-natured, peace-loving men.

No two men, however, could have been more unlike in outward aspect. The prince was, if we may say so, built on the Gothic model—fair, blue-eyed, bulky of limb, huge, muscular, massive, with a soft beard and moustache—for he had not yet seen twenty-four summers—and hair that fell like rippling gold on his shoulders. Captain Arkal, on the contrary, was dark, with a thick reddish beard, luxuriant brown hair, piercing black eyes, and limbs that were hardened as well as darkened by thirty years of constant exposure to elemental and other warfare.

"I hope that I may be of some use to you," said the prince, "though I profess not to know more of seamanship than I acquired during my voyage hither, and as that voyage occurred six years ago, it may be that I have lost the little I had learned. But if pirates should assail us, perhaps I may do you some service."

"Little fear I have of that," returned the captain with an approving nod. "Now, bid your comrades farewell and get on board, for the wind is failing fast, and it behoves us to get well forward on our voyage before night."

It was evident that the leave-taking which ensued was not merely formal, for the youths from whom Bladud was parting had been his companions in study for six years, as well as his competitors in all the manly games of the period, and as he excelled them all in most things—especially in athletics—some looked up to the young prince from Albion as a sort of demi-god, while others to whom he had been helpful in many ways regarded him with the warmest affection.

"Come here aside with me; I must have a few last words with you alone," said Bladud, taking young Dromas by the arm and leading him aside.

The prince's other friends made no objection to this evidence of preference, for Dromas had shared the same apartment with him while in Athens, and engaged in similar studies with Bladud for several years; had travelled with him in the East, and sailed over the sea in his company, even as far as Egypt, besides having been second to him in most of the games practised by the young men. Indeed, at the high jump he equalled, and at the short race had even excelled him.

"Dromas," said the prince impressively—"Come, now, my old friend and comrade," interrupted the Greek youth lightly, "don't put on such a long face. I foresee that you are about to give me a lecture, and I don't want the tone of remonstrance to be the last that I shall hear. I know that I'm a wild, good-for-nothing fellow, and can guess all you would say to me. Let us rather talk of your speedy return to Hellas, for, to tell you the truth, I feel as if the loss of you would leave me like a poor man who has been crippled in the wars. I shall be a mere shadow till you return."

There was a slight tremor in the voice, which showed that much of the gaiety of the young man was forced.

"Nay, I have no mind to give you a lecture," returned Bladud, "I only ask you to grant me two requests."

"Granted, before mentioned, for you have ever been a

reasonable creature, Bladud, and I trust you to retain your character on the present occasion."

"Well, then, my first request is that you will often remember the many talks that you and I have had about the gods, and the future life, and the perplexing conditions in which we now live."

"Remember them," exclaimed Dromas with animation, "my difficulty would be to forget them! The questions which you have propounded and attempted to answer—for I do not admit that you have been quite successful in the attempt—have started up and rung in my ears at all kinds of unseasonable times. They haunt me often in my dreams—though, to say truth, I dream but little, save when good fellowship has led me to run supper into breakfast—they worry me during my studies, which, you know, are frequent though not prolonged; they come between me and the worthy rhapsodist when he is in the middle of the most interesting—or least wearisome—passage of the poem, and they even intrude on me at the games. The very last race I ran was lost, only by a few inches, because our recent talk on the future of cats caused a touch of internal laughter which checked my pace at the most critical moment. You may rest assured that I cannot avoid granting your first request. What is your second?"

"That you promise to visit me in my home in Albion. You know that it will be impossible for me ever again to re-visit these shores, where I have been so happy. My father, if he forgives my running away from him, will expect me to help him in the management of his affairs. But you have nothing particular to detain you here—"

"You forget—the old woman," interrupted Dromas gravely.

"What old woman?" asked Bladud in surprise.

"My mother!" returned his friend.

The prince looked a little confused and hastened to apologise. Dromas' mother was one of those unfortunate people who existed in the olden time as well as in modern days, though perhaps not so numerously. She was a confirmed invalid, who rarely quitted her house, and was seldom seen by any one save her most intimate friends, so that she was apt to be forgotten—out of sight out of mind, then as now.

"Forgive me, Dromas—," began Bladud, but his friend interrupted him.

"I cannot forgive when I have nothing to forgive! Say no more about that. But, now I come to consider of it, I grant your second request conditionally. If my mother agrees to accompany me to Albion, you may expect to see me some day or other—perhaps a year or two hence. You see, since my father and brother were slain in the last fight with our neighbours, I am the only one left to comfort her, so I cannot forsake her."

"Then this will be our final parting," returned Bladud, sadly, "for your mother will never consent to leave home."

"I don't know that," returned Dromas with a laugh. "The dear old soul is intensely adventurous, like myself, and I do believe would venture on a voyage to the Cassiterides, if the fancy were strong upon her. You have no idea how powerfully I can work upon her feelings. I won't say that I can make much impression on her intellect. Indeed, I have reason to know that she does not believe in intellect except as an unavoidable doorway leading into the feelings. The fact is, I tried her the other day with the future of cats, and do you know, instead of treating that subject with the gravity it merits, she laughed in my face and called me names—not exactly bad names, such as the gods might object to—but names that were not creditable to the intelligence of her first-born. Now," continued Dromas with increasing gravity, "when I paint to her the beauty of your native land; the splendour of your father's court; the kindliness of your mother, and the exceeding beauty of your sister—fair like yourself, blue-eyed, tall—you said she was tall, I think?"

"Yes—rather tall."

"Of course not *quite* so tall as yourself, say six feet or so, with a slight, feminine beard—no? you shake your head; well, smooth-faced and rosy, immense breadth of shoulders—ah! I have often pictured to myself that sister of yours—"

"Hilloa!" shouted Captain Arkal in a nautical tone that might almost have been styled modern British in its character.

It was an opportune interruption, for Dromas had been running on with his jesting remarks for the sole purpose of crushing down the feelings that almost unmanned him.

With few but fervently uttered words the final farewells were at last spoken. The oars were dipped; the vessel shot from the land, swept out upon the blue waves of the Aegean, the sail was hoisted, and thus began the long voyage to the almost unknown islands of the far North-West.

CHAPTER TWO

TEMPORARY DELAY THROUGH ELEMENTS AND PIRATES

But it is not our purpose to inflict the entire log of that voyage on our reader, adventurous though the voyage was. Matter of much greater importance claims our regard. Still it would be unjust to our voyagers to pass it over in absolute silence.

At the very commencement of it, there occurred one of those incidents to which all voyagers are more or less subject. A gale arose the very evening of the day on which they left port, which all but swamped the little vessel, and the violence of the wind was so great that their huge sail was split from top to bottom. In spite of the darkness and the confusion that ensued, Captain Arkal, by his prompt action and skilful management, saved the vessel from immediate destruction. Fortunately the gale did not last long, and, during the calm that followed, the rent was repaired and the sail re-set.

Then occurred another incident that threatened to cut short the voyage even more disastrously than by swamping.

The sea over which they steered swarmed with pirates at the

R. M. Ballantyne

time we write of, as it continued to swarm during many centuries after. Merchantmen, fully aware of the fact, were in those days also men of war. They went forth on their voyages fully armed with sword, javelin, and shield, as well as with the simple artillery of the period—bows and arrows, slings and stones.

On the afternoon of the day that followed the gale, the vessel—which her captain and owner had named the *Penelope* in honour of his wife—was running before a light breeze, along the coast of one of the islands with which that sea is studded.

Bladud and some of the crew were listening at the time to an account given by a small seaman named Maikar, of a recent adventure on the sea, when a galley about as large as their own was seen to shoot suddenly from the mouth of a cavern in the cliffs in which it had lain concealed. It was double-banked and full of armed men, and was rowed in such a way as to cut in advance of the *Penelope*. The vigour with which the oars were plied, and the rapidity with which the sail was run up, left no doubt as to the nature of the craft or the intentions of those who manned it.

"The rascals!" growled Arkal with a dark frown, "I more than half expected to find them here."

"Pirates, I suppose?" said Bladud.

"Ay—and not much chance of escaping them. Give another haul on the sail-rope, mate, and pull, men, pull, if you would save your liberty—for these brutes have no mercy."

The sail was tightened up a few inches, and the vessel was put more directly before the wind. The way in which the slaves bent to the oars showed that the poor fellows fully understood the situation.

For a few minutes Captain Arkal watched the result in stern silence. Then, with an unwonted look and tone of bitterness, he said in a low voice—

"No—I thought as much. She sails faster than we do. Now, friend Bladud, you shall presently have a chance of proving whether your royal blood is better than that of other men."

To this remark the prince made no other reply than by a good-natured smile as he took up the bronze helmet which lay beside his sword on the thwart and placed it on his head.

Captain Arkal regarded him with a sort of grim satisfaction as he followed up the action by buckling on his sword.

The sword in question was noteworthy. It was a single-handed weapon of iron, made in Egypt, to suit the size and strength of its owner, and was large enough to have served as a two-handed sword for most men.

"You can throw a javelin, no doubt?" asked the captain, as he watched the young man's leisurely preparations for the expected combat.

"Yes, I have practised throwing the spear a good deal—both in peace and war."

"Good. I have got one here that will suit you. It belonged to my grandfather, who was a stout man, and made powerful play with it during a neighbouring tribe's raid—when I was a baby—to the discomfort, I have been told, and surprise of his foes. I always keep it by me for luck, and have myself used it on occasion, though I prefer a lighter one for ordinary use. Here it is—a pretty weapon," he continued, drawing a javelin

R. M. Ballantyne

of gigantic proportions from under the gunwale and handing it to Bladud. "But we must proceed with caution in this matter. Take off your helmet at present, and try to look frightened if you can."

"I fear me that will be difficult, captain."

"Not in the least. Look here, nothing is easier when you get used to it."

As he spoke Arkal caused his stern visage to relax into a look of such amiable sheepishness that Bladud could not repress a sudden laugh which recalled and intensified the captain's fierce expression instantly.

"Learn to subdue yourself, young man," he muttered sternly. "If these pirates hear laughter, do you think they can be made to believe we are afraid of them?"

"Forgive me, captain; if you had seen your own face, you would have joined in the laugh. I will be more careful. But how do you mean to proceed, and what do you wish me to do?"

Captain Arkal, who was restored to good-humour by this compliment to his power of expression, as well as by the modesty with which the prince received his rebuke, explained his intentions—in low, earnest tones, however, for they were by that time drawing near to the piratical craft.

Having got well ahead of the *Penelope*, it had backed its sail and lay still, awaiting her coming up.

"Creep to the bow, Bladud, with your helmet off, and show as little of your bulk as may be. Show only your head above the bulwarks, and look as miserable as I did just now—more so if you can. Take your sword, javelin, and shield with you. I need say no more to a man of war. Use them when you see your opportunity."

Bladud received his orders in silence, and obeyed them with that unquestioning and unhesitating promptitude which is one of the surest evidences of fitness to command. Meanwhile the mate, who was accustomed to his captain's habits, and needed no instructions, had caused the sailors to lay their shields and swords out of sight at their feet, so that they might approach the pirates in the character of simple traders who were completely cowed by the appearance of the foe. To increase this aspect of fear, the sail was lowered as they drew near, and the oars were used to complete the distance that yet intervened between the two vessels.

This humble and submissive approach did not, however, throw the pirates quite off their guard. They stood to their arms and prepared to spring on board their victim when close enough. As the pirate vessel lay motionless on the water she presented her broadside to the trader. The captain took care to steer so that this relative position should be maintained. The pirate chief, a huge man in rude armour, with a breast-plate of thick bull-hide and a shield of the same on his left arm, gave orders to pull the oars on one side of his vessel so that the two might be brought alongside.

They were about fifty yards apart at the moment. Before the order could be carried into effect, however, Arkal uttered a low hiss. Instantly the double banks of oars bent almost to the breaking point, and the *Penelope* leaped forward like a sentient creature. Each man seized sword and shield and sprang up, and Bladud, forgetting both helmet and shield in the hurry of the moment, poised the mighty javelin which had so astonished its owner's enemies in days gone by, and in another moment hurled it shrieking through the air. It flew

R. M. Ballantyne

straight as a thunderbolt at the pirate chief; pierced through shield and breastplate, and came out at his back, sending him headlong into the arms of his horrified crew.

The whole incident was so sudden that the pirates had scarcely time to recover from their surprise when the bow of the *Penelope* crashed into the side of their vessel and stove it in, for the trader, like some of the war-vessels of the period, was provided with a ram for this very purpose.

As the *Penelope* recoiled from the shock, a yell of rage burst from the pirates, and a volley of javelins and stones followed, but, owing to the confusion resulting from the shock, these were ill-directed, and such of them as found their mark were caught on the shields. Before another discharge could be made, the pirate vessel heeled over and sank, leaving her crew of miscreants struggling in the sea. Some of them—being, strange to say, unable to swim—were drowned. Others were killed in the water, while a few, taking their swords in their teeth, swam to the trader and made desperate attempts to climb on board. Of course they failed, and in a few minutes nothing remained of the pirate vessel to tell of the tragedy that had been enacted, except an oar or two and a few spars left floating on the sea.

"Would that all the sea-robbers in these parts could be as easily and thoroughly disposed of," remarked the captain, as he gave orders to re-hoist the sail. "Ho! Bladud, my worthy prince, come aft here. What detains you?"

But Bladud did not answer to the call. A stone from the enemy had fallen on his defenceless head and knocked him down insensible.

Four of the men now raised him up. As they did so, one of the men—the small seaman, Maikar—was found underneath him in a state of semi-consciousness. While they carried Bladud aft, the little sailor began to gasp and sneeze.

"Not killed, I see," remarked the mate, looking into his face with some anxiety.

"No, not quite," sighed Maikar, drawing a long breath, and raising himself on one elbow, with a slightly dazed look, "but I never was so nearly burst in all my life. If an ox had fallen on me he could not have squeezed me flatter. Do, two of you, squeeze me the other way, to open me out a little; there's no room in me left to breathe—scarcely room to think."

"Oh! your battles are not yet over, I see," said the mate, going off to the stern of the vessel, where he found Bladud just recovering consciousness and smiling at the remarks of the captain, who busied himself in stanching the wound, just over his frontal bone, from which blood was flowing freely.

"H'm! this comes of sheer recklessness. I told you to take off your helmet, but I did not tell you to keep it off. Man, you launched that javelin well!—better than I could have done it myself. Indeed, I doubt if my old grandfather could have done it with such telling effect—straight through and through. I saw full a hand-breadth come out at the villain's back. What say you, mate? Little Maikar wounded?"

"No, not wounded, but nearly burst, as he says himself; and no wonder, for Bladud fell upon him."

"Didn't I tell you, mate," said the captain, looking up with a grin, "that nothing will kill little Maikar? Go to, man, you pretend to be a judge of men; yet you grumbled at me for engaging him as one of our crew. Do you feel better now, prince?"

R. M. Ballantyne

"Ay, greatly better, thank you," replied Bladud, putting his hand gently on the bandages with which the captain had skilfully bound his head.

"That is well. I think, now, that food will do you service. What say you?"

"Nay, with your leave, I prefer sleep," said the prince, stretching himself out on the deck. "A little rest will suffice, for my head is noted for its thickness, and my brain for its solidity—at least so my good father was wont to say; and I've always had great respect for his opinion."

"Ah, save when it ran counter to your own," suggested Arkal; "and especially that time when you ran away from home and came out here in the long ship of my trading friend."

"I have regretted that many a time since then, and I am now returning home to offer submission."

"D'you think that he'll forgive you?"

"I am sure he will, for he is a kind man; and I know he loves me, though he has never said so."

"I should like to know that father of yours. I like your description of him—so stern of face, yet so kind of heart, and with such an unchangeable will when he sees what is right. But what *is* right, and what is wrong?"

"Ay—what is—who can tell? Some people believe that the gods make their will known to man through the Delphic Oracle."

"Boh!" exclaimed the captain with a look of supreme contempt.

The turn of thought silenced both speakers for a time; and when Captain Arkal turned to resume the conversation, he found that his friend was sound asleep.

R. M. Ballantyne

CHAPTER THREE

ON THE VOYAGE

Weather has always been, and, we suppose, always will be, capricious. Its uncertainty of character—in the Levant, as in the Atlantic, in days of old as now, was always the same—smiling to-day; frowning to-morrow; playful as a lamb one day; raging like a lion the next.

After the rough handling experienced by the *Penelope* at the beginning of her voyage, rude Boreas kindly retired, and spicy breezes from Africa rippled the sea with just sufficient force to intensify its heavenly blue, and fill out the great square-sail so that there was no occasion to ply the oars. One dark, starlight but moonless night, a time of quiet talk prevailed from stem to stern of the vessel as the grizzled mariners spun long yarns of their prowess and experiences on the deep, for the benefit of awe-stricken and youthful shipmates whose careers were only commencing.

"You've heard, no doubt, of the great sea-serpent?" observed little Maikar, who had speedily recovered from the flattening to which Bladud had subjected him, and was busy enlivening a knot of young fellows in the bow of the ship.

"Of course we have!" cried one; "father used to tell me about it when I was but a small boy. He never saw it himself, though he had been to the Tin Isles and Albion more than once; but he said he had met with men who had spoken with shipmates who had heard of it from men who had seen it only a few days before, and who described it exactly."

"Ah!" remarked another, "but I have met a man who had seen it himself on his first voyage, when he was quite a youth; and he said it had a bull's head and horns, with a dreadful long body all over scales, and something like an ass's tail at the end."

"Pooh!—nonsense!" exclaimed little Maikar, twirling his thumbs, for smoking had not been introduced into the world at that period—and thumb-twirling would seem to have served the ancient world for leisurely pastime quite as well, if not better—at least we are led to infer so from the fact that Herodotus makes no mention of anything like a vague, mysterious sensation of unsatisfied desire to fill the mouth with smoke in those early ages, which he would certainly have done had the taste for smoke been a natural craving, and thumb-twirling an unsatisfactory occupation. This absolute silence of the "Father of History," we think, almost proves our point. "Nonsense!" repeated little Maikar. "The youth of the man who told you about the serpent accounts for his wild description, for youth is prone to strange imaginings and—"

"It seems to me," interrupted a grave man, who twirled his thumbs in that slow, deliberate way in which a contemplative man smokes—"it seems to me that there's no more truth about the great sea-serpent than there is about the golden fleece. I don't believe in either of them."

"Don't you? Well, all I can say is," returned the little man, gazing fixedly in the grave comrade's face, "that I saw the great sea-serpent with my own eyes!"

"No! did you?" exclaimed the group, drawing their heads closer together with looks of expectancy.

"Ay, that did I, mates; but you mustn't expect wild descriptions about monsters with bulls' horns and asses' tails from me. I like truth, and the truth is, that the brute was so far away at the time we saw it, that not a man of us could tell exactly what it was like, and when we tried the description, we were all so different, that we gave it up; but we were all agreed on this point, that it certainly *was* the serpent."

The listeners seemed rather disappointed at this meagre account and sudden conclusion of what had bidden fair to become a stirring tale of the sea; but Maikar re-aroused their expectations by stating his firm belief that it was all nonsense about there being only one sea-serpent.

"Why, how could there be only one?" he demanded, ceasing to twirl, in order that he might clench his fist and smite his knee with emphasis. "Haven't you got a grandfather?" he asked, turning suddenly to the grave man.

"Certainly, I've got two of them if you come to that," he answered, taken rather aback by the brusque and apparently irrelevant nature of the question.

"Just so—two of them," repeated the little man, "and don't you think it likely that the sea serpent must have had two grandfathers also?"

"Undoubtedly—and two grandmothers as well. Perhaps he's got them yet," replied the grave man with a contemplative look over the side, where the rippling sea gleamed with phosphoric brilliancy.

"Exactly so," continued Maikar in an eager tone, "and of

course these also must have had two grandfathers besides a mother each, and it is more than likely that the great sea-serpent himself is the father of a large family."

"Which implies a wife," suggested one of the seamen.

"Not necessarily," objected an elderly seaman, who had once been to the lands lying far to the north of Albion, and had acquired something of that tendency to object to everything at all times which is said to characterise the people of the far North. "Not necessarily," he repeated, "for the serpent may be a bachelor with no family at all."

There was a short laugh at this, and an illogical man of the group made some irrelevant observation which led the conversation into a totally different channel, and relegated the great sea-serpent, for the time being, to oblivion!

While the men were thus engaged philosophising in the bow, Bladud and the captain were chatting in subdued voices in the stern.

"It is impossible," said the latter, in reply to a remark made by the former, "it is impossible for me to visit your father's court this year, though it would please me much to do so, but my cargo is intended for the south-western Cassiterides. To get round to the river on the banks of which your home stands would oblige me to run far towards the cold regions, into waters which I have not yet visited—though I know them pretty well by hearsay. On another voyage I may accomplish it, but not on this one."

"I am sorry for that, Arkal, because things that are put off to another time are often put off altogether. But the men of the Tin Isles often visit my father's town in their boats with copper and tin, and there are tracks through the forest which horses can traverse. Could you not visit us overland? It would not be a journey of many weeks, and your trusty mate might look after the ship in your absence. Besides, the diggers may not have enough of the metal ready to fill your ship, so you may be idle a long time. What say you?"

Captain Arkal frowned, as was his wont when considering a knotty question, and shook his head.

"I doubt if I should be wise to venture so much," he said; "moreover, we are not yet at the end of our voyage. It is of little use troubling one's-self about the end of anything while we are only at the beginning."

"Nevertheless," rejoined Bladud, "to consider the possible end while yet at the beginning, seems not unreasonable, though, undoubtedly, we may never reach the end. Many a fair ship sets sail and never returns."

"Ay, that is true, as I know to my cost," returned the captain, "for this is not my first venture. A long time ago I loaded a ship about the size of this one, and sent her under command of one of my best friends to the Euxine sea for gold. I now think that that old story about Jason and his ship *Argo* sailing in search of the golden fleece was running too strong in my youthful brain. Besides that, of course I had heard the report that there is much gold in that direction, and my hopes were strong, for you know all the world runs after gold. Anyhow, my ship sailed and I never saw her or my friend again. Since then I have contented myself with copper and tin."

A slight increase in the wind at that moment caused the captain to dismiss his golden and other memories, and look inquiringly to windward.

"A squall, methinks?" said Bladud.

"No, only a puff," replied his friend, ordering the steersman to alter the course a little.

The squall or puff was only strong enough to cause the *Penelope* to make a graceful bow to the controlling element and cleave the sparkling water with her prow so swiftly that she left a gleaming wake as of lambent fire astern. It was short-lived, however, and was followed by a calm which obliged little Maikar and his comrades to cease their story-telling and ply their fifty oars. Thus the pace was kept going, though not quite so swiftly as if they were running before a stiff breeze.

"The gods are propitious," said the captain; "we are going to have a prosperous voyage."

"How many gods are propitious?" asked Bladud.

"That is a question much too deep for me to answer."

"But not too deep to think of—is it?"

"Of what use would be my thinking?" returned the captain, lightly. "I leave such matters to the learned."

"Now, mate," he added, turning to his subordinate, "I'm going to rest a while. See that you keep an open eye for squalls and pirates. Both are apt to come down on you when you least expect them."

But neither squalls nor pirates were destined to interfere with the *Penelope* during the greater part of that voyage. Day after day the skies were clear, the sea comparatively smooth, and the winds favourable. Sometimes they put ashore, when the weather became stormy and circumstances were favourable. On such occasions they lighted camp-fires under the trees, the ruddy light of which glowed with a grand effect on the picturesque sailors as they sat, stood, or reclined around them.

At other times they were obliged to keep more in the open sea, and occasionally met with traders like themselves returning home, with whom, of course, they were glad to fraternise for a time and exchange views.

Once only did they meet with anything like a piratical vessel, but as that happened to be late in the evening, they managed, by plying the oars vigorously, and under the shade of night, to escape a second encounter with those robbers of the sea.

Thus, in course of time, the length of the great inland sea was traversed, the southern coast of what is now known as France was reached, and the captain's prophecy with regard to a prosperous voyage was thus far fulfilled.

CHAPTER FOUR

THE STORM AND WRECK

It was near daybreak on the morning of a night of unclouded splendour when the mate of the *Penelope* aroused his chief with the information that appearances to windward betokened a change of some sort in the weather.

"If there is a change at all it must be for the worse," said Arkal, raising himself on one elbow, rubbing his eyes, yawning, and then casting a glance over the side where the rippling foam told that the wind was increasing. Raising his eyes to the windward horizon, he threw aside the sheepskin blanket that covered him and rose up quickly.

"There is indeed a change coming. Rouse the men and reduce the sail, mate. Bestir you! The squalls are sudden here."

The orders were obeyed with promptitude. In a few minutes the sail was reduced to its smallest size, and all loose articles about the vessel were made fast.

"You expect a gale, captain?" asked Bladud, who was aroused by the noise of the preparations.

"Ay—or something like one. When a cloud like that rises up

on the horizon there is usually something more than a puff coming. You had better keep well under the lee of the bulwarks when it strikes us."

Bladud's nautical experience had already taught him what to expect and how to act in the circumstance that threatened. Standing close to the side of the ship, he laid hold of a stanchion and looked out to windward, as most of the crew were by that time doing. Captain Arkal himself took the helm.

The increasing daylight showed them that the bank of cloud was spreading quickly over the sky towards the zenith, while a soft hissing sound told of the approaching wind. Soon the blackness on the sea intensified, and white gleams as of flashing light showed where the waves were torn into foam by the rushing wind.

With a warning to "hold on fast!" the captain turned the vessel's head so as to meet the blast. So fierce was it that it cut off the crests of the wavelets, blowing the sea almost flat for a time, and producing what is known as a white squall. The sail was kept fluttering until the fury of the onset was over, then the wind was allowed to fill it; the *Penelope* bent down until the sea began to bubble over the lee bulwarks, and in a few moments more she was springing over the fast rising waves like a nautical racehorse.

Every moment the gale increased, obliging the mariners to show but a corner of the sail. Even this had at last to be taken in, and, during the whole of that dismal day and of the black night which followed, the *Penelope* drove helplessly before the wind under a bare pole. Fortunately the gale was favourable, so that they were enabled to lay their course, but it required all the skill and seamanship of Captain Arkal to prevent their being pooped and swamped by the waves that rolled hissing after them as if hungering mightily to swallow them up.

To have the right man in the right place at such times of imminent danger is all-important, not only to the safety of the craft, but to the peace of mind of those whose lives are in jeopardy. All on board the little vessel during that hurricane felt much comforted by the knowledge that their captain was in the right place. Although a "square man," he had by no means been fitted into a round hole! Knowing this, Prince Bladud felt no anxiety as to the management of the craft, and gave himself up to contemplate the grandeur of the storm, for the howling blast, creaking spars, and bursts of rattling thunder, rendered conversation out of the question.

During a slight lull, however, Bladud asked the question whether the captain knew on what part of the coast they were running.

"Not exactly," he replied, "we have been running so long in darkness that I can only guess. If it holds on much longer like this I shall have to put her head to wind and wait for more light. It may be that we have been driven too far to the left, and there are islands hereabouts that we must keep well clear of. I would that we had put into some bay for shelter before this befell us. Ho! mate."

"Ay, captain."

"See that you put our sharpest pair of eyes in the bow, and let a second pair watch the first, lest the owner of them should go to sleep."

"Little Maikar is there, sir," shouted the mate, "and I am watching him myself."

R. M. Ballantyne

"We shall do well with Maikar in the bow, for he sees like a weasel, and is trustworthy," muttered the captain as he glanced uneasily over the stern, where the hungry waves were still hissing tumultuously after them, as if rendered furious by the delayed meal.

At daybreak on the second day the gale moderated a little, and they were enabled once more to show a corner of their sail, and to encourage the hope that the worst was over. But a fresh outburst, of greater fury than before, soon dashed these hopes, and obliged the captain to throw overboard all the spare spars and some of the heaviest part of the cargo. Still the gale increased, and the impatient waves began to lip over the poop occasionally as if unable to refrain from tasting!

"More cargo must go," muttered the captain, with a gloomy frown. Being resolute, he gave orders to that effect.

Presently the order was given to take soundings. When this was done it was found that they were in twenty fathoms water. On taking another cast, the depth reported was fifteen fathoms.

There were no charts covered with soundings to guide the mariner in those days, but it did not require much experience to convince a seaman that land was probably too near, with such a sudden change from twenty to fifteen fathoms. Arkal was, however, not unprepared for it, and quickly gave orders to stand by to let go the anchors. At that moment the voice of little Maikar was heard shouting, in stentorian tones, "Land ahead!"

The captain replied with a sharp "let go!" and four anchors were promptly dropped from the stern. At the same moment he placed the helm fair amidships, and made it fast with rudder-bands. As the stern of the *Penelope* was formed like the bow, a sharp cut-water was by this means instantly presented to the sea, thus avoiding the necessity and danger incurred by modern ships, in similar circumstances, of anchoring by the head and swinging round.

The hungry waves hissed tumultuously on, but were cleft and passed under the ship disappointed, for there was still enough of water beneath to permit of her tossing to and fro and rising to them like a duck, as she strained and tugged at the anchors.

Just as these operations had been performed, the mists of darkness seemed to lift a little and revealed a wild rocky line of coast, against which the waves were breaking madly.

"Now all hope is over; pray to your gods, men," said the mate, whose courage was not quite equal to his position.

"There are no gods!" growled the captain bitterly, for he saw that he was now a ruined man, even though he should escape with life.

"There is *one* God," said Bladud quietly, "and He does all things well."

As he spoke, the captain, whose eyes had not ceased to look searchingly along the coast, observed something like a bay a short way to the left of the place where they lay.

"It looks like a sandy bay," he said.

"It *is* a sandy bay," exclaimed the anxious mate; "let us up anchors and run into it."

"Have an easy mind and keep your advice till asked for," returned the captain with a look of scorn. "If we are destined

R. M. Ballantyne

to escape, we *shall* escape without making haste. If we are doomed to die, nothing can save us, and it is more manly to die in a leisurely way than in a hurry. When we can see clearly we shall know better how to act."

Although this manner of submitting to the inevitable did not quite suit the mate, he felt constrained to repress his impatience, while the coolness of the captain had a quieting effect on some of the men who were inclined to give way to panic. The sight of Bladud—as he sat there leaning on the hilt of his sword with an expression of what appeared to be serene contentment—had also a quieting effect on the men.

When the increasing light showed that the sandy bay was a spot that might possibly be reached in safety, orders were given to cut the cables, loose the rudder-bands and hoist the sail. For a few minutes the vessel ran swiftly towards the bay, but before reaching the shore she struck with violence. The fore part of the *Penelope* stuck fast immovably, and then, at last, the ravenous waves attained their longed-for meal. They burst over the stern, swept the decks, tore up the fastenings, revelled among the tackling and began tumultuously to break up the ship.

"Launch the skiff," shouted the captain, hastening to lend a hand in the operation.

The men were not slow to obey, and when it touched the water they swarmed into it, so that, being overloaded, it upset and left its occupants struggling in the water. A number of the men who could swim, immediately jumped overboard and tried to right the skiff, but they failed, and, in the effort to do so, broke the rope that held it. Some clung to it. Others turned and swam for the shore.

A good many of the men, however, still remained in the

wreck, which was fast breaking up. To these the captain turned.

"Now, men," he said, "those of you who can swim would do well to take to the water at once, for it is clear that we shall not have a plank left to stand on soon. Come, mate, show them an example."

The man, though not very courageous, as his pale face betrayed, happened to be a good swimmer, and at once leaped into the sea. He was followed by all who could swim. Those who could not, were encouraged to make the attempt with planks and oars to aid them. As for Bladud, he busied himself like the captain in giving heart to the non-swimmers and showing them how best to use their floats.

The last of the men to leave was little Maikar.

He stood at the bow with his arms crossed on his chest and a look of melancholy interest on his countenance.

"What! not gone yet?" exclaimed the captain, turning to him.

"I cannot swim," said the man.

"But neither can these," returned the captain, pointing to the men who had left last.

"My father used to say," rejoined Maikar, as if murmuring to himself, "that I was born to be drowned, and I'm inclined to think he was right."

"Surely you are not afraid," said Arkal.

"Afraid!" exclaimed Maikar, with a sarcastic laugh. "No, captain, but I'm sorry to part with you, because you've been a good captain to me."

"An' I bear no ill-will to you, Bladud, though you *did* squeeze most of the life out of me once. Farewell, both."

As he spoke the little man seized an oar, leaped overboard, and, after some trouble in steadying himself and pointing the oar in the right direction, struck out for the shore.

It was a long way off, and often, while this scene was being enacted, was heard the bubbling cry of men whose powers were failing them. Some were carried by currents against a point to the westward and, apparently, dashed against the rocks. Others sank before half the distance had been traversed.

Bladud and the captain looked at each other when Maikar had left them.

"Can you swim?" asked the captain. "Like a duck," returned the prince, "and I can help you if required."

"I swim like a fish," returned the captain, "but it is hard to part from my *Penelope*! She has never failed me till now, and as this venture contains all my goods, I am a ruined man."

"But your life still remains," said the prince. "Be of good cheer, captain. A stout man can make his fortune more than once. Come, let us go."

A loud cry from Maikar at that moment hastened their deliberations.

"Are you going to cumber yourself with your weapons?" asked Arkal, as they were about to spring from the side, observing that his friend took up his sword and shield.

"Ay—that am I. It is not a small matter that will part my good sword and me."

Both men sprang overboard at the same moment, and made for the spot where little Maikar was still giving vent to bubbling yells and struggling with his oar.

Bladud was soon alongside of him, and, seizing his hair, raised him out of the water.

"Got the cramp," he shouted.

"Keep still, then, and do what I tell ye," said the prince, in a tone of stern command.

He caught the poor man under the armpits with both hands, turned on his back and drew him on to his chest. Swimming thus on his back, with Captain Arkal leading so as to keep them in the right direction, the three were ultimately cast, in a rather exhausted condition, on the shore of the little bay.

R. M. Ballantyne

CHAPTER FIVE

AFTER THE WRECK

It was on the southern shore of what is now known as France that our hero and his comrades in misfortune were cast.

At the time we write of, we need hardly say, the land was nameless. Even her old Roman name of Gaul had not yet been given to her, for Rome itself had not been founded. The fair land was a vast wilderness, known only—and but slightly—to the adventurous mariners of the east, who, with the spirit of Columbus, had pushed their discoveries and trade far beyond the Pillars of Hercules.

Of course the land was a vast solitude, inhabited, sparsely, by a few of those wandering tribes which had been driven westward—by conquest or by that desire for adventure which has characterised the human race, we suppose, ever since Adam and Eve began to explore the regions beyond Eden. Like the great wilderness lying to the north of Canada at the present time, it was also the home of innumerable wild animals which afforded to its uncivilised inhabitants both food and clothing.

Captain Arkal was the only one of the three survivors of the wreck who had seen that coast before or knew anything about it, for, when Bladud had entered the Mediterranean many years before, he had passed too far to the southward to see the northern land.

As they staggered up the beach to a place where the thundering waves sent only their spray, Bladud looked round with some anxiety.

"Surely," he said, "some of the crew must have escaped. It can hardly be that we three are the only survivors out of so many."

The party halted and looked back at the seething waves from which they had just escaped.

"It would be foul shame to us," said the captain, "if we did not try to lend a helping hand to our comrades; but we shall find none of them here. I observed when they started that, in spite of my warning, they made straight for the land, instead of keeping well to windward to avoid being swept round that point of rock to the west. I led you in the right direction, and that is why we alone are here. If any of the others have been saved, they must be on the other side of that point."

While he was speaking, the captain had hurried into the woods, intending to cross the neck of land which separated them from the bay beyond the point referred to.

Their strength returned as they ran, for their intense desire to render aid to those of their late comrades who might stand in need of it seemed to serve them in the stead of rest.

"Come, quick!" cried little Maikar, whose catlike activity and strength enabled him to outrun his more bulky companions. "We may be too late; and some of them can't swim—I know."

R. M. Ballantyne

They reached the crest of a ridge a few minutes later, and, halting, looked at each other in dismay, for the bay beyond the point was full of great rocks and boulders, among which the waves rushed with such fury that they spouted in jets into the air, and covered the sea with foam.

"No living soul can have landed there," said the captain, in a tone that showed clearly he had given up all hope.

"But some may have been swept round the next point," suggested Maikar eagerly, commencing to run forward as he spoke.

Bladud followed at once, and so did the captain, but it was evident that he regarded any further effort as useless.

It proved a longer and more toilsome march than they had expected to pass beyond the second point, and when at last it was reached, there was not a speck at all resembling a human being to be seen on the coast, in all its length of many miles.

"No hope," murmured Bladud.

"None," returned the captain.

Little Maikar did not speak, but the expression of his countenance showed that he was of the same opinion.

"Now," resumed the captain, after a brief silence, "if we would not starve we must go straight back, and see whether any provisions have been washed ashore."

They did not, however, return to the spot where they had landed, for they knew that the same current which had carried their hapless comrades to the westward must have borne the remains of the wreck in the same direction.

Descending, therefore, to the foam-covered bay before referred to, they searched its margin carefully, but for some time found nothing—not even a scrap of wreck.

At last, just as they were about to give up in despair, and turn to some other method of obtaining food, they observed a portion of the wreck that had been driven high up on the beach into a cleft of rock. Running eagerly towards it, they found that it was only a plank.

Bladud and the captain looked at it for a moment or two in silence, and Maikar gave vent to a groan of disappointment.

"Never mind," said the prince, lifting the plank and laying it on his shoulder, in the quiet thoughtful way that was peculiar to him, "it will serve to make a fire and keep us warm."

"But we need not to be kept warm, for the weather is fine and hot," said Maikar, with a rueful expression. "Moreover, we need food, and we cannot eat a plank!"

The prince did not reply, but led the way towards a neighbouring cliff.

"Don't you think we had better make our fire in the woods, Bladud?" asked the captain.

"That would oblige one of us to watch in case natives or wolves should attack us, and none of us are in a fit state to watch. We must sleep."

"But I can't sleep without first eating," said Maikar in a remonstrative tone. "Should we not go to the woods first and try to catch something?"

"Can you on foot run down the hare, the deer, the bear, the

wild-boar, or even the rabbit?"

"Not I. My legs are swift enough, though short, but they are not equal to that."

"Well, then, as we have neither bow nor shaft, and my good sword would be of little use against such game, why waste our time and strength in the woods?"

"But we might find honey," suggested Maikar.

"And if we did not find honey, what then?"

"Berries," answered the little man.

"Berries are not nearly ripe yet."

"True, I forgot that."

"Say you did not know it, man," interposed the captain with a laugh; "never be ashamed of confessing ignorance in regard to things that you're not bound to know. Lead on, Bladud, we will follow. You know more of woodcraft than either of us. If it were the sea we had to do battle with I would claim to lead. On land, being only a babe, I freely resign the helm to one who knows how to steer."

Agreeing to this arrangement, Bladud led his companions up the steep face of a cliff until a projecting ledge was reached, which was just wide enough to form a camping-ground with a perpendicular cliff at the back, and with its other sides so precipitous as to render the approach of enemies—whether two or four-legged—exceedingly difficult. By piling a few stones at the head of the path by which it was reached, they rendered it impossible for any one to approach without awakening the sleepers.

Bladud then, using his sword as a hatchet, chipped off some pieces of the plank, and directed his companions to cut away the wet parts of these and reduce the dry parts to shavings.

They obeyed this order in silence, and wonderingly, for a fire seemed useless, their encampment being well sheltered from the wind, and, as we have said, the weather was warm. By means of a cord, a rude bow, and a drill made of a piece of dry wood, their leader soon procured fire, and, in a few minutes, a bright flame illumined their persons and the cliff behind them.

As the shades of evening were falling by that time, the aspect of things was much improved by the change.

"Now, comrades," said the prince, undoing the breast of his tunic, and drawing from either side a flat mass of dark substance that resembled old dried cow-hide, "we shall have supper, and then—to rest."

"Dried meat!" exclaimed little Maikar, his eyes—and indeed his whole visage—blazing with delighted surprise.

"Right. Maikar. I knew that you would be hungry when we got ashore, so I caught up two pieces of meat and stuffed them into my breast just as we were leaving—one for Arkal and me; the other for you. It may not be quite enough, perhaps, but will do, I hope, to keep you quiet till morning."

"Nay, I shall content me with my fair share, it I may claim a share at all of what I had no hand in procuring. It was wise of you to do this. How came you to think of it?"

"To say truth, I can lay claim to neither wisdom nor forethought," answered the prince, dividing the food into equal portions. "The meat chanced to be lying close to my hand as I was about to leap into the sea. Had I seen it sooner, I would have advised all to take some in the same way. There, now, set to and cook it. For myself, I feel so sleepy that I'm half inclined to eat it raw."

The jerked or dried meat which had been thus opportunely brought away, may be said to have been half cooked in the drying process, and indeed, was sometimes eaten in its dried condition, when it was inconvenient to cook it. In a few minutes, therefore, the supper was ready, and, in a few minutes more, it was disposed of—for strong jaws, sound teeth and good appetite make short work of victuals.

By that time the night had set in; the gale was moderating; the stars had come out, and there seemed every prospect of a speedy and favourable change in the weather. With darkness came the wolves and other creatures of the night, both furred and feathered. Against the former the party was protected by the steep ascent and the barricade, but the latter kept swooping down out of darkness, ever and anon, glaring at them for a moment with round inquiring eyes and sweeping off, as if affrighted, in unearthly silence.

Little heed was paid to these sights and sounds, however, by our adventurers, who were filled with sadness at the loss of their ship and comrades.

They spoke but little during the meal, and, after partially drying themselves, lay down with their feet towards the fire, and almost instantly fell asleep. Being trained to a hardy life, they did not feel the want of couch or covering, and healthy exhaustion prevented dreams from disturbing their repose.

Gradually the fire died down; the howling of the wolves ceased; the night-birds betook them to their haunts, and no sound was heard in or around the camp except the soft breathing of the sleepers and the booming of the distant waves.

R. M. Ballantyne

CHAPTER SIX

FIRST ANXIETIES AND TROUBLES

The day that followed the wreck was well advanced before the sleepers awakened.

Their first thoughts were those of thankfulness for having escaped with life. Then arose feelings of loneliness and sorrow at the sad fate of the crew of the *Penelope*, for though it was just possible that some of their comrades had reached the shore on the beach that extended to the westward, such an event was not very probable. Still the bare hope of this induced them to rise in haste. After a hurried breakfast on the remnants of the previous night's supper, they proceeded along the coast for several miles, carefully searching the shores of every bay.

About noon they halted. A few scraps of the dried meat still remained, and on these they dined, sitting on a grassy slope, while they consulted as to their future proceedings.

"What is now to be done?" asked the captain of Bladud, after they had been seated in silence for some minutes.

"I would rather hear your opinion first," returned his friend. "You must still continue to act as captain, for it is fitting that age should sit at the helm, while I will act the part of guide and forester, seeing that I am somewhat accustomed to woodcraft."

"And the remainder of our band," said little Maikar, wiping his mouth after finishing the last morsel, "will sit in judgment on your deliberations."

"Be it so," returned Bladud. "Wisdom, it is said, lies in small compass, so we should find it in you."

Captain Arkal, whose knitted brows and downcast eyes showed that his thoughts were busy, looked up suddenly.

"It is not likely," he said, "that any ships will come near this coast, for the gale has driven us far out of the usual track of trading ships, and there are no towns here, large or small, that I know of. It would be useless, therefore, to remain where we are in the hope of being picked up by a passing vessel. To walk back to our home in the east is next to impossible, for it is not only far distant, but there lie between us and Hellas far-reaching gulfs and bays, besides great mountain ranges, which have never yet been crossed, for their tops are in the clouds and covered, summer and winter, with eternal snow."

"Then no hope remains to us," said Maikar, with a sigh, "except to join ourselves to the wild people of the land—if there be any people at all in it—and live and die like savages."

"Patience, Maikar, I have not yet finished."

"Besides," interpolated Bladud, "a wise judge never delivers an opinion until he has heard both sides of a question."

"Now, from my knowledge of the lie of coast-lands, I feel sure that the Isles of the Cassiterides must lie there," continued the captain, pointing westward, "and if we travel diligently, it is not unlikely that we shall come down upon the coast of this land almost opposite to them. There we may find, or perhaps make, a boat in which we could cross over— for the sea at that part is narrow, and the white cliffs of the land will be easily distinguished. Once there, I have no doubt that we shall find a ship belonging to one of my countrymen which will take Maikar and me back to our homes, while you, prince, will doubtless be able to return to your father's court on foot."

It will be seen from this speech that the Phoenician captain included the southern shore of England in his idea of the Cassiterides. His notion of the direction in which the islands lay, however, was somewhat incorrect, being founded partly on experience, but partly also on a misconception prevalent at the time that the islands referred to lay only a little way to the north of Spain.

"Your plan seems to me a good one," said Bladud, after some thought, "but I cannot help thinking that you are not quite right in your notion as to the direction of the tin islands. When I left Albion, I kept a careful note of our daily runs— being somewhat curious on such points—and it is my opinion that they lie *there*."

He pointed almost due north. The captain smiled and shook his head. Bladud looked at Maikar, who also smiled and shook his head.

"If you want my opinion," said the little man, gravely, "it is that when two great, good and wise men differ so widely, it is more than likely the truth lies somewhere between them. In *my* judgment, therefore, the Cassiterides lie yonder."

He pointed with an air of confidence in a north-west direction.

"It does seem to me," said Bladud, "that Maikar is right, for as you and I seem to be equally confident in our views, captain, a middle course may be the safest. However, if you decide otherwise, I of course submit."

"Nay," returned the captain, "I will not abuse the power you have given me. Let us decide the matter by lot."

"Ay, let us draw lots," echoed Maikar, "and so shove the matter off our shoulders on to the shoulders of chance."

"There is, there can be, no such thing as chance," said Bladud in a soliloquising tone. "However, let it be as you wish. I recognise the justice of two voices overriding one."

Lots were drawn accordingly, and the longest fell to the little seaman. Without further discussion, therefore, the course suggested by him was adopted.

"And now, comrades," said the prince, rising and drawing his knife—which, like his sword, had been procured in Egypt, and was of white metal—"we must set to work to make bows and arrows, for animals are not wont to walk up to man and request to be killed and cooked, and it won't be long before Maikar is shouting for food."

"Sorry am I that the good javelin of my grandfather went down in the carcase of the pirate chief," remarked the captain, also rising, "for it seems to me by the way you handled it, Bladud, that you could have killed deer with it as well as men."

"I have killed deer with such before now, truly, but the arrow is handier and surer."

"Ay, in a sure hand, with a good eye to direct it," returned Arkal, "but I make no pretence to either. A ship, indeed, I can manage to hit—when I am cool, which is not often the case in a fight—and if there are men in it, my shafts are not quite thrown away, but as to deer, boars, and birds, I can make nothing of them. If I mistake not, Maikar is not much better than myself with the bow."

"I am worse," observed the little man quietly.

"Well then," said Bladud, with a laugh, "you must make me hunter to the party."

While conversing thus they had entered the forest, and soon found trees suitable to their purpose, from which they cut boughs,—using their swords as hatchets.

We have already shown that the prince had brought his sword, shield, and knife on shore with him. Captain Arkal and Maikar had also saved their swords and knives, these having been attached to their girdles at the time they leaped from the wreck. They were somewhat inferior weapons to those worn by Bladud, being made of bronze. The swords of the seamen, unlike that of the prince, were short and double-edged, shaped somewhat like those used long afterwards by the Romans, and they made up in weight for what they lacked in sharpness.

It did not take many hours for the party, under the direction of the prince, to form three strong and serviceable bows, with several arrows, the latter being feathered with dropped plumes, and shod with flint, according to the fashion of the times. Bowstrings had to be made at first out of the tough fibrous roots of a tree, split into threads and plaited together.

"Of course they are not so good as deer-sinews for the purpose," remarked Bladud, stringing one of the bows and fitting an arrow to it, "but we must be content until we kill a deer or some other animal. Perhaps we shall have an opportunity soon."

The remark seemed to have been prophetic, for, as the last word passed his lips, a fawn trotted out of a glade right in front of the party and stood as if paralysed with surprise. The captain and Maikar were reduced to much the same condition, for they made no attempt to use their bows.

"Ho!—" exclaimed the former, but he got no further, for at the moment Bladud's bow twanged, and an arrow quivered in the breast of the fawn, which fell dead without a struggle.

"Well done!" exclaimed the captain heartily. "If such luck always attends you, prince, we shall fare well on our journey."

"It was not altogether luck," returned the other. "See you that spot on the bark of yonder tree—about the size of Maikar's mouth as it now gapes in astonishment?"

"I see it, clear enough—just over the—"

He stopped abruptly, for while he was yet speaking an arrow quivered in the centre of the spot referred to.

After that the captain talked no more about "luck," and Maikar, shutting his mouth with a snap, as if he felt that no words could do justice to his feelings, sprang up and hastened to commence the operation of flaying and cutting up the fawn.

Having thus provided themselves with food, they spent the

rest of the day in preparing it for the journey by drying it in the sun; in making tough and serviceable bowstrings out of the sinews of the fawn, fitting on arrow-heads and feathers, and otherwise arranging for a prolonged march through a country which was entirely unknown to them, both as to its character and its inhabitants.

"It comes into my head," said the captain, "that Maikar and I must provide ourselves with shields and spears of some sort, for if the people of the land are warlike, we may have to defend ourselves."

"That is as you say," returned the prince, rising as he spoke and going towards a long straight bough of a neighbouring tree, on which he had fixed a critical gaze.

With one sweep of his heavy sword he severed it from the stem and returned to his companions.

"Have you taken an ill-will at that tree, or were you only testing the strength of your arm?" asked Maikar.

"Neither, my friend; but I must have a javelin to make my equipment complete, and I would advise you and the captain to provide yourselves with like weapons, for we may meet with four-footed as well as two-legged foes in these parts. I will show you how to point the things with flint."

"That is well said," returned the seaman, rising and going into the woods in search of a suitable branch, followed by the captain.

It was late that night before the weapons were shaped and pointed with flint and all ready for a start on the following morning—the only thing wanting to complete their armament being a couple of shields.

"We are sure to meet with a wild boar or a bull before long, or it may be a bear," said Maikar, "and the hides of any of these will serve our purpose well."

"That is, if we use them well," remarked the captain.

"No one said otherwise," retorted Maikar. "Some people are so full of wise thoughts that they blurt them out, without reason, apparently to get rid of them."

"Just so, Maikar, therefore blurt out no more, but hold thy tongue and go to sleep. Good-night."

R. M. Ballantyne

CHAPTER SEVEN

CONVERSE AND ADVENTURES BY THE WAY

Day was just beginning to break in the east when the prince raised his head from the bundle of leaves that had formed his pillow, and looked sleepily around him.

His companions lay still, sound asleep and sprawling, in all the *abandon* characteristic of the heroes of antiquity.

Some of these characteristics were wonderfully similar to those of modern heroes. For instance, the captain lay flat on his back with his mouth wide open, and a musical solo proceeding from his nose; while Maikar lay on his side with his knees doubled up, his arms extended at full length in front of him, and his hands tightly clasped as if, while pleading with some one for mercy, he was suddenly petrified and had fallen over on his side.

Rising softly, Bladud took up his bow and quiver, and, buckling on his sword, left the encampment without disturbing the sleepers. He had not proceeded more than a mile when he startled several wild turkeys or birds of that species from their rest. One of these he instantly brought down. Following them up he soon shot another, and returned to camp, where he found his comrades as he had left them—

the musical nose being if anything more emphatic than before.

Although naturally a grave man, Bladud was by no means destitute of a sense of humour, or disinclined on occasion to perpetrate a practical joke. After contemplating the sleepers for a moment he retired a few paces and concealed himself in the long grass, from which position he pitched one of the huge birds into the air, so that it fell on the captain's upturned visage. The snore changed at once into a yell of alarm, as the mariner sprang up and grasped his sword, which, of course, lay handy beside him.

Electrified by the yell, Maikar also leaped to his feet, sword in hand.

"What d'ye mean by that?" cried the captain, turning on him fiercely.

"What mean *you* by it?" replied Maikar with equal ferocity.

He had barely uttered the words, when the second turkey hit him full in the face and tumbled him over the ashes of the fortunately extinguished fire.

"Come, come!" interposed the prince, stepping forward with a deprecating smile; "there should be no quarrelling among friends, especially at the beginning of a long journey. See, I have fetched your breakfast for you. Instead of tumbling on the fire and putting it out, Maikar, I think it would be wiser to see if there is a spark left and blow it into a flame. Quick! I am hungry."

It need hardly be said that these orders were received with a laugh and a prompt obedience on the part of the little man.

"Yes—there is fire," he said, blowing with tremendous energy until flame was produced. "And, do you know, there is something within me that has a loud voice, but only utters one word—'Food! food! food!' There, now, you may get the birds ready, for the fire will be ready for them in two winks."

There was no occasion, however, to give this advice to his friends, for already the birds had been plucked, split open at the breast, laid flat, and their interiors scraped out in a summary manner. The plucking was not, indeed, all that could be wished, but what fingers failed to do a singe in the flames accomplished to the perfect satisfaction of men who were in no way particular. Sharp-pointed sticks were then thrust through the expanded carcases, and they were stuck up in front of the blaze to roast.

Underdone meat is an abomination to some, a luxury to others—reminding one of that very ancient proverb, "Tastes differ." We cannot say whether on this occasion the uniformity of action in our heroes was the result of taste or haste, but certain it is that before the fowls were only half-roasted on one side, they were turned over so as to let the fire get at the other, and breakfast was begun while the meat was yet frightfully underdone.

Thereafter the three men arose, like giants refreshed—if we may say so, for Maikar was indeed mentally, though not physically, a giant—buckled on their swords, slung bows and quivers on their backs, along with the turkey remains, and took up shields and javelins. Having laid their course by the stars the night before, they set out on their journey through the unknown wilderness.

The part of the country through which they passed at the beginning of the march was broken and diversified by hill and dale; in some places clothed with forests, in others covered with grass, on which many wild animals were seen browsing. These, however, were remarkably timid, and fled at the first sign of the approaching travellers, so that it was impossible to get within bow-shot of them.

"From this I judge that they are much hunted," said Bladud, halting on a ridge to note the wild flight, of a herd of deer which had just caught eight of them.

"If so, we are likely to fall in with the hunters before long, I fear," remarked the captain.

"Why do you fear?" asked Maikar.

"Because they may be numerous and savage, and may take a fancy to make slaves of us, and as we number only three we could not resist their fancy without losing our lives."

"That would be a pity," returned Maikar, "for we have only one life to lose."

"No; we have three lives to lose amongst us," objected the captain.

"Which makes one each, does it not?" retorted the seaman.

"True, Maikar, and we must lose them all, and more if we had them, rather than become slaves."

"You are right, captain. We never, *never* shall be slaves," said Bladud.

They say that history repeats itself. Perhaps sentiment does the same. At all events, the British prince gave utterance that day to a well-known sentiment, which has been embalmed in modern song and shouted by many a Briton with tremendous enthusiasm—though not absolute truth.

"Captain Arkal," said the little seaman, as they jogged quietly down the sunny slope of a hill, at the bottom of which was a marsh full of rushes, "how do you manage to find your way through such a tangled country as this?"

"By observing the stars," answered the captain.

"But I have observed the stars since I was a little boy," objected Maikar, "and I see nothing but a wild confusion of shining points. How can these guide you? Besides, there are no stars in the daytime."

"True, Maikar; but we have the sun during the day."

Maikar shook his head perplexedly.

"Listen," said the captain, "and I will try to enlighten your dark mind; but don't object else you'll never understand. All stars are not alike—d'ye understand that?"

"Any fool could understand that!"

"Well, then, of course *you* can understand it. Now, you have noticed, no doubt, that some stars are in groups, which groups may alter their position with regard to other groups, but which never change with regard to each other."

"Each other," repeated Maikar, checking off each statement with a nod and a wave of his javelin.

"Well," continued the captain, "there's one group of stars— about six—plainly to be seen on most fine nights, two stars of which are always pretty much in a line with a little star a short way in front of them—d'ye see?"

"Yes."

"Well, that star shows exactly where the cold regions lie—over *there* (extending his arm and pointing), and of course if you know that the cold regions lie *there*, you know that the hot regions must lie at your back—there, and it follows that the Pillars of Hercules lie *there* (pointing west), and home lies somewhere about *there* (pointing eastward)."

"Stop!" cried Maikar in great perplexity—for although a seaman he was densely ignorant. "Hot regions, *there*, cold, *there*, home and the Pillars, *there*, and *there*, and *there* (thrusting his arms out in all directions). I've no more idea of where you've got me to now than—than—"

"Oh, never mind," interrupted the captain, "it doesn't matter, as you are not our guide. But, ho! look! look! down in the hollow there—among the rushes. What's that?"

"A boar!" said Bladud, in a low whisper, as he unslung his bow. "Come, now, it will take all our united force to slay that brute, for, if I have not lost my power of judging such game, I'm pretty sure that he's a very big old boar with formidable tusks."

While the prince was speaking, his comrades had also prepared their weapons, and looked to their guide for directions.

These were hastily but clearly given. As the boar was evidently asleep in his lair, it was arranged that the three friends should stalk him, as the broken ground was specially favourable for such a mode of attack.

"We will advance together," said Bladud, "with our bows ready. I will lead; you follow close. When we get within range you will do as you see me do, and be sure that you aim at the brute's side—not at his head. Send your arrows with all the force you can. Then drop the bows and get your javelins ready."

With eager looks the captain and little sailor nodded assent. They were much excited, having often heard tales of boar-hunting, though neither of them had ever taken part in that work.

A few minutes' walk brought them to the edge of the rushes, where they had a fair view of the monstrous animal as it lay fully extended on its side, and not more than thirty yards distant.

"Take him just behind the fore-leg," whispered Bladud, as he drew his bow. His companions followed his example. Two of the bows twanged simultaneously, but the third—that of Maikar—was pulled with such vigour that it broke with a crash that would have awakened the sleepiest of wild boars, had there been nothing else to arouse him. As it was, other things helped to quicken his sensibilities. Bladud's unfailing arrow went indeed straight for the heart, but a strong rib caught and checked its progress. The captain's shaft, probably by good luck, entered deep into the creature's flank not far from the tail.

To say that the forest was instantly filled with ear-splitting shrieks is to express the result but feebly. We might put it as a sort of indefinite question in the rule of three, thus—if an ordinary civilised pig with injured feelings can yell as we all know how, what must have been the explosion of a wild-boar of the eighth century BuCu, in circumstances such as we have described? Railway whistles of the nineteenth century, intermittently explosive, is the only possible answer to the question, and that is but an approximation to the truth.

For one instant the infuriated creature paused to look for its assailants. Catching sight of them as they were fitting arrows to their bows, it gave vent to a prolonged locomotive-express yell, and charged. Bladud's arrow hit it fair between the eyes, but stuck in the impenetrable skull. The shaft of the captain missed, and the javelin of Maikar went wildly wide of the mark.

By order of Bladud the three had separated a few yards from each other. Even in its rage the monster was perplexed by this, for it evidently perceived the impossibility of attacking three foes at the same moment. Which to go for was the question. Like an experienced warrior it went for the "little one."

Maikar had drawn his last weapon—the short sword of bronze—and, like a brave man as he was, "prepared to receive boarelry." Another instant and the enemy was upon him. More than that, it was over him, for, trusting to his agility—for which he was famed—he tried to leap to one side, intending to make a vigorous thrust at the same moment. In doing so his foot slipped; he fell flat on his side, and the boar, tripping over him, just missed ripping him with its fearful tusks. It fell, with a bursting squeak, beyond.

To leap up and turn was the work of an instant for the boar, and would have been the same for the man if he had not been partially stunned by the fall. As it was, the captain, who was nearest, proved equal to the emergency, for, using his javelin as a spear, he plunged it into the boar's side. But that side was tougher than he had expected. The spear was broken by a sharp twist as the animal turned on its new foe, who now stood disarmed and at its mercy. Bladud's ponderous sword, however, flashed in the air at that moment, and fell on the creature's neck with a force that would have made Hercules envious if he had been there. Deep into the brawn it cut, through muscle, fat, and spine, almost slicing the head from the trunk, and putting a sudden stop to the last yell when it reached the windpipe. The boar rolled head over heels like a shot hare, almost overturning Bladud as it wrenched the sword from his hand, and swept the captain off his legs, carrying him along with it in a confusion of blood and bristles.

It was truly a terrific encounter, and as the prince stood observing the effect of his blow, he would probably have burst into a fit of laughter, had he not been somewhat solemnised by Captain Arkal's fearful appearance, as he arose ensanguined, but uninjured, from the ground.

CHAPTER EIGHT

DISCOVERY AND FLIGHT

Being now provided with material for making shields, they resolved to spend a day in camp. This was all the more necessary, that the shoes or sandals which they had worn at sea were not well suited for the rough travelling which they had now to undertake.

Accordingly they selected a spot on the brow of a hill from which the surrounding country could be seen in nearly all directions. But they were careful also to see that several bushes shielded themselves from view, for it was a matter of uncertainty whether or where natives might make their appearance.

Here, bathed in glorious sunshine, with a lovely prospect of land and water, tangled wood and flowery plains, to gladden their eyes, and the savoury smell of pork chops and turkey to tickle their nostrils, they spent two days in manufacturing the various necessary articles. Captain Arkal provided himself with a new javelin.

Maikar made another bow, and both fabricated tough round shields with double plies of the boar's hide. Out of the same substance Bladud made a pair of shoes for each of them.

"The sandals you wear at home," he said, "are not so good as those used by us in Albion. They don't cover the feet sufficiently, and they expose the toes too much. Yet our sandals are easily and quickly made. Look here—I will show you."

His companions paused in their labour and looked on, while the prince took up an oblong piece of boar-hide, over a foot in length and six inches broad, which had been soaking in water till it had become quite soft and limp. Placing one of his feet on this he drew the pattern of it on the skin with a pointed stick. Around this pattern, and about a couple of inches from it, he bored a row of holes an inch or so apart. Through these holes he rove a thong of hide, and then rounded away the corners of the piece.

"There," said he, placing his foot in the centre of it and drawing the thong, "my sandal is ready."

The tightening of the thong drew up the edges of the shoe until they overlapped and entirely encased his foot.

"Good," said the captain, "but that kind of sandal is not new to me. I've seen it before, not only in your country, but in other lands."

"Indeed? Well, after all, it is so simple, and so likely to hit the minds of thoughtful men, that I doubt not it is used wherever travelling is bad or weather cold. We shall need such sandals in this land, for there is, no doubt, great variety of country, also of weather, and many thorns."

While our travellers were thus labouring and commenting on their work, unseen eyes were gazing at them with profound interest and curiosity.

A boy, or youth just emerging from the state of boyhood, lay low in a neighbouring thicket with his head just elevated sufficiently above the grass to enable his black eyes to peer over it. He was what we of the nineteenth century term a savage. That is to say, he was unkempt, unwashed, and almost naked—but not uneducated, though books had nothing to do with his training.

The prince chanced to look round, and saw the black eyes instantly, but being, as we have said, an adept in woodcraft—including savage warfare—he did not permit the slightest evidence of recognition to escape him. He continued his gaze in the same direction, allowing his eyes slowly to ascend, as if he were looking through the tree-tops at the sky. Then turning his head quietly round he resumed his work and whistled—for whistling had been invented even before that time.

"Comrades," he said, after a few minutes, "don't look up from your work, but listen. We are watched. You go on with your occupations as if all was right, and leave me to deal with the watcher."

His comrades took the hint at once and went quietly on with their labours, while the prince arose, stretched himself, as if weary of his work. After a few minutes of looking about him, as though undecided what to do next, he sauntered into the bush at the side of their encampment opposite to that where the watcher lay.

The moment he got out of range of the boy's eyes, however, his careless air vanished, and he sped through the underwood with the quietness and something of the gait of a panther—stooping low and avoiding to tread on dead twigs. Making a wide circle, he came round behind the spot where the watcher was hid. But, trained though he had been in the art

R. M. Ballantyne

of savage warfare, the boy was equal to him. From the first he had observed in Bladud's acting the absence of that "touch of nature which makes the whole world kin," and kept a bright look-out to his rear as well as in his front, so that when Bladud, despite his care, trod on a dry stick the boy heard it. Next moment he was off, and a moment after that he was seen bounding down the hill like a wild-cat.

The prince, knowing the danger of letting the boy escape and carry information to his friends, dashed after him at full speed—and the rate of his running may be estimated when it is remembered that many a time he had defeated men who had been victors at the Olympic games. But the young savage was nearly his match. Feeling, however, that he was being slowly yet surely overtaken, the boy doubled like a hare and made for a ridge that lay on his left. By that time the chase was in full view of the two men in camp, who rose and craned their necks in some excitement to watch it.

"He's after something," said the captain.

"A boy!" said Maikar.

"Ay, and running him down, hand over hand."

"There seems to be no one else in sight, so we don't need to go to his help."

"If he needs our help he'll come for it," returned the captain with a laugh, "and it will puzzle the swiftest runner in the land to beat his long legs. See, he's close on the lad now."

"True," responded the other, with a sigh of disappointment, "but we shan't see the end of it, for the boy will be over the ridge and out of sight before he is caught."

Maikar was right. Even while he spoke the youthful savage gained the summit, where his slim, agile figure was clearly depicted against the sky. Bladud was running at full speed, not a hundred yards behind him, yet, to the amazement of the spectators, the boy suddenly stopped, turned round, and waved his hand with a shout of defiance. Next moment he was over the ridge and gone. A few seconds later the prince was seen to halt at the same point, but instead of continuing the pursuit, he remained immovable for a few minutes gazing in front of him. Then he returned toward the encampment with a somewhat dejected air.

"No wonder you look surprised," he said, on arriving. "The other side of that ridge is a sheer precipice, down which I might have gone if I had possessed wings. There was no track visible anywhere, but of course there must have been a well-concealed one somewhere, for soon after I reached the top I saw the young wild-cat running over the plain far below. On coming to the edge of a long stretch of forest, he stopped and capered about like a monkey. I could see, even at that distance, that he was making faces at me by way of saying farewell. Then he entered the woods, and that was the end of him."

"I wish it was the end of him," observed the captain, with something like a growl—for his voice was very deep, and he had a tendency to mutter when disturbed in temper. "The monkey will be sure to run home and tell what he's seen, and so bring all his tribe about our ears."

"Ay, not only his tribe," remarked Maikar, "but his uncles, brothers, fathers, nephews, and all his kin to the latest walkable generation."

"Are your weapons ready?" asked Bladud, taking up his sword and putting on his helmet.

"All ready," answered the captain, beginning to collect things—"I have just finished two head-pieces out of the boar-hide for myself and Maikar, which will turn an arrow or a sword-cut, unless delivered by a strong arm. Don't you think them handsome?"

"They are suitable, at any rate," said Maikar, "for they are as ugly as our faces."

"Come, then, we must make haste, for wild men are not slow to act," rejoined Bladud. "By good fortune our way does not lie in the direction the boy took. We shall get as far away from them as possible, and travel during the night."

In a few minutes the little party—by that time fully equipped for the chase or war—were hurrying down the hillside in the direction of the setting sun. It was growing late in the evening, and as they reached the bottom, they had to cross a meadow which was rather swampy, so that their feet sank in some parts over the ankles.

"I say, guide," observed Maikar, who, like his nautical commander, had small respect for rank, and addressed the prince by what he deemed an appropriate title, "it has just come into my head that we are leaving a tremendous trail behind us. We seafaring men are not used to trouble our heads on that score, for our ships leave no track on the waves, but it is not so on the land. Won't these naked fellows follow us up and kill us, mayhap, when we're asleep?"

"Doubtless they will try," answered Bladud, "but we land-faring men are in the habit of troubling our heads on that score, and guarding against it. Do you see yonder stream, or, rather, the line of bushes that mark its course?"

"Ay, plainly."

"Well, when we reach that, you shall see and understand without explanation."

On reaching the stream referred to, they found that it was a small, shallow one, with a sluggish current, for the plain through which it flowed was almost flat.

"You see," said Bladud, pausing on the brink, "that it flows towards the sea in the direction we have come from. Now step into the water and follow me down stream."

"Down?" exclaimed the captain in surprise, and with some hesitation. "We don't want to return to the sea whence we have just come, do we?"

"Captain Arkal," returned Bladud, sternly, "when you give orders on board ship, do you expect to have them questioned, or obeyed?"

"Lead on, guide," returned the captain, stepping promptly into the water.

For about a quarter of a mile the prince led his followers in silence and with much care, for it was growing very dark. Presently they came to a place where the banks were swampy and the stream deep. Here their guide landed and continued to walk a short distance down the bank, ordering his followers to conceal their track as much as possible, by closing the long grass over each footprint. The result, even to the unpractised eyes of the seamen, did not seem satisfactory, but their leader made no comment. After proceeding about fifty yards further, he re-entered the stream and continued the descent for about a mile. Then he stopped abruptly, and, turning round, said, "Now, comrades, we will land for a moment, then re-enter the stream and ascend."

The astonishment of Captain Arkal was so great, that he was again on the point of asking an explanation, for it seemed to him that wandering down the bed of a stream for the mere purpose of turning and wandering up it, when haste was urgent, could only be accounted for on the supposition that the prince had gone mad. Remembering his previous rebuff, however, he kept silence.

On reaching the swampy part of the bank their leader did not land, but held straight on, though the water reached nearly to their armpits. They were somewhat cooled, but not disagreeably so, for the night was warm.

In course of time they reached the spot where they had first entered the stream. Passing it, without landing, they held on their course for a considerable distance, until they came to a place where the stream was not more than ankle-deep. Here Bladud paused a few moments and turned to his companions.

"Now, captain," he said, with a smile that may be said to have been almost audible though not visible, "do you understand my proceedings?"

"Not quite, though, to say truth, I begin to think you are not just so mad as you seemed at first."

"Don't you see," continued the prince, "that when we first came to the stream, I entered it so that our footprints on the bank would show clearly that we had gone downwards. This will show our pursuers, when they arrive here, that, though we are wise enough to take to the water because it leaves no footprints, we are not experienced enough to be careful as to concealing the direction we have taken. When they reach the swampy bank and deep water, they will be led to think we did not like getting wet, and the effort made to cover our footprints, will make them think that we are very ignorant woodsmen. Then, with much confidence, they will continue to follow down stream, looking on the banks now and then for our footprints, until they begin to wonder whether we intend to make a highroad of the river all the way to the sea. After that they will become perplexed, astonished, suspicious as to our stupidity, and will scurry round in all directions, or hold a council, and, finally they will try up stream; but it will be too late, for by that time we shall be far away on our road towards the setting sun."

"Good!" ejaculated Maikar, when this explanation was finished.

"Good!" echoed the captain, with an approving nod. "You understand your business, I see. Shove out your oars. We follow."

Without further remark Bladud continued his progress up stream. It was necessarily slow at first, but as night advanced the moon rose, in her first quarter, and shed a feeble but sufficient light on their watery path.

At last they came to a place where the leader's sharp eye observed signs of the presence of man. Stopping short and listening intently, they heard subdued voices not far from the spot where they stood.

"Stay where you are," whispered Bladud. "Don't move. I'll return immediately."

He entered the bushes cautiously and disappeared. Standing there without moving, and in profound silence, under the dark shadow of an overhanging bush, it is no wonder that the captain and his comrade began to think the time very long, yet it was only a few minutes after he had left them that their guide returned.

"Only a single family," he whispered—"three men, two women, and four children. We have nothing to fear, but we must pass on in silence."

The discovery of those natives obliged them to continue the march up the bed of the stream much longer than they had intended, and the night was far advanced before they thought it prudent to leave the water and pursue the journey on dry land.

Fortunately the country was open and comparatively free from underwood, so that they made progress much more rapidly; nevertheless, it was not thought safe to take rest until they had placed many a mile between them and the natives, who, it was thought probable, would be started in pursuit of them by the youth to whom Bladud had given chase.

Much wearied, and almost falling asleep while they advanced, the travellers halted at last in a dense thicket, and there, lying down without food or fire, they were soon buried in profound repose.

CHAPTER NINE

HOMECOMING

It is beyond the scope of this tale to describe minutely all that befell our adventurers on their long, fatiguing, and dangerous march through ancient Gaul, which land at that time had neither name nor history.

Suffice it to say that, after numerous adventures with savage beasts, and scarcely less savage men, and many hair-breadth escapes and thrilling incidents by flood and field, they at last found themselves on the shores of that narrow channel which separated the northern coast of Gaul from the white cliffs of Old Albion. They were guided thereto, as we have said, by the Pole-star, which shone in our sky in those days with its wonted brilliancy, though, probably, astronomers had not yet given to it a local habitation in their systems or a distinctive name.

Of course their passage through the land had been attended with great variety of fortune, good and bad. In some parts they met with natives who received them hospitably and sent them on their way rejoicing. Elsewhere they found banditti, fortunately in small bands, with whom they had to fight, and once they were seized and imprisoned by a tribe of inhospitable savages, from whom they escaped, as it were, by the skin of their teeth.

In all these vicissitudes the gigantic frame and the mild, kindly looks of Bladud went far to conciliate the uncertain, attract the friendly, and alarm the savage, for it is a curious fact, explain it how we may, that the union of immense physical power with childlike sweetness of countenance, has a wonderful influence in cowing angry spirits. It may be that strong, angry, blustering men are capable only of understanding each other. When they meet with strong men with womanlike tenderness they are puzzled, and puzzlement, we think, goes a long way to shake the nerves even of the brave. At all events it is well known that a sudden burst of wrath from one whose state of temper is usually serene, exerts a surprising and powerful effect on average mankind.

Whatever be the truth as to these things, it is certain that nearly every one who looked up at the face of Bladud liked him, and more than once when his ponderous sword sprang from its sheath, and his blue eyes flashed, and his fair face flushed, and his magnificent teeth went together with a snap, he has been known to cause a dozen men to turn and flee rather than encounter the shock of his onset.

Little Maikar, who was himself as brave as a lion, nearly lost his life on one occasion, because he was so taken up and charmed with the sight of one of Bladud's rushes, that he utterly forgot what he was about, and would have been crushed by the smite of a savage club, if the captain had not promptly turned aside the blow and struck the club-man down.

"At last!" exclaimed the prince, with a gaze of enthusiasm at the opposite cliffs, "my native land! Well do I love it and well do I know it, for I have stood on this shore and seen it from this very spot when I was quite a boy."

"Indeed! How was that?" asked Arkal.

"I used to be fond of the sea, and was wont to travel far from my father's home to reach it. I made friends with the fishermen, and used to go off with them in their little skiffs. One day a storm arose suddenly, blew us off shore, and, when we were yet a long distance from this coast, overturned our skiff. What became of my companions I know not. Probably they were drowned, for I never more saw them; but I swam ashore, where I think I should have died of exhaustion if I had not been picked up by an old fisherman of this land, who carried me to his hut and took care of me. With the old man I remained several months, for the fishermen on the two sides of the channel had been quarrelling at the time, and the old man did not dare to venture across. I did not care much, for I enjoyed playing with his grandson, and soon learned their language. After a time the quarrelling ceased, and the old man landed me on my own side."

"That is interesting. I only wish the old fisherman was here now with his skiff, for there is no village in sight and no skiff to be seen, so how we are to get over I cannot tell,— swimming being impossible and wings out of the question."

"Ay, except in the case of fish and birds," observed Maikar.

"True, and as we are neither fish nor birds," rejoined the captain, "what is to be done?"

"We must find a skiff," said the prince.

"Good, but where?"

"On the other side of yon bluff cape," replied Bladud. "It was there that my friend the old fisherman lived. Mayhap he may live there still."

Pushing on along shore they passed the bold cape referred to, and there, sure enough, they found the old man's hut, and the old man himself was seated on a boulder outside enjoying the sunshine.

Great was his surprise on seeing the three strangers approach, but greater was his joy on learning that the biggest of the three was the boy whom he had succoured many years before.

After the first greetings were over, Bladud asked if he and his friends could be taken across in a skiff.

The old man shook his head.

"All that I possess," he said, "you are welcome to, but my skiff is not here, and if it was I am too old to manage it now. My son, your old companion, has had it away these two days, and I don't expect him home till to-morrow. But you can rest in my poor hut till he comes."

As there seemed nothing better to be done, the travellers agreed to this. Next day the son arrived, but was so changed in appearance, that Bladud would not have recognised his old playmate had not his father called him by name.

The skiff, although primitive and rude in its construction, was comparatively large, and a considerable advance on the dug-outs, or wooden canoes, and the skin coracles of the period. It had a square or lug-sail, and was steered by a rudder.

"My son is a strange man," remarked the old fisherman, as the party sauntered down to the shore, up which the skiff had been dragged. "He invented that skiff as well as made it, and the curious little thing behind that steers it."

"Able and strange men seem to work their minds in the same way," returned Bladud; "for the thing is not altogether new. I have seen something very like it in the East; and, to my mind, it is a great improvement on the long oar when the boat is driven through the water, but it is of no use at all when there is no motion."

"No; neither is it of use when one wishes to sweep round in a hurry," observed the captain, when this was translated to him. "If it had not been for my steering-oar bringing you sharp round when we were attacking the pirate, you would hardly have managed to spit the chief as you did, strong though you be."

It was found that the new style of skiff was a good sailer, for, although the wind was light, her lug-sail carried her over to the coast of Albion in about four hours.

"There has been some bad feeling of late between the men from the islands and the men of our side—there often is," said the young fisherman, who steered. "I am not sure that it will be safe to land here."

"If that be so, hold on close along the shore in the direction of the setting sun," returned Bladud, "and land us after nightfall. I know the whole country well, and can easily guide my comrades through the woods to my father's town on the great river."

The young fisherman did not reply for a few seconds. He seemed in doubt as to this proposal.

"There has been war lately," he said, "between your father

and the southern tribes, and it may be dangerous for so small a party to traverse the lands of the enemy. I would gladly go and help you, but what could one arm more do to aid you against a host? Besides, my father is dependent on me now for food. I may not forsake the old one who has fed and guarded me since I was a little boy."

"Concern yourself not about that, friend," replied the prince. "We need no help. During many days we have travelled safely enough through the great woods of the interior, and have held our own against all foes."

"Without doubt we are well able to take care of ourselves," remarked the captain, "though it is but fair to admit that we have had some trouble in doing so."

"Ay, and some starvation, too," added Maikar; "but having come safe over the mainland, we are not afraid to face the dangers of the isles, young man."

"I said not that you were afraid," rejoined the fisherman, with something of dignified reproof in his manner; "but it is not disgraceful for brave men to act with caution."

"Well said, my old comrade!" exclaimed Bladud; "and so we shall be pleased if you will land us here. But your speech leads me to understand that you have had news of my father's doings lately. Is the old man well?"

"Ay, King Hudibras is well, and as fond of fighting as ever, besides being well able for it. I am not sure that he would be pleased if he heard you call him the 'old man.'"

"Indeed? Yet nearly fifty winters have passed over his head, and that is somewhat old for a warrior. And my mother and sister—have you heard of them?"

"Excellently well, I believe. At least, so I have been told by the Hebrew merchant who came over sea with one of the Phoenician ships, and wanders over the whole land with his pack of golden ornaments—which so take the fancy of the women, indeed of the men also. How the fellow escapes being robbed on his journeys is more than I can tell. It is said that he travels by night and sleeps in caves during the day. Some people even think that he is in league with evil spirits. I doubt that; but he told me the other day, when I met him on our side of the channel, that your sister is about to be married to a neighbouring chief—I forget his name—Gunrig, I think—with whom your father wishes to be on friendly terms."

"Married!" exclaimed Bladud, with a troubled look.

"Ay, and it is said she does not like the match."

"Does my mother approve of it?"

"I think not, though the Hebrew did not seem to feel quite sure on that point. But your father seems resolved on it, and you know he is not easily turned from his purpose when determined to have his way. He is more difficult to move than a woman in that matter."

"Come, friend," said Bladud gravely, "don't be too free in your remarks on my father."

"And don't be too hard on the women-folk," added the captain, with a grim smile, "they are not all alike. At least there is one that I know of in the East, whose spirit is like that of the lamb, and her voice like the notes of the songbird."

Maikar looked as if he were on the point of adding something to the conversation, but his thoughts seemed too deep for utterance, for he only sighed.

R. M. Ballantyne

"Land us in yon creek," said Bladud promptly. "It seems that I have not returned home a moment too soon. There, under the cliff—so."

The skiff ran alongside of a ledge of rock as he spoke, and next moment the prince leaped upon the shores of his native land.

With a brief farewell to his old playmate, he turned, led his companions up the neighbouring cliff, and, plunging into the forest, set off at a pace which betrayed the urgency of his desire to reach home.

Although they travelled almost night and day, it took them the better part of two weeks to reach the river, on the banks of which King Hudibras' chief town was built. They arrived at the eastern bank without mishap, and found that people were crowding over from the western side to attend some display or fete which was obviously going on there. Mingling with the crowd they went to the river's edge, where numerous wooden canoes and coracles were busily engaged in ferrying the people over.

Approaching a man, whose apparel betokened him one of the poorer class, Bladud addressed him—

"Can you tell me, friend, what is going on here to-day?"

"Truly you must be a stranger if you know not, for every one—far and near—has heard of the wedding of our king's pretty daughter."

"Is she, then, married?" asked the prince, scarcely able to conceal his anxiety.

"Not yet, but she is to be married to-morrow—if no

champion comes to claim her."

"How? What mean you?"

"I mean what I say. Gunrig, the great chief whom she is to wed, is a proud and a stout man. Many chiefs have been courting the fair princess, and, in his pride of heart and strength, Gunrig has challenged any one to fight him in single combat, promising that the bride shall be given to the conqueror."

"And does my—does the king agree to such a base proposal?"

"Well, he objected to it at first, but Gunrig is such a dangerous enemy, and his tribe so powerful, that the king has given in at last. Besides, he knows that the chief is so strong and big, and so well able to use his weapons, that none of the other chiefs are likely to venture a trial with him, or, if they do, they are sure to get the worst of it."

"You don't seem to like this Gunrig, I think."

"No. I hate him. Everybody hates him; he is such a proud brute, but what can *we* do? when the king commands, all must obey. If I was as big and stout as you are," added the man with a steady gaze at the prince, "I'd go at this fellow and win the fair princess myself."

"Perchance I may have a try," returned Bladud with a light laugh. "Does the princess hate him? and the queen?"

"Ay, worse than poison."

"Come, let us go and see the sport," said the prince to his companions, as he hurried away from the river. "You know our language well enough, I think, captain, to understand what has been said?"

"Ay, the most of it; and there is no doubt you are much wanted at this feast."

In a few minutes our travellers arrived at the suburbs of the little town, which was embosomed among trees and green fields.

As hundreds of people had come in from all the country round, and some of them were Phoenician mariners from ships then in port, our three adventurers might not have attracted much attention, had it not been for the towering height, stalwart frame, and noble bearing of Bladud. As it was, people commented on them, bestowing looks of admiration particularly on the prince, but they did not address or molest them in any way—supposing, of course, that they had come from a distance to see the show; though many wondered that such a strapping fellow as the tall one could have come to the land without having been heard of.

"Perhaps he has only just arrived in one of the ships," was the sagacious remark of one.

"But the ships have been here a long time, and we have seen all their crews," was the comment of another.

On arriving at the scene of festivities, they found that an immense assemblage encircled the arena, in which a number of young men were competing in athletic sports. The captain and Maikar gently elbowed their way to the front, where they could see what was going on.

"I will remain in the back row where I can see well enough," said Bladud. "Keep a look-out for me when you feel lost. I don't mean to make myself known just yet."

CHAPTER TEN

THE SPORTS

At the further end of the ground enclosed for the sports, a slightly raised platform had been prepared for the king and his household. The royal party ascended it soon after the travellers arrived, but the distance was too great to permit of faces being distinguished. Bladud could easily perceive, however, the tall form of his father, and the graceful figure of his mother, as they took their places, closely followed by the chief warriors. These, however, did not bring their women—that privilege being reserved for the household of the king only. Close behind the king and queen walked the young Princess Hafrydda. She was not only graceful, but beautiful, being very fair like her mother, with light-blue eyes like those of her brother Bladud; she had peach-bloom cheeks, and a brow of snow, save where her cap failed to protect it from the sun.

After the princess, and shrinking behind her as if to escape the gaze of the courtiers, or rather warriors, who crowded the platform, came a girl of about nineteen summers, the companion of Hafrydda. Branwen was a complete contrast to her friend in complexion. She was the daughter of a famous northern chief, and was quite as beautiful as the princess, while her jet-black eyes and curly brown hair gave more of

R. M. Ballantyne

force and character to features which were delicately moulded.

There was reason for poor Branwen's desire to escape observation, for the proud Gunrig was paying her attentions which were far too pointed and familiar in one who was about to marry the king's daughter. Indeed, it was whispered that he had changed his mind since he had seen Branwen, and would have even resigned the princess in her favour, if he had dared to offer such an affront to the king.

Hudibras himself was the last to ascend the platform. He was a fine-looking, portly man, with a great shock of black hair, a long beard, and limbs so well proportioned that he did not seem taller than other men until he stood beside them. He was a worthy sire of such a son as Bladud, though three inches shorter.

There was a sort of barbaric splendour in the costumes of both men and women, combined with some degree of graceful simplicity. The king was clothed in a softly-dressed deer-skin jacket, over which he wore a wolf-skin with the hair outside. A tunic of purple cotton, brought by Phoenician ships from the far East, covered him as far down as the knees, which were bare, while his lower limbs were swathed in strips of scarlet cloth. Leather sandals, resembling those made by Bladud while in Gaul, protected his feet. No crown or other token of royalty rested on his brow, but over his dark and grizzled locks he wore a species of leather skull-cap which, being exceeding tough, served the purpose of a helmet. On his breast was a profusion of ornaments in the form of beads and bosses of gold and tin, the former of which had been brought from the East, the latter from the mines of his native land. A bronze sword with an ivory sheath, inlaid with gold, hung at his left side, and a knife of the same material at his right. Altogether King Hudibras, being broad and strong in proportion to his height, presented a very regal appearance indeed, and bore himself with becoming dignity. He had married the daughter of a Norse Jarl; and his two children, Bladud and Hafrydda, had taken after their gentle mother in complexion and disposition, though they were not altogether destitute of a sub-current of their father's passionate nature.

The nobles, or rather warriors—for ability to fight constituted nobility in those days—were clothed in garments which, with sundry modifications, resembled those of the king. As for the women of the court, their costumes were what may be styled flowing, and therefore graceful, though difficult to describe. Like their lords, they were profusely ornamented with precious metals and bands and loops of coloured cloth. Hafrydda and her companion Branwen allowed their hair to fall, after the manner of the times, in unrestrained freedom over their shoulders—that of the former resembling a cataract of rippling gold, while that of the latter was a wavy mass of auburn. Both girls wore wild flowers among their tresses. Of course the queen had rolled up her slightly grey hair in the simple knot at the back of the head, which is more becoming to age, and she wore no ornament of any kind on her head.

Public games are pretty much the same in all lands, and have probably been similar in all times. We shall not weary the reader by describing minutely all that went on. There was racing, of course, and jumping both with and without a run, as well as over a willow-wand held high. There was also throwing the heavy stone, but the method pursued in this feat was not in accordance with modern practice, inasmuch as the competitor turned his back to the direction in which the stone was to be thrown, heeled instead of toed the line, seized the stone with both hands and hurled it backwards over his head.

R. M. Ballantyne

As the games proceeded it was evident that the concourse became much excited and deeply interested in the efforts of the various competitors—the king and his court not less so than the people.

After the conclusion of one of the races, Captain Arkal left the front row, and pushing his way towards Bladud, whispered—

"It seems to me that you could easily beat the winner of that race, smart though he be. What say you? Will you try?"

"I fear being discovered by my father if I go so prominently before him, and I wish to announce myself in private."

"Pooh! discovery is impossible! Have you not told me that you were a smooth-chinned boy, and not grown to near your present height when you left home? How can they ever recognise one who returns a sunburnt giant, with a beard that covers half his face?"

"Perhaps you are right," returned the prince, looking as if uncertain how to act; but the advice of little Maikar corresponding with that of the captain decided him.

In those primitive times the rules and ceremonies connected with games were few and simple. "Entries" were not arranged beforehand; men came and went, and competed or refrained, as they pleased, though, of course, there were a few well-known greyhound-like men and athletes who competed more or less in all games of the various districts around, and whose superlative powers prevented other ambitious men from becoming too numerous. These were, we may say, the "professionals" of the time.

No special costumes were worn. Each man, as he stepped to

the front, divested himself of wolf-skin, deer-skin, boar-skin, or cat-skin mantle, and, perchance, also of his upper coat, and stood forth in attire sufficiently light and simple to leave his limbs unhampered.

A long race—ten times round the course—was about to come off, and the men were being placed by the judges, when Bladud pushed through the crowd and made his way to the starting-point. There was a murmur of admiration as his tall and graceful figure was seen to join the group of competitors in front of the royal stand. He gave the Greek letter Omicron as his name, and no further questions were asked him. Divesting himself of the rug or mantle, which he wore thrown over one shoulder after the manner of a plaid, he stood forth in the thin loose tunic which formed his only garment, and tightened his belt as he toed the line.

It was with a feeling of satisfaction that he observed several of the king's warriors among the runners, and one of these was Gunrig. Being an agile as well as a stout man, he did not consider it beneath his dignity to join in the sports.

The king himself gave the signal to start. He descended from his stand for the purpose, and Bladud was greatly pleased to find that though he looked at him he evidently failed to recognise him.

At the signal, about twenty powerful fellows—mostly young, though some were in the prime of life—started out at full speed for a short distance, as if to test each other; then they began to slow, so as not to break their wind by over-exertion at the beginning. Bladud felt at once that he was more than a match for the best of them, unless any one should turn out to have been concealing his powers. He therefore placed himself alongside of Gunrig, and kept at his elbow about half a foot behind him the first two rounds of the course.

R. M. Ballantyne

At first Gunrig took no notice of this, but when he perceived that the tall stranger continued to keep the same position, he held back a little, intending to reverse the position for a time. But Bladud also held back and frustrated his intention. Exasperated by this, Gunrig put on what we in these times call a "spurt," and went ahead at a pace which, in a few seconds, left most of the runners a good way behind. This was received by the spectators with a cheer, in which surprise was fully as prominent as satisfaction, for although they knew that the chief was celebrated for his speed of foot, few of them had actually seen him run before that day, and it at once became evident that if his endurance was equal to his speed, it would go hard with his competitors.

Bladud was left behind a few yards, but, without making a spurt, he lengthened his stride a little, and in a moment or two had resumed his former position at his rival's elbow.

A wild cheer of delight ensued, for now it was recognised that in all probability the race would lie between these two. As, however, all this occurred in the third round of the course, and all the other runners seemed to be doing their work with steady resolution, there was still the possibility of one or more of them proving themselves, by endurance perhaps, more than a match for the swift-footed. The excitement, therefore, became intense, and, as round after round of the course was completed the relative position of the various men changed considerably.

At the seventh round some, who had been husbanding their strength, let out, and, passing others with great ease, came close upon the heels of Gunrig and Bladud. This was, of course, a signal for enthusiastic cheering. Others of the runners, feeling that their chance of taking a respectable place was hopeless, dropped out of the race altogether and were cheered vociferously as they retired.

At last, in the eighth round, it became practically, as had been anticipated, a race between the leading two, for they were far ahead of all the others by that time, but occupied exactly the same relative position as before. Gunrig became so exasperated at this, that on commencing the ninth round, he made a sudden effort which carried him five or six yards ahead of his rival.

The spectators could not avoid cheering him at this, but the cheer was feeble.

"The tall man is losing wind," cried one in a disappointed tone.

"I feared his legs were too long," observed another. Most of the people, however, looked on in anxious silence.

"I did not think he would give in so easily," murmured little Maikar regretfully.

"He has not given in yet," returned the captain, with a satisfied nod. "See—he pulls up!"

This was true. To the unbounded surprise of the spectators, Bladud had actually stopped a moment to tighten his belt at the beginning of the tenth round. Then, to their still greater amazement, he put on what we may call an Olympic spurt, so that he overtook his rival in less than a quarter of a minute; passed him easily, ran over the rest of the course at a rate which had not been equalled since Old Albion was created, and passed the winning-post full five hundred yards in advance of Gunrig, amid yells of delight and roars of laughter, which continued for some time—bursting forth again and again as the novelty and surprise of the thing became more and more forced home to the spectators' minds.

R. M. Ballantyne

"You have met more than your match to-day, Gunrig," remarked the king, with a laugh, as the defeated man strode angrily up to the platform.

"I have met foul play," replied the chief angrily. "He pretended that he could not run, else would I have put on more force. But it matters not. I will have another opportunity of trying him. Meanwhile, there is yet the heavy stone to throw. How now, wench?" he added, turning fiercely on Branwen, who had nearly hidden her face in her shawl, "do you try to hide that you are laughing at me?"

Poor Branwen was in anything but a laughing mood. She was too much afraid of the fiery chief for that, and had merely covered her face, as a modern beauty might drop her veil, to avoid his gaze.

The fair-haired Hafrydda, however, was not so timid, her smile was evidently one of amusement at his defeat, which angered him all the more.

"Gunrig," said the king, drawing himself up, and speaking impressively, "remember that you are my guest, and that it ill becomes you to insult my women before my face."

"Pardon me," replied the chief, with an effort to recover himself. "You must remember that I am not accustomed to defeat."

"True," returned the king blandly, "so now you had better take to the heavy stone and come off the victor."

Gunrig at once went down into the arena and sent a challenge to Bladud.

The latter had returned to his place among the spectators, but his height rendered him easy to find. He accepted the challenge at once, and, as no other competitor for the heavy stone offered, the two had it all to themselves. This was no matter of wonder, for the heaviest stone among those laid out for trial was of a weight that many of the young men or warriors could barely lift, while the stoutest of them could not have thrown it more than a few feet.

Boiling over as he was with indignation, Gunrig felt as if he was endued with more than usual strength. He lifted the stone with ease, faced the platform, heeled the line, and hurled the stone violently over his head, so that it fell with a heavy thud far behind him. Then Bladud took it up.

"Oh! what a stout man he is!" whispered Branwen to Hafrydda, "and what a handsome face!"

"That is true; and I hope he will win," replied the princess.

"Hush! child, the king will be displeased if he hears you," said her mother earnestly. "What ever you think, keep silence."

The queen spoke with such unwonted energy that Hafrydda was surprised, but her thoughts were instantly diverted to Bladud, who made a magnificent cast and sent the stone a yard further than his opponent. But Gunrig seized it again and hurled it a foot beyond that.

"Well done," said the king. "Go on. It is the best in three heaves that wins."

Bladud grasped the stone and hurled it back over his head with all his force. Up and up it went as if it had resolved to become an aerolite and visit the moon! Then down it came with a mighty thud ten yards beyond Gunrig's mark.

Once more the air rang with the enthusiastic plaudits of the multitude, while the king ordered the victor to approach the stand.

Bladud did so with some trepidation, for now he knew that he would have to speak, and feared that though his appearance had not betrayed him, his voice would probably do so.

CHAPTER ELEVEN

A NOTABLE DUEL FOLLOWED BY
CHANGES AND PLOTS

Every eye was riveted with admiration and curiosity on the young stranger as he approached.

"You have acquitted yourself well, young man," said the king, "and it becomes us to invite you to our palace and to ask if we can serve you in any way."

Bladud had a deep voice, and, by way of increasing his chances of concealing his identity, he pitched it a note or two lower than usual as he replied.

"I thank you, sir, for your hospitality and gladly accept it. As to your offer to serve me, I would count it a favour if you will permit me to enter into combat with one of your friends."

"Indeed!" exclaimed the king, in great surprise, "that is a strange request, but I may not deny you. Which of my warriors may it be?"

"It is none of your warriors, sir," answered Bladud, "but one of your guests who has, I am told, challenged whoever will to fight him for the hand of your fair daughter. I am here now to accept that challenge and to fight with Gunrig if he will."

"Assuredly, young man, your ambition or presumption seems equal to your prowess," returned the king with an offended look; "know ye not that this challenge was delivered to chiefs of this country, not to unknown strangers, and although I admit that your tongue seems well accustomed to our language, it has a foreign smack about it which does not belong to those who are home-bred."

"I am a chief," answered Bladud, proudly, "and this is my native land."

"What is your name, then, and where come ye from?" demanded the king.

"That I may not answer just now, but I am here, in your power, if what I say be not found true, you may do what you will with me. Meanwhile I ask permission to accept the challenge."

At this point Gunrig, unable to restrain himself longer, sprang forward.

"Grant him permission, king," he cried. "If I were not ready to abide by my word I were not worth my salt. Nay, indeed, whether you grant him permission or not I will fight him, for he has twice beaten me this day, and now insults me, therefore there is a deadly feud between us."

"You were always a hot-head, Gunrig," replied the king, with a grim smile. "But have your way. Only it does not follow that if you lose the day I will give my child to the conqueror."

"Be that as you choose," said Gunrig, "I am now ready."

As he spoke the fiery chief grasped his shield, leaped down into the arena and drew his sword.

Bladud was not slow to follow. In those days action usually followed close on the heels of purpose, and as the laws of chivalry had not yet been formulated there was no braying of trumpets or tedious ceremonial to delay the combat.

"Oh! I do hope he will conquer," whispered the Princess Hafrydda to her dark-eyed companion, "and save me from that horrid man."

"I hope so too," returned Branwen, in a subdued voice, "but—"

She stopped abruptly, and a blush deepened the rich colour of her cheek, which she sought to conceal by drawing her shawl still closer over it. This was needless, for the clash of swords at the moment, as the combatants met in deadly conflict, claimed the exclusive attention of the damsels, and caused the entire concourse to press close around the barricades with eager interest.

"A strange way to mark his home-coming," muttered Captain Arkal, thrusting himself as near to the scene of action as possible, closely followed by Maikar, who, being little, kept easily in his wake.

"He knows well what he's about," returned the little man, whose admiration for Bladud was great, and his belief in him unbounded.

Maikar was one of those men—of whom there are no doubt thousands—who powerfully appreciate, almost venerate, and always recognise, the spirit of justice when displayed by their fellows, although they may not always be aware of the fact that they do recognise it—hence his belief in the prince.

"A good day for the land if that long-legged fellow slays him," remarked one of the crowd.

"That's true," said another.

Indeed, this seemed to be the opinion of most of the spectators; there was also a general expression of confidence that the stranger was sure to be victorious, but some objectors—of whom there are, and necessarily must be a considerable number in the world—held that Gunrig was a stout man to tackle, and it was not always length of limb that gained the day.

Such comments, however, were not numerous, for the concourse soon became too deeply absorbed to indulge in speech.

The fight that now ensued gave some weight to the objectors' views.

At first the combatants rushed at each other with the ferocity of men who mean to settle a dispute by instant and mutual destruction, and there was a sort of gasp of excited surprise among the people as the two swords fell at the same moment with something like a thunderclap on the respective shields. Feeling that neither could overcome the other by the might of a resistless blow, each, after one or two rapid cuts, thrusts, and guards, ascertained that his adversary was so nearly his match as to render great care needful. They retired a few paces, and then advancing, settled down to their work, point to point and foot to foot.

Gunrig, although inferior in stature to the prince, was about equal to him in strength and weight, and, being a trained warrior in the prime of life, was possessed of a sturdy endurance which, to some extent, made up for the other's superior agility. In other respects they seemed well matched, for each was highly trained and expert in the use of his weapons.

After a second onset, somewhat similar to the first, and with much the same result, the two went at each other with cut and thrust so rapidly that it was almost impossible to distinguish their swords as they flashed like gleaming flames in the sunshine.

Suddenly Gunrig drew back, and, springing at the prince with uplifted weapon, as if to cut him down, changed the attack into a quick thrust which, passing under the youth's uplifted shield, went straight to his breast. But the quick eye of Bladud detected the intention in time. Leaping lightly backward, he caused the thrust to come short; at the same time he returned with a quick thrust at the chief's right shoulder which took effect slightly. Giving him no time to recover, he made a sweeping cut at Gunrig's neck, which, had it fallen, would have shorn his head from his shoulders, but the chief, instead of guarding it, suddenly stooped, and, as the sword passed whistling above him, returned with a thrust so fierce that it pierced right through the thick shield opposed to it.

Here was an opportunity of which Bladud was not slow to avail himself. Although the arm which held it was slightly wounded, he gave the shield a violent and sudden twist, which not only held the weapon fast but nearly wrenched it out of the chief's hand. An ordinary sword would have been snapped, but Gunrig's weapon was a big bronze one that had done service in many a fray, and its owner's hand was strong.

R. M. Ballantyne

He held it fast, but before he could withdraw it and recover himself Bladud cut him fair over the head. Whether it was accident or design no one could tell, but the flat instead of the edge of his sword descended on the headpiece, and the blow which should otherwise have cleft his adversary to the chin only stretched him insensible on the field.

A great sigh of relief, mingled with wild cheers of satisfaction, greeted this effective termination of the fight, and the king was evidently not ill-pleased.

"Pick him up, some of you," he said, pointing to the prostrate Gunrig, "and carry him to the palace. See that he is well cared for. Go, Branwen, and see that everything is properly done for him."

Branwen at once left the stand, and the king, descending into the arena, proceeded to congratulate the victor.

Before he could do so, however, to his unbounded surprise, the queen also descended with her daughter and threw her arms round the prince's neck, while Hafrydda seized his hand and covered it with kisses.

"Body of me! am I dreaming?" cried the king, after a few moments of speechless amazement.

"Oh! Bladud," exclaimed the queen, looking up in his smiling face, "did you really think you could deceive your own mother? Fie, fie, I would have recognised you if you had come with your face painted black."

By this time the king had recovered, and realised the fact that his long-lost son had returned home. He strode towards him, and, grasping his hand, essayed to speak, but something in his throat rendered speech impossible. King Hudibras was a stern man, however, and scorned to show womanly weakness before his people. He turned suddenly round, kicked a few courtiers out of his way, remounted the platform, and, in a loud voice, announced the conclusion of the sports.

Great was the rejoicing among the people assembled there, when the news spread that the long-lost Prince Bladud had returned home, and that the tall youth who had defeated Gunrig was he, and they cheered him with even more zest and energy than they had at the moment of his victory.

Meanwhile Gunrig, having been conveyed to the residence of the king, was laid on a couch. The palace was, we need scarcely say, very unlike our modern palaces, being merely a large hut or rude shanty of logs, surrounded by hundreds of similar but smaller huts, which composed this primitive town. The couch on which the chief lay was composed of brushwood and leaves. But Gunrig did not lie long upon it. He was a tough man, as well as a stout, and he had almost recovered consciousness when the princess, returning from the games, arrived to assist her friend in attending to the king's commands.

She found Branwen about to enter the chamber, in which the chief lay, with a bandage.

"Hast heard the news?" she asked, with a gladsome smile.

"Not I," replied Branwen, in a rather sharp tone.

"Whatever it is, it seems to have made you happy."

"Truly it has. But let us go in with the bandages first. The news is too good to be told in a hurry."

R. M. Ballantyne

The sound of their voices as they entered aroused Gunrig completely, and he rose up as they approached.

"My father sent us," said the princess in some confusion, "to see that you are well cared for. Your wounds, I hope, are not dangerous?"

"Dangerous, no; and they will not prevent me from speedily avenging myself on the young upstart who has appeared so suddenly to claim you for a bride. Stay, you need not go so quickly, or toss your head in pride. I will stand by my word, and let him keep who wins. But I have a word to say to you, Branwen. Come along with me."

Wooers among the ancient Albionites were not, it would seem, celebrated for politeness—some of them, at least! The chief seized the shrinking girl by the wrist as he spoke, and led her out of the house and into a neighbouring thicket, where he bade her sit down on a fallen tree.

"Now," he said, sitting down beside her, and putting his arm round her waist, despite her objections, "this young turkey-cock has fairly won Hafrydda, and he is welcome to her for all that I care—that is, if he lives to claim her hand after our next meeting, for, since I've seen your pretty face, Branwen, I would rather wed you than the fairest lass that ever owned to Norland blood. What say you to take the princess's place and become my wife?"

"Oh! no, no," exclaimed Branwen, in great distress, trying to disengage his arm, "you love Hafrydda, and it is impossible that you can love us both! Let me go."

"I'm not so sure that I ever really cared for the princess," replied the chief; "but of this I am quite sure, that I never loved her half as much as I love you, Branwen."

The girl tore herself away from him, and, standing up with flushed face and flashing eyes, exclaimed—

"Shame would crush you, if you were a brave man, for uttering such a speech. But you are *not* brave; you are a coward, and your late opponent will teach you that. Be sure that I will never consent to wed one who is a disgrace to manhood."

A fierce scowl crossed Gunrig's swarthy countenance, but it passed in a moment, and a look of admiration replaced it as he looked up with a smile.

"I like maids with your temper," he said, still keeping his seat, "but you forget that if the king so wills it, you shall be compelled to accept me, and I think the king will scarce dare to thwart my wishes, especially now that another man has a right to the princess."

"I defy you," returned the girl, still at a white heat of indignation, "and if the king tries to force me to wed you, I will defy him too! The young stranger will be my champion— or, if he should refuse, there are other ways by which a helpless girl may escape from tyrants."

She turned with these words and fled. Gunrig sprang up to pursue, but, fortunately for the girl, a modest bramble, that scarce ventured to raise its branches above the ground, caught his foot and sent him headlong into a rotten stump, which seemed only too ready to receive him. Extracting his head from its embrace, he stood up in a bewildered frame of mind, found that the light-footed Branwen had escaped him, and sat down again on the fallen tree to recover his equanimity.

Meanwhile the poor girl ran back to the palace, rushed into

R. M. Ballantyne

Hafrydda's room, threw herself on a couch, and burst into tears.

This was such an unwonted exhibition of weakness in Branwen that the princess stood looking at her for a few moments in silent surprise. Then she sought to comfort her, and made her relate, bit by bit, with many a sob between, what had occurred.

"But why do you cry so bitterly?" asked Hafrydda. "It is so unlike you to give way to despair. Besides, you defied him, you say, and you were right to do so, for my dear father will never force you to wed against your wishes."

"I know better," returned the other, with some bitterness. "Did he not intend to make *you* wed against your wishes?"

"That is true," replied the gentle Hafrydda, with a sigh. "But I am saved from that now," she added, brightening up suddenly, "and that reminds me of the good news. Do you know who the handsome youth is who rescued me from this monster?"

"No, I don't; and I'm sure I don't care," answered Branwen, with a touch of petulance. "At all events, I suppose you will be glad of the change of husbands."

"He will never be my husband," returned the princess, somewhat amused by her friend's tone, for she suspected the cause. "He is my brother Bladud—my long-lost brother!"

The change that came over Branwen's pretty face on hearing this was remarkable.

"Your brother!" she exclaimed. "No wonder that he is beautiful, as well as brave!"

A merry laugh broke from the princess as she kissed her friend. "Well, but," she said, "what will you do? You know that always, when I have been perplexed or in trouble, I have come to you for help and advice. Now that things are turned the other way, I know not what advice to give you."

"I have settled what to do," answered Branwen, drying her eyes, and looking up with the air of one whose mind has been suddenly and firmly made up. "Your father, I know, will consent to Gunrig's wishes. If he did not, there would be war again—horrible war—between the tribes. I will never be the cause of that if I can help it. At the same time, it would kill me to wed with Gunrig. I would rather die than that; therefore—I will run away."

"And leave me?" exclaimed the princess anxiously.

"Well, I should have to leave you, at any rate, if I stay and am compelled to marry Gunrig."

"But where will you run to?"

"That I will not tell, lest you should be tempted to tell lies to your father. Just be content to know that I shall not be far away, and that in good time you shall hear from me. Farewell, dear Hafrydda, I dare not stay, for that—that monster will not be long in hatching and carrying out some vile plot—farewell."

CHAPTER TWELVE

PLOTS AND PLANS

About three miles beyond the outskirts of King Hudibras' town—the name of which has now, like many other things, been lost in the proverbial mists of antiquity—an old man dwelt in a sequestered part of the forest. His residence was a dry cave at the foot of a cliff, or, rather, a rude hut which, resting against the cliff, absorbed the cave, so to speak, into its rear premises.

The old man had a somewhat aquiline nose, a long white beard, and a grave, but kindly, expression of countenance. He was one of the sons of Israel—at that time *not* a despised race. Although aged he was neither bowed nor weak, but bore himself with the uprightness and vigour of a man in his prime. When at home, this man seemed to occupy his time chiefly in gathering firewood, cooking food, sleeping, and reading in a small roll of Egyptian papyrus which he carried constantly in his bosom.

He was well known, far and near, as Beniah the merchant, who trafficked with the Phoenician shipmen; was a sort of go-between with them and the surrounding tribes, and carried his wares from place to place far and wide through the land. He was possessed of a wonderful amount of curious knowledge, and, although he spoke little, he contrived in the little he said to make a favourable impression on men and women. Being obliging as well as kind, and also exceedingly useful, people not only respected Beniah, but treated him as a sort of semi-sacred being who was not to be interfered with in any way. Even robbers—of whom there were not a few in those days—respected the Hebrew's property; passed by his hut with looks of solemnity, if not of awe, and allowed him to come and go unchallenged.

Most people liked Beniah. A few feared him, and a still smaller number—cynics, who have existed since the days of Adam—held him to be in league with evil spirits. He was a tall, stalwart man, and carried a staff of oak about six feet long, as a support during his travels. It had somehow come to be understood that, although Beniah was pre-eminently a man of peace, it was nevertheless advisable to treat him with civility or to keep well out of the range of that oaken staff. Possibly this opinion may have been founded on the fact that, on one occasion, three big runaway Phoenician seamen, who thought they would prefer a life in the woods to a life on the ocean wave, had one evening been directed to Beniah's hut as a place where strangers were never refused hospitality when they asked it with civility. As those three seamen made their appearance in the town that same evening, in a very sulky state of mind, with three broken heads, it was conjectured that they had omitted the civility—either on purpose or by accident. Be this as it may, Beniah and his six-foot staff had become objects of profound respect.

Evening was drawing on and Beniah was sitting on a stool beside his open door, enjoying the sunshine that penetrated his umbrageous retreat, and reading the papyrus scroll already referred to, when the figure of a woman approached him with timid, hesitating steps. At first the Hebrew did not observe her, but, as she drew nearer, the crackling of branches under her light footsteps aroused him. He looked up quickly, and the woman, running forward, stood before him with clasped hands.

"Oh! sir," she exclaimed, "have pity on me! I come to claim your protection."

"Such protection as you need and I can give you shall have, my daughter; but it is a strange request to make of such a man, in such a place, and at such a time. Moreover, your voice is not quite strange to me," added the old man with a perplexed look. "Surely I have heard it before?"

"Ay, Beniah, you know my voice and have seen my face," said the woman, suddenly removing her shawl and revealing to the astonished eyes of the old man the pretty head and face of Branwen with her wealth of curling auburn hair.

"Child," exclaimed the Hebrew, rising and letting fall his roll, while he took her hand in both of his, "what folly have you been guilty of, for surely nothing but folly could move you thus to forsake the house of your friends?"

"Ay, father, you say truth," returned the girl, her courage returning as she noted the kindly tone of the old man's voice. "Folly is indeed the cause of it, but it is the folly of man, not of women."

Branwen then gave him a detailed account of the duel between Bladud and Gunrig, as well as of the subsequent proceedings of the latter, with regard to herself.

The face of the old man elongated as she proceeded with her narration, and as it was long by nature—the face, not the narration—its appearance when she had concluded was solemnising in the extreme.

"Assuredly you are right, my child, for it is amazing folly in such a man as Gunrig to suppose he is a fitting mate for you,—though it is no folly in him to wish to get you for a wife,—and it is no folly in you to flee from such an undesirable union. But how to help you in this matter is more difficult to conceive than anything that has puzzled my brain since the day I left Tyre."

"Can you not conceal me here till we have time to think what is best to be done?" asked Branwen simply, "for I will die rather than wed this—this monster Gunrig!"

The Hebrew smiled pitifully, for he saw in the maiden's face and bearing evidence of a brave, resolute spirit, which would not condescend to boasting, and had no thought of using exaggerated language.

"Truly I will conceal you—for a time. But I cannot leave you here alone when I go on my wanderings. Besides, the king will send out his hunters all over the land—men who are trained to note the slightest track of bear, deer, and wolf, and they will find it easy work to discover your little footprints. No doubt, near the town, and even here where many wanderers come and go, they will fail to pick up the trail, but if you venture into the lonely woods the footmarks will certainly betray you, and if I go with you, my doom will be fixed, for my big sandal is as well known to the king's hunters as the big nose on my face, or the white beard on my chin."

Poor Branwen became, and looked, very miserable on hearing this, for the idea of hunters and footprints had not once occurred to her.

"Oh what, then, is to be done?" she asked with a helpless yet eager look.

For some time the old man sat in silence, with closed eyes as if in meditation. Then he said, with a sad smile, that he supposed there was nothing for it but to reveal one of his secrets to her.

"I have not many secrets, Branwen," he said, "but the one which I am about to reveal to you is important. To make it known would be the ruin of me. Yet I feel that I may trust you, for surely you are a good girl."

"No, I'm *not*," cried Branwen, with a look of firmness, yet of transparent honesty, that amused her companion greatly; "at least," she continued in a quieter tone, "I don't *feel* good, and the queen often tells me that I am *very* naughty, though I sometimes think she doesn't mean it. But when I think of that—that monster and his insult to my dear Hafrydda, and his impudence in wanting me. Oh! I could tear him limb from limb, and put the bits in the fire so that they could never come together again!"

"My dear child," returned Beniah remonstratively, while she paused with flashing eyes and parted lips, as though she had not yet given vent to half her wrath, "whatever other folk may say or think of you, you are good enough in my esteem, but it is wrong to give way thus to wrath. Come, I will reveal my little secret, and it behoves us to be quick, for they will soon miss you and send the hunters on your track."

As he spoke the Hebrew led the refugee through his hut and into the cave beyond, the darkness at the further end of which was so great, that it would have been impossible to see but for a stone lamp which stood in a recess in the wall. This revealed the fact that the place was used as a kitchen.

"That is my chimney," said Beniah, taking up the lamp and holding it so that a large natural hole or crack could be seen overhead, it formed an outlet to the forest above—though the opening was beyond the reach of vision. The same crack extended below in the form of a yawning chasm, five or six feet wide. There seemed to be nothing on the other side of this chasm except the wall of the cliffs; but on closer inspection, a narrow ledge was seen with a small recess beyond. Across the chasm lay a plank which rested on the ledge.

"This is my secret—at least part of it," said the Hebrew, pointing to the plank which bridged the chasm. "Give me your hand; we must cross it."

Branwen possessed a steady as well as a pretty head. Placing her hand unhesitatingly in that of her guide, she quickly stood on the ledge, close to a short narrow passage, by which they reached a smaller cave or natural chamber in the solid rock. Here, to the girl's intense surprise, she found herself surrounded by objects, many of which she had never seen before, while others were familiar enough. Against the wall were piled webs of cloth of brilliant colours, and garments of various kinds. In one corner was a heap of bronze and iron weapons, shields and other pieces of Eastern armour, while in a recess lay piled in a confused heap many Phoenician ornaments of gold, silver, and bronze, similar to those which were worn by the warriors and chief men of King Hudibras' court. It was, in fact, the stock in trade of the Hebrew—the fount at which he replenished his travelling pack; a pack which was a great mystery to most of his friends, for, however much they might purchase out of it, there seemed to be no end to its inexhaustible power of reproduction.

"Here," said Beniah, amused at the girl's gaze of astonishment, "ye will be safe from all your foes till a Higher Power directs us what shall be done with you, for, to say truth, at this moment my mind is a blank. However, our present duty is not action but concealment. Water and dried fruit you will find in this corner. Keep quiet. Let not curiosity tempt you to examine these things—they might fall and cause noise that would betray us. When danger is past, I will come again. Meanwhile, observe now what I am about to do, and try to imitate me."

He returned to the entrance, and, taking up the plank-bridge, drew it into the passage, guiding its outer end on a slight branch, which seemed to have fallen across the chasm accidentally, but which in reality had been placed there for this purpose. Then, sliding it out again, he refixed it in position.

"Is that too hard for you? Try."

Branwen obeyed, and succeeded so well, that old Beniah commended her on her aptitude to learn.

"Now be careful," he added, when about to re-cross the bridge. "Your life may depend on your attention to my instructions."

"But what if I should let the plank slip?" said she in sudden anxiety.

"There is another in the cave on the floor. Besides, I have two or three planks in the forest ready against such a mishap. Fear not, but commit yourself to the All-seeing One."

He crossed over alone, leaving the girl on the other side, and waited till she had withdrawn the bridge, when he returned to the mouth of the outer cave, and sat down to continue the perusal of his roll. Branwen meanwhile returned to the inner cave, or store, and sat down to meditate on thoughts which had been awakened by the Hebrew's reference to the All-seeing One. She wondered if there was an All-seeing One at all, and, if there was, did He see all the wickedness that was done by men—ay, and even by women! and did He see the thoughts of her mind and the feelings of her heart?

It will be gathered from this, that the maiden was considerably in advance of the uncivilised age in which she lived, for the ancient inhabitants of Albion were not addicted to the study of theology, either natural or speculative.

"If I but knew of such an All-seeing One," she murmured, "I would ask Him to help me."

Raising her eyes as she spoke, she observed the goods piled round the walls, and the light of the lamp—which had been left with her—glittered on the trinkets opposite. This was too much for her. It must be remembered that, besides living in a barbarous age, she was an untutored maiden, and possessed of a large share of that love for "pretty things," which is—rightly or wrongly—believed to be a peculiar characteristic of the fair sex. Theology, speculative and otherwise, vanished, she leaped up and, forgetting her host's warning, began to inspect the goods.

At first conscience—for she had an active little one—remonstrated.

"But," she replied, silently, with a very natural tendency to self-justification, "although Beniah told me not to touch things, I did not *promise* not to do so?"

"True, but your silence was equivalent to a promise," said something within her.

"No, it wasn't," she replied aloud.

"Yes, it was," retorted the something within her in a tone of exasperating contradiction.

This was much too subtle a discussion to be continued. She brushed it aside with a laugh, and proceeded to turn over the things with eager admiration on her expressive face. Catching up a bright blue-and-scarlet shawl, large enough to cover her person, she threw it over her and made great, and not quite successful, efforts to see her own back. Suddenly she became motionless, and fixed her lustrous brown eyes on the roof with almost petrified attention.

A thought had struck her! And she resolved to strike it back in the sense of pursuing it to a conclusion.

"The very thing," she said, recovering from petrification, "and I'll *do* it!"

The preliminary step to doing it seemed to be a general turn over of the Hebrew's shawls, all of which, though many were beautiful, she rejected one after another until she found an old and considerably worn grey one. This she shook out and examined with approving nods, as if it were the finest fabric that ever had issued from the looms of Cashmere. Tying her luxuriant hair into a tight knot behind, and smoothing it down on each side of her face, and well back so as not to be obtrusive, she flung the old shawl over her head, induced a series of wrinkles to corrugate her fair brow; drew in her lips so as to conceal her teeth, and, by the same action, to give an aquiline turn to her nose; bowed her back, and, in short, converted herself into a little old woman!

At court, Branwen had been celebrated for her powers of mimicry, and had been a source of great amusement to her companions in the use—sometimes the abuse—of these powers; but this was the first occasion on which she had thought of personating an old woman.

Having thus metamorphosed herself, she looked eagerly round as if in search of a mirror. It need scarcely be said that glass had not been heard of by the natives of the Tin Islands or of Albion at that time, nevertheless, mirrors were not unknown. Espying in a corner, a great bronze shield, that might once have flashed terror at the siege of Troy—who knows—she set it up against the wall. It was oval in shape, and presented her face with such a wide expanse of cheeks, that she laughed lightly and turned it the other way. This arrangement gave her visage such lengthened astonishment of expression, that she laughed again, but was not ill pleased at her appearance on the whole.

To make the illusion perfect, she sought and found an article of dress, of which the Albionic name has been forgotten, but which is known to modern women as a petticoat. It was reddish brown in colour, and, so far, in keeping with the grey old shawl.

While she was busy tying on this garment, and otherwise completing her costume, almost quite forgetful in her amusement of the danger which had driven her to that strange place, she heard voices in the outer cave, and among them one which turned her cheeks pale, and banished every thought of fun out of her heart. It was the voice of Gunrig!

That doughty warrior—after having partially regained the equanimity which he had sat down on the fallen tree to recover—arose, and returned to his apartment in the palace for the double purpose of feeding and meditation. Being a robust man, he did not feel much the worse for the events of the morning, and attacked a rib of roast beef with gusto. Hearing, with great surprise, that his late antagonist was no other than Bladud, the long-lost son of the king, he comforted himself with another rib of roast beef, and with the reflection that a prince, not less than a man-at-arms, is bound to fight a duel when required to do so. Having finished his meal, he quaffed a huge goblet of spring water, and went out to walk up and down with his hands behind his back.

Doubtless, had he lived in modern days, he would have solaced himself with a glass of bitter and a pipe, but strong drink had not been discovered in those islands at the time, and smoking had not been invented. Yet it is generally believed, though we have no authentic record of the fact, that our ancestors got on pretty well without these comforts. We refrain, however, from dogmatising on the point, but it is our duty to state that Gunrig, at all events, got on swimmingly without them. It is also our duty to be just to opponents, and to admit that a pipe might possibly have soothed his wrath.

Of course, on hearing of Branwen's flight, the indignant king summoned his hunters at once, and, putting the enraged Gunrig himself at the head of them, sent him fuming into the woods in search of the runaway. They did not strike the trail at once, because of, as already explained, the innumerable footprints in the neighbourhood of the town.

"We can't be long of finding them now," remarked the chief to the principal huntsman, as they passed the entrance to Beniah's retreat.

"It may be as well to run up and ask the old man who lives here if he has seen her," replied the huntsman. "He is a man with sharp eyes for his years."

"As you will," said Gunrig sternly, for his wrath had not yet been appreciably toned down by exercise.

They found the Hebrew reading at his door.

"Ho! Beniah, hast seen the girl Branwen pass this way to-day?" cried Gunrig as he came up.

"I have not seen her pass," replied the Hebrew, in a tone so mild that the angry chief suspected him.

"She's not in your hut, I suppose?" he added sharply.

"The door is open, you may search it if you doubt me," returned the Hebrew with a look of dignity, which he knew well how to assume.

The chief entered at once, and, after glancing sharply round the outer room entered the kitchen. Here Beniah showed him the chimney, pointed out the yawning chasm below, and commented on the danger of falling into it in the dark.

"And what is there beyond, Hebrew?" asked the chief.

Beniah held up the lamp.

"You see," he said, "the rock against which my poor hut rests."

Then the old man referred to the advantages of the situation for supplying himself with food by hunting in the forest, as well as by cultivating the patch of garden beside the hut, until his visitor began to show signs of impatience, when he apologised for intruding his domestic affairs at such a time, and finally offered to join and aid the search party.

"Aid us!" exclaimed Gunrig in contempt. "Surely we need no aid from you, when we have the king's head-huntsman as our guide."

"That may be true, chief, nevertheless in the neighbourhood

of my own hut I could guide you, if I chose, to secret and retired spots, which it would puzzle even the head-huntsman to find. But I will not thrust my services upon you."

"You are over-proud for your station," returned the chief angrily, "and were it not for your years I would teach you to moderate your language and tone."

For a moment the eyes of the old man flashed, and his brows contracted, as he steadily returned the gaze of Gunrig. In his youth he had been a man of war, and, as we have said, his strength was not yet much abated by age, but years and deep thought had brought wisdom to some extent. With an evident effort he restrained himself, and made no reply. The chief, deeming his silence to be the result of fear, turned contemptuously away, and left the hut with his followers.

During this colloquy, poor Branwen had stood in the dark passage, listening and trembling lest her hiding-place should be discovered. She was a strange compound of reckless courage and timidity—if such a compound be possible. Indignation at the man who had slighted her bosom friend Hafrydda, besides insulting herself, caused her to feel at times like a raging lion. The comparative weakness of her slight and graceful frame made her at other times feel like a helpless lamb. It was an exasperating condition! When she thought of Gunrig, she wished with all her heart and soul that she had been born a big brawny man. When she thought of Bladud, nothing could make her wish to be other than a woman!

As she stood there listening, there occurred a slight desire to clear her throat, and she almost coughed. The feeling came upon her like a shock—what if she had let it out! But a sneeze! It was well known that sneezes came even to people the most healthy, and at moments the most inopportune, and well she knew from experience that to repress a sneeze would ensure an explosion fit to blow the little nose off her face. If a sneeze should come at that moment, she was lost!

But a sneeze did not come. The olfactory nerves remained placid, until the visitors had departed. Then she retreated to the inner cave, drew the grey shawl over her head, and awaited the development of her plans.

Presently she heard footsteps, and the voice of the Hebrew calling to her softly, but she took no notice. After a moment or two it sounded again, somewhat louder.

Still no answer.

Then Beniah shouted, with just a shade of anxiety, "Branwen!"

Receiving no reply, he ran in much alarm for one of his spare planks; thrust it over the chasm; crossed, and next moment stood in the inner cave the very embodiment of astonished consternation, for Branwen was gone, and in her place stood a little old woman, with a bowed form, and a puckered-up mouth, gazing at him with half-closed but piercingly dark eyes!

The Hebrew was almost destitute of superstition, and a man of great courage, but this proved too much for him. His eyes opened with amazement; so did his mouth, and he grew visibly pale.

The tables were turned at this point. The man's appearance proved too much for the girl. Her eyes opened wide, her brilliant teeth appeared, and, standing erect, she burst into a fit of merry laughter.

R. M. Ballantyne

"Child!" exclaimed Beniah, his usually grave mouth relaxing into a broad smile, which proved that his teeth were not less sound than his constitution, "you have shown to me that fear, or something marvellously like it, is capable of lurking within my old heart. What mean you by this?"

"I mean that there is an idea come into my head which I shall carry out—if you will allow me. I had thought at first of staying with you as your grand-daughter or your niece, but then it came into my head that I could not live long here in such a character without some one who knew me seeing me and finding me out—though, let me tell you, it would not be easy to find me out, for I can change my look and voice so that none but those who know me well could discover me. Then the idea of being an old woman came into my head, and—you can speak to my success. There is nothing more natural than that you should have an old woman to take care of your house while you go on your travels; so I can stay till you go and see my father and tell him to send for me."

"Your father lives very far from here," returned the Hebrew, with the lines of perplexity still resting on his brow.

"That is true; but Beniah's legs are long and his body is strong. He can soon let my father know of his daughter's misfortune. You know that my father is a powerful chief, though his tribe is not so strong in numbers as the tribe of King Hudibras, or that—that fiend Gunrig. But his young men and my brothers are very brave."

"Well, let it be as you say, for the present, my child, and you may consider this cave your private chamber while you remain in my house. But let me advise you to keep close when I am absent, and do not be tempted to prove the strength of your disguise. It may not be as perfect as you think, and your voice may betray you."

Having agreed upon this temporary plan, the Hebrew departed to make preparations for a long journey, while Branwen busied herself in arranging the apartment in which, for some time at least, she hoped to remain in hiding.

CHAPTER THIRTEEN

MOTHER AND SON

We need scarcely say that the search for Branwen proved fruitless. Gunrig and the hunters returned to town crestfallen at being unable to discover the trail of a girl, and the chief went off in undiminished wrath to his own home—which was distant about a day's journey on foot from the capital of King Hudibras.

Even in those savage times warriors were not above taking counsel, occasionally, with women. The king went to consult on the situation with the queen, the princess, and Bladud; while Gunrig sought advice and consolation from his mother. Of course neither of these men would for a moment have admitted that he needed advice. They only condescended to let their women-folk know what had occurred, and hear what they had to say!

"Why, do you think, has the ungrateful child fled?" asked the king in some indignation.

"I cannot imagine," answered the queen. "We have all been so kind to her, and she was so fond of us and we of her. Besides, her visit was not half over, and her father would not be pleased if she were to return home so soon and so unexpectedly."

Of course Hafrydda knew the cause, but she maintained a discreet silence.

"Return home!" echoed the king in contempt, "how can a little delicate thing like her return home through miles and miles of forest swarming with wild beasts and not a few wilder men? Impossible! My hunters must go out again, every day, till she is found. I will lead them myself since they seem to have lost the power of their craft."

"Is this 'little delicate thing' as beautiful as my sister describes her to be?" asked Bladud, somewhat amused by his father's tone and manner.

"Ay, that she is," answered the king. "Beautiful enough to set not a few of my young men by the ears. Did you not see her on the platform at the games—or were you too much taken up with the scowling looks of Gunrig?"

"I saw the figure of a young woman," answered the prince, "but she kept a shawl so close round her head that I failed to see her face. As to Gunrig, I did not think it worth my while to mind him at all, so I saw not whether his looks were scowling or pleased."

"Ha! boy—he gave you some trouble, notwithstanding."

"He has gone away in anger at present, however, so we will let him be till he returns for another fight."

Gunrig, meanwhile, having reached his town or village, went straight to the hut in which his mother dwelt and laid his troubles before her. She was a calm, thoughtful woman, very unlike her passionate son.

"It is a bad business," she remarked, after the chief had

R. M. Ballantyne

described the situation to her, and was striding up and down the little room with his hands behind his back, "and will require much care in management, for King Hudibras, as you know, is very fierce when roused, and although he is somewhat afraid of you, he is like to be roused to anger when he comes to understand that you have jilted his daughter."

"But I have not jilted her," said Gunrig, stopping abruptly in his walk, and looking down upon his parent. "That ass Bladud won her, and although he does turn out to be her brother, that does not interfere with his right to break off the engagement if so disposed. Besides, I do not want to wed the princess now. I have quite changed my mind."

"Why have you changed your mind, my son?"

"Because I never cared for her much; and since I went to visit her father I have seen another girl who is far more beautiful; far more clever; more winning, in every way."

The woman looked sharply at the flushed countenance of her son.

"You love her?" she asked.

"Ay, that do I, as I never loved woman before, and, truly, as I think I never shall love again."

"Then you must get her to wife, my son, for there is no cure for love."

"Oh, yes, there is, mother," was the light reply of the chief, as he recommenced to pace the floor. "Death is a pretty sure and sharp cure for love."

"Surely you would not kill yourself because of a girl?"

Gunrig burst into a loud laugh, and said, "Nay, truly, but death may take the girl, or death may take me—for, as you know, there is plenty of fighting among the tribes, and my day will surely come, sooner or later. In either case love will be cured."

"Can you guess why this girl has fled?" asked the woman.

Gunrig's brows contracted, and a grim smile played on his lips as he replied, after a brief pause—

"Well, I am not quite sure, mother. It may be that she is not too fond of me—which only shows her want of taste. But that can be cured when she finds out what a fine man I am! Anyhow, I will have her, if I should have to hunt the forest for a hundred moons, and fight all the tribes put together."

"And how do you propose to go about it, my son?"

"That is the very thing I want you to tell me. If it were fighting that had to be done I would not trouble you—but this is a matter that goes beyond the wisdom of a plain warrior."

"Then, if you would gain your end, my son, I should advise you to send a message to King Hudibras by one of your most trusty men; and let the message be that you are deeply grieved at the loss of his daughter's hand; that—"

"But I'm nothing of the kind, mother, so that would not be true."

"What does it matter whether true or not, if the king only believes it to be true?"

R. M. Ballantyne

"I don't quite agree, mother, with your notions about truth. To my mind a warrior should always be straightforward and say what he means."

"Then go, my son, and tell the king what you have just told me, and he will cut your head off," replied the dame in a tone of sarcasm.

"If I act on that advice, I will take my warriors with me and carry my sword in my hand, so that his head would stand as good a chance of falling as mine," returned Gunrig with a laugh. "But go on with your advice, mother."

"Well, say that you feel in honour bound to give up all claim to his daughter's hand, but that, as you want a wife very much to keep your house as your mother is getting too old, you will be content to take his visitor, Branwen, and will be glad to help in the search for her. Will you send that message?"

"It may be that I will. In any case I'll send something like it."

So saying the chief turned abruptly on his heel and left the room.

CHAPTER FOURTEEN

A TERRIBLE CALAMITY

It may be imagined that the return home of Prince Bladud was the cause of much rejoicing in the whole district as well as in his father's house. At *first* the king, being, as we have said, a very stern man, felt disposed to stand upon his dignity, and severely rebuke the son who had run away from home and remained away so long. But an undercurrent of tenderness, and pride in the youth's grand appearance, and great prowess, induced him to give in with a good grace and extend to him unreserved forgiveness.

As for the queen, she made no attempt to conceal her joy and pride, and the same may be said of the princess.

There was instituted a series of fetes and games in honour of the return of the prodigal, at which he was made—not unwillingly—to show the skill which he had acquired from practising with the competitors at the Olympic games, about which the islanders had heard from Phoenician traders from time to time, and great was the interest thus created, especially when he showed them, among other arts, how to use their fists in boxing, and their swords in guarding so as to enable them to dispense with a shield. But these festivities did not prevent him from taking an interest in the search that his father and the hunters were still making for Branwen.

When many days had passed, however, and no word of her whereabouts was forthcoming, it was at last arranged that a message regarding her disappearance should be sent to her father's tribe by a party of warriors who were to be led by the prince himself.

"I will go gladly," he said to his sister, a day or two before the party was to set out. "For your sake, Hafrydda, I will do my best to clear up the mystery; and I think it highly probable that I shall find the runaway safely lodged in her father's house."

"I fear not," returned Hafrydda, with a sad look. "It seems impossible that she could have made her way so far alone through the wild forests."

"But she may not have been alone. Friends may have helped her."

"She had no friends in the town, having been here but a short time," objected the princess. "But do your best to find her, Bladud, for I feel quite sure that you will fall in love with her when you see her."

The youth laughed.

"No fear of that," he said, "many a pretty girl have I seen in the East; nevertheless I have, as you see, left them all without a thought of ever returning again."

"But I did not say you would fall in love with Branwen because she is pretty. I feel sure that you will, because she is sweet, and merry, and good—yet thoughtful—wonderfully thoughtful!"

"Ay, and you may add," said the queen, who came into the room just then, "that she is sometimes thoughtless and wonderfully full of mischief."

"Nay, mother, you are not just," returned the princess. "Her mischief is only on the surface, her thoughtfulness lies deep down."

"Well, well, whatever may be the truth regarding her, I shall not trouble my head about her; for I have never yet felt what men call love, and I feel sure I never shall."

"I like to hear you say that, brother," rejoined Hafrydda; "for I have noticed, young though I am, that when men say they will never fall in love or marry, they are always pretty near the point of doing one or both."

But poor Bladud was destined to do neither at that time, for an event was hanging over him, though he knew it not, which was to affect very seriously the whole of his after life.

For several days previous to the above conversation, he had felt a sensation that was almost new to him—namely, that of being slightly ill. Whether it was the unwonted exertions consequent on his efforts at the games, or the excitement of the return home, we cannot say, but headache, accompanied by a slight degree of fever, had troubled him. Like most strong men in the circumstances, he adopted the Samsonian and useless method of "shaking it off"! He went down into the arena and performed feats of strength and agility that surprised even himself; but the fever which enabled him to do so, asserted itself at last, and finally compelled him to do what he should have done at first—pocket his pride and give in.

Of course we do not suggest that giving in to little sensations of ailment is either wise or manly. There are duties which

R. M. Ballantyne

call on men to fight even in sickness—ay, in spite of sickness—but "showing off" in the arena was not one of these.

Be this as it may, Bladud came at last to the condition of feeling weak—an incomprehensible state of feeling to him. He thereupon went straight home, and, flinging himself half petulantly on a couch, exclaimed—"Mother, I am ill!"

"My son, I have seen that for many days past, and have waited with some anxiety till you should come to the point of admitting it."

"And now that I have admitted it," returned the youth with a languid smile, "what is to be done?"

The answer to that question was not the simple one of modern days, "Send for the doctor," because no doctors worthy of the name existed. There was, indeed, a solemn-visaged, long-headed, elderly man among King Hudibras' followers who was known as the medicine-man to the royal household, but his services were not often in request, because people were seldom ill, save when they were going to die, and when that time came it was generally thought best to let them die in peace. This medicine-man, though a quack in regard to physic, was, however, a true man, as far as his knowledge went in surgery—that is to say, he was expert at the setting of broken bones, when the fractures were not too compound; he could bandage ordinary wounds; he had even ventured into the realm of experimental surgery so far as to knock out a decayed back tooth with a bronze chisel and a big stone. But his knowledge of drugs was naturally slight, and his power of diagnosis feeble. Still, unworthy though he may be of the title, we will for convenience style him the doctor.

"My poor boy," said the queen, in answer to his question,

and laying her hand on his hot brow, "I am so sorry that we cannot have the services of our doctor, for he is away hunting just now—you know he is very fond of the bow and line. Perhaps he may—"

"Oh, never mind the doctor, mother," said Bladud impatiently, with that slighting reference to the faculty which is but too characteristic of youth; "what do *you* think ought to be done? You were always doctor enough for me when I was little; you'll do equally well now that I am big."

"Be not hasty, my son. You were always hot-headed and—"

"I'm hot-headed *now*, at all events, and argument won't tend to cool it. Do what you will with it, for I can stand this no longer. Cut it off if you like, mother, only use a sharp knife and be quick about it."

In those days, far more than in this our homeopathic era, it was the habit of the mothers of families to keep in store certain herbs and roots, etcetera, which, doubtless, contained the essences now held in modern globules. With these they contrived decoctions that were unquestionably more or less beneficial to patients when wisely applied. To the compounding of something of this sort the queen now addressed herself. After swallowing it, the prince fell asleep.

This was so far well; but in the morning he was still so far from well, that the visit to Branwen's father had to be postponed. Several days elapsed before the doctor returned from his hunting expedition. By that time the fever had left the prince. He began to get somewhat better, and to go about, but still felt very unlike his old self. During this what we may style semi-convalescent period, Captain Arkal and little Maikar proved of great use and comfort to him, for they not only brought him information about the games—which were

R. M. Ballantyne

still kept up—but cheered him with gossipy news of the town in general, and with interesting reminiscences of their late voyage and the Eastern lands they had so recently left.

One day these faithful friends, as well as the queen and princess, were sitting by Bladud's couch—to which unaccountable fits of laziness confined him a good deal—when the medicine-man was announced.

He proceeded at once to examine the patient, while the others stood aside and looked on with that profound respect which ignorance sometimes, though not always, assumes in the presence of knowledge.

The doctor laid his hand on Bladud's brow, and looked earnestly into his eyes. Then he tapped his back and chest, as if to induce some one in his interior to open a door and let him in—very much as doctors do now-a-days. Then he made him remove his upper garments, and examined his broad and brawny shoulders. A mark, or spot, of a whitish appearance between the left shoulder and the elbow, at once riveted his attention, and caused an almost startled expression on his grave countenance. But the expression was momentary. It passed away and left the visage grave and thoughtful—if possible, more thoughtful than before.

"That will do," he said, turning to the queen. "Your treatment was the best that could have been applied. I must now see his father, the king."

"Alone?" asked the queen.

"Alone," replied the doctor.

"Well, what think ye of Bladud?" asked the king, when his physician entered his chamber, and carefully shut the door.

"He is smitten with a fatal disease," said the doctor in a low, earnest voice.

"Not absolutely fatal?" cried the king, with sudden anxiety.

"As far as I know it is so. There is no cure that I ever heard of. Bladud is smitten with leprosy. It may be years before it kills him, but it will surely do so at last."

"Impossible—impossible!" cried the king, becoming fierce and unbelieving in his horror. "You are too confident, my medicine-man. You may, you must, be mistaken. There is a cure for everything!"

"Not for leprosy," returned the doctor, with sad but firm emphasis. "At least I never heard of a cure being effected, except by some of the Eastern wise men."

"Then, by all the gods that protect our race and family, my son shall return to the East and one of these wise men shall cure him—else—else—Have ye told the queen?"

"Not yet."

"That is well. I will myself tell her. Go!" This summary dismissal was nothing new to the doctor, who understood the king well, and sympathised with his obvious distress. Pausing at the door, however, he said—

"I have often talked with Phoenician captains about this disease, and they tell me that it is terribly infectious, insomuch that those who are smitten with it are compelled to live apart and keep away from men. If Bladud remains here the disease will surely spread through the house, and thence through the town."

R. M. Ballantyne

Poor Hudibras fell into a chair, and covered his face with both hands, while the doctor quietly retired.

It is impossible to describe the consternation that ensued when the terrible fact was made known. Of course the news spread into the town, and the alarm became general, for at various times the Phoenician mariners had entertained the islanders with graphic descriptions of the horrors connected with this loathsome disease, and it soon became evident, that even if the king and his family were willing to run the risk of infection by keeping Bladud near them, his people and warriors would insist on the banishment of the smitten man.

To Bladud himself the blow was almost overwhelming—almost, but not quite, for the youth was possessed of that unselfish, self-sacrificing spirit which, in all ages of the world's history, has bid defiance to misfortune, by bowing the head in humble submission to the will of God. He knew well the nature of the dread disease by which he had been attacked, and he shuddered at the thought that, however long he might be spared to live, it would sap his strength, disfigure his person, and ultimately render his face hideous to look upon, while a life of absolute solitude must from that day forward be his portion. No wonder that in the first rush of his dismay, he entertained a wild thought of putting an end to his own existence. There was only one gleam of comfort to him, and that was, the recollection that he had caught the disease in a good cause—in the rescue of a poor old woman from destruction. The comfort of the thought was not indeed great, still it was something in the awful desolation that overwhelmed him at the time.

While travelling in the East, a short time previous to setting sail for home, he had come across an old woman who was being chased by a wild bull. Her flight would have been short-lived in any case, for there chanced to be a steep precipice not far from her, towards which she ran in her terror and scrambled hastily down until she reached a spot where she could go no further without losing her foothold. To the rock she clung and screamed in her despair.

It was her screams that first attracted Bladud's attention. Rushing forward, he was just in time to see the bull—which could not check its mad career—plunge over the cliff, at the bottom of which it was killed by the fall.

Bladud at once began to descend to the help of the poor woman. As he did so, the words "unclean! unclean!" met his ear. The woman was a leper, and, even in her dire extremity, the force of habit caused her to give the usual warning which the Eastern law requires. A shudder passed through the prince's frame, for he knew well the meaning of the cry—but as he looked down and saw the disfigured face and the appealing eyes turned towards him, a gush of intense pity, and of that disregard of self which is more or less characteristic of all noble natures, induced him to continue his descent until he reached the poor creature. Grasping her tightly round the waist, he assisted her up the perilous ascent, and finally placed her in safety at the top of the cliff.

For a time Bladud felt some anxiety as to the result of the risk he had run, but did not mention his adventure to any one. Gradually the fear wore off, and at length that feeling of invulnerability which is so strong in youth, induced him to dismiss the subject from his thoughts altogether. He had quite forgotten it until the doctor's statement fell upon him with the stunning violence of a thunder-clap.

It is usually when deep sorrows and great difficulties are sent to them, that men and women find out the quality of their natures. Despair, followed by listless apathy, might well have seized on one who, a few days before, possessed all the

R. M. Ballantyne

advantages of great physical strength and manly beauty, with what appeared to be sound health and a bright life before him. But, instead of giving way, he silently braced himself for a lifelong conflict. He did not turn, in his extremity, to the gods of his fathers—whatever these might be—for he did not believe in them, but he did believe in one good supreme Being. To Him he raised his heart, offered an unspoken prayer, and felt comforted as well as strengthened in the act.

Then, being a man of prompt action, he thoughtfully but quickly formed his plans, having previously made fast his door—for well he knew that although his strong-minded father might keep him at arm's-length, his loving mother and sister would not only come to talk with him, but would, despite all risks, insist on embracing him.

That he was not far wrong was proved the same evening, for when the king revealed the terrible news to his wife and daughter, they went straight to Bladud's door and knocked for admission.

"Who goes there?" demanded the prince.

"Your mother. Let me in, Bladud."

"I may not do so just now, dear mother. Tomorrow you shall know all. Rest content. I feel better."

In the dead of night Bladud went out softly and sought the hut where Captain Arkal and Maikar slept. He found them conversing in great sorrow about the terrible calamity that had overtaken their friend when he entered. They started up in surprise to receive him.

"Keep off," he said, shrinking back. "Touch me not! I know not whether the disease may not be catching even at its present stage. Sit down. I will stand here and tell you what I want you to tell my mother in the morning."

The two men silently obeyed, and the prince continued.

"I am on the point of leaving home—it may be for ever. The Disposer of all things knows that. The disease, as you know, is thought to be incurable. If so, I shall die where no one shall find me. If health returns I shall come back. It will be of no use to search for me; but I think that will not be attempted. Indeed, I know that my father would be compelled to banish me if I wished to remain at home. It is partly to spare him the pain of doing so that I banish myself of my own accord; and partly to avoid leaving infection behind me that I go without farewell. Let my dear mother and sister understand this clearly—and—comfort them if you can."

"But where will you go to and what will you do?" asked the captain anxiously.

"That I do not yet know. The forests are wide. There is plenty of room for man and beast. This only will I reveal to you. To-night I shall call at the hut of Beniah the Hebrew. He is a wise man and will advise me. If I send news of myself it shall be through him. But tell not this to any one. It would only bring trouble on the old man. Farewell, my comrades. I will remember you as brothers—always. May the All-powerful One watch over us."

Unable to restrain himself, little Maikar sprang up with the obvious intention of rushing at his friend and seizing his hand, but the prince stepped back, shut the door against him, and, in another moment, was gone.

R. M. Ballantyne

CHAPTER FIFTEEN

AN EAVESDROPPER IN THE CAVE

An hour later Beniah the Hebrew, who had been obliged to postpone for a time his journey to the North, was startled by hearing footsteps approaching his hut in the dell. It was so unusual an event at that hour of the night, that he arose quickly and grasped the six-foot staff which was his only weapon.

At a much earlier hour Branwen had retired to rest in the inner cave, and was buried in that profound sleep which proverbially accompanies innocence and youth. The noise in the outer cave partially aroused her, but, turning on her other side with a profound sigh, she prepared for a little more of the perquisites of innocence and youth. Presently she was startled into a condition of absolute wide-awakeness by the sound of a well-known voice, but it suddenly changed into that of the Hebrew.

"I've dreamt it, I suppose," she muttered, in a tone of regret; nevertheless, she listened.

"Come in," said Beniah, evidently to some one outside of his door.

"I may not enter—I am a leper," answered the first voice; and Branwen sat up, with her great beautiful eyes opened to the utmost, and listening intently, though she could not make out clearly what was said.

"It matters not; I have no fear. Come in. What! Prince Bladud!" exclaimed Beniah in astonishment as our hero entered.

"Even so. But how is it that you know me?"

"I saw you once, and, once seen, you are not easily forgotten. But what mean ye about being a leper?"

"Keep at a safe distance, and I will tell you."

Hereupon the prince began to give the old man an account of his illness; the opinion expressed by the doctor as to its nature; and the determination he had formed of forsaking home, and retiring to the solitude of some unfrequented part of the forest for the remainder of his life.

It would have been a sight worth looking at—had there been light to see it—the vision of Branwen, as she stood in the passage in partial *deshabille*, with her eyes wide, her lips parted, her heart beating, and a wealth of auburn hair curling down her back, listening, as it were, with every power of her soul and body. But she could not hear distinctly. Only a disconnected word reached her now and then. In a state of desperate curiosity she returned to her cave.

A few minutes later a noise was heard by the two men in the outer cave; and a little old woman in a grey shawl was seen to thrust a plank over the chasm and totter across towards them.

Poor Beniah was horrified. He did not know what to do or say. Happily he was one of those men whose feelings are never betrayed by their faces.

The old woman hobbled forward and sat down on a stool close to them. Looking up in their faces, she smiled and nodded.

In doing so she revealed the fact that, besides having contorted her face into an unrecognisable shape, she had soiled it in several places with streaks of charcoal and earth.

"Who is this?" asked Bladud in surprise. Before the old man could reply, the old woman put her hand to her ear, and, looking up in the prince's face, shouted, in tones that were so unlike to her own natural voice that Beniah could scarce believe his ears—

"What say you, young man? Speak out; I'm very deaf."

With a benignant smile Bladud said that he had merely asked who she was.

"Haven't you got eyes, young man? Don't you see that I'm a little old woman?"

"I see that," returned the prince, with a good-humoured laugh; "and I fear you're a deaf old woman, too."

"Eh?" she said, advancing her head, with her hand up at the ear.

"You seem indeed to be extremely deaf," shouted the prince.

"What does he say?" demanded the old woman, turning to the Hebrew.

By this time Beniah had recovered his self-possession. Perceiving that the maiden was bent on carrying out her *role*, and that he might as well help her, he put his mouth close to her ear, and shouted in a voice that bid fair to render her absolutely deaf—

"He says he thinks you are extremely deaf; so I think you had better hold your tongue and let us go on with our conversation."

"Deaf, indeed!" returned the woman in a querulous tone; "so I am, though I hear you well enough when you shout like that. Perhaps he'll be as deaf as I am when he's as old. There's nothing like youth for pride and impudence. But go on, never mind me."

"She's a poor creature who has sought refuge with me from her persecutors," said Beniah, turning to the prince, while the old woman fell to crooning a wild song in a low voice, accompanying the music—if such it may be called—by a swaying motion of her body to and fro.

Seeing that she meant to sit there, and that she apparently heard nothing, Bladud resumed the conversation where it had been interrupted.

"Now, as I was saying, you know the country in all directions, and can tell me of the most likely part where I can find what I want—a solitude where I shall be able to escape from the face of man, and build a hut to live in till I die. It may be long, it may be short, before death relieves me. Meanwhile, I can hunt and provide myself with food till the time comes."

The crooning of the old woman stopped at this point, and she sank her face on her hands as if she had fallen asleep.

R. M. Ballantyne

"I know of a man—a hunter," said Beniah, "a wild sort of being, who lives a long way from here, in a beautiful part of the land, where there is a wonderful swamp with a hot spring in the midst of it. Besides hunting, the man who lives there cultivates the ground a little, and keeps a few cattle and pigs. It may be that he can put you in the way of finding what you want; and you need not tell him about your disease, for you are not yet sure about it. Thus you will have an opportunity of keeping out of the way of men until you find out whether the doctor is right about it. He may be wrong, you know. Diseases sometimes resemble each other without being the same."

Bladud shook his head.

"There can be no doubt that I am doomed," he said. "I know the disease too well."

The Hebrew also believed that, if the doctor was right in his opinion, there was no hope for the youth. Being unwilling, however, to dwell upon this point, he asked—

"How did you come by it?"

"Very simply," answered the prince, who thereupon entered into a graphic account of the incident which we have already recorded. Having done so, he made up his mind, after some further talk, to pay a visit to the hunter who dwelt in the region of the Hot Swamp.

"But you will not surely go without arms?" said Beniah.

"Why not? If I am doomed to die at any rate, why should I take the life of any man to save my own?"

"Let me at least give you a bow and a sheaf of arrows. You

cannot procure food without these."

"Well, you are right. I will accept your kind offer. To say truth, my heart was so crushed at first by this blow, that such matters did not occur to me when I left; for it is terrible to think of having to die of a slow disease without father, mother, or sister to comfort one!"

"It is indeed, my son," returned Beniah with much feeling. "If you will accept it, I can give you a word of comfort."

"Give it me," said Bladud; "for I need it much,—if it be but true."

"It is true," returned the Hebrew earnestly; "for in one of the books of our holy men who spoke for the All-Father, it is written, 'When my father and my mother forsake me, then the Lord will take me up.'"

"It is a good word," returned the prince; "and I can well believe it comes from the All-Father, for is He not also All-Good? Yet I can scarcely claim it as mine, for my father and mother have not forsaken me, but I them."

A few minutes more, and Bladud rose to depart. He took the bow and arrows in his left hand, and, totally forgetting for the moment the duty of keeping himself aloof from his fellow-men, he shook hands warmly with Beniah, patted the old woman kindly on the shoulder, and went out into the dark night.

The moment he was gone Branwen started up with flashing eyes that were still bedewed with tears, and seized the old man's hand.

"Child," he said, "thou hast been weeping."

"Who could listen to his telling of that old woman's escape from the bull and the precipice without tears?" she replied. "But tell me, what is this terrible disease that has smitten the prince?"

"It is one well known and much dreaded in the East—called leprosy."

Here the Hebrew went into a painfully graphic account of the disease; the frightful disfigurement it caused, and its almost, if not quite, certain termination in death.

"And have the queen and Hudibras actually let him go away to die alone?" she exclaimed.

"Not so, my child. Before you interrupted us he told me that he had left home by stealth on purpose. But, Branwen," continued the old man with some severity, "how could you run such a risk of being discovered?"

"I ran no risk," she replied, with a laugh.

"Besides, it was not fair to pretend to be deaf and thus obtain all his secrets."

"I don't care whether it was fair or not," replied the girl with a wilful shake of her head. "And was it fair of you to back me up as you did?"

"Your rebuke is just, yet it savours of ingratitude. I should not have done so, but I was completely taken aback. Do you know that your face is dirty?"

"I know it. I made it so on purpose. Now tell me—when are you going away to tell my father and brothers about me?"

"I shall probably start to-morrow. But many days must pass before I can bring them here, for, as you know, their town is a long way off. But, child, you do not seem to reflect that you have betrayed me."

"How?" asked Branwen, wonderingly.

"Did you not thrust out the plank and cross over before the very eyes of Bladud?"

Branwen pursed her lips into the form of an O and opened her eyes wide.

"I never thought of that!" she said. "But after all it does not matter, for the prince took no notice of the plank, and *he* is not the man to go and betray secrets!"

The Hebrew laughed, patted the girl on the head and sent her off to rest. Then he busied himself in making preparation for his too long-delayed journey.

Next morning, before daybreak, he set off, leaving Branwen in charge of the hut, with strict orders to keep well out of sight. If any one should come to it she was to retreat to the inner cavern and withdraw the bridge.

"They may do as seemeth to them good in the outer hut. There is nothing there worth stealing, and they are welcome to make themselves at home."

The Hebrew went on his mission; arrived in due time at his journey's end; reported Branwen's dilemma; guided a party of stout warriors under her father Gadarn, and led them to his hut in the dell in the dead of a dark night, for it was no part of the programme to abduct the girl by main force, unless peaceful or stealthy measures should prove unsuccessful.

When, however, he reached the dell and entered his dwelling, he found that the bird had flown! Every nook and cranny of the place was carefully searched; but, to the consternation of the Hebrew, and the wrath of Gadarn and his men, not a vestige of Branwen was to be found.

CHAPTER SIXTEEN

ADVENTURES IN THE FORESTS

Poor Branwen! it was an unfortunate day for her when, in her youthful ignorance and recklessness, she took to the wild woods, resolved to follow Bladud to his destination and secretly wait there and watch over him like a guardian angel, as it were, until the terrible disease should lay him on his deathbed, when she would reveal herself and nurse him to the end!

Let not the reader suppose there was any lack of maiden modesty in this resolve. It must be borne in mind that Branwen was little more than a child in experience; that she was of an age at which the world, with all its affairs, is enveloped in a halo of romance; that her soul had been deeply stirred by the story of the rescue of the leprous old woman, and her pity powerfully aroused by the calm, though hopeless, tones of the doomed man when he spoke of his blighted prospects. Rather than leave him to die in absolute solitude she would sacrifice everything, and, in spite of infection and disfigurement, and the horrible nature of a disease which eats away the features before it kills, she would soothe his dying hours. Besides this, it must be remembered that our ancestors' notions of propriety were somewhat different from ours, and—well, it was about eight hundred years BuC!

Whether love was a factor in her resolve we cannot say, but we are firmly convinced that, if it were, she was ignorant of the fact.

It is, however, one thing to resolve—quite another thing to carry resolution into effect. Branwen had, in an incidental way, obtained from her protector, Beniah, information as to the direction in which the hunter of the Hot Swamp lived, and the distance to his dwelling; but when she actually found herself in the forest, with nothing to guide her save the position of the sun—and, on cloudy days not even that—she began to realise somewhat of the difficulties that attended her enterprise, and when, on the first night, she crouched among the forked branches of an old oak, and heard the cries of wolves and other wild creatures, and even saw them prowling about by the light of the moon as it flickered through the foliage, she began to appreciate the dangers.

She had not, indeed, been so foolish as to set out on her expedition without a certain amount of forethought—what she deemed careful and wise consideration. She knew that by noting the position of the sun when at its highest point in the sky she could follow pretty closely the direction which Beniah had pointed out to her. She was quite aware that food was absolutely necessary to life, and had packed up a large bundle of dried meat, and also provided herself with one of her host's bows and a sheaf of arrows. Besides this, she knew, like every girl of the period, how to snare rabbits, and was even expert in throwing stones, so that, if it should come to the worst, she could manage to subsist on little birds. As to sleeping at night, she had been accustomed, as a little girl, to climb trees, which faculty had not yet departed from her, and she knew well that among the branches of many kinds of trees there were cosy resting-places where neither man nor beast would be likely to discover her. She had also some idea of what it is to follow a trail, for she had often heard the king's chief hunter refer to the process. As it was certain that Bladud, being an enormously big man, would leave a very obvious trail behind him, she would follow that—of course keeping well in the rear, so that he might never dream of her existence or intentions until the fatal time arrived when she should have to appear like a guardian angel and nurse him till he died.

Poor Branwen felt dreadfully depressed when she thought of this termination, and was quite unlike her gay reckless self for a time; but a vague feeling of unbelief in such a catastrophe, and a determination to hope against hope kept her from giving way to absolute despair, and nerved her to vigorous exertion.

It was in this state of mind that she had set the Hebrew's house in order; carried everything of value to the inner cave; removed the plank bridge; closed the outer door, and had taken her departure.

As already said, she concealed herself among the branches of an old oak the first night, and, although somewhat alarmed by the cries of wild animals, as well as by the appalling solitude and darkness around, she managed to make a fair supper of the dried meat. Then,—she could not tell when,—she fell into a profound slumber, which was not broken until the sun had risen high, and the birds were whistling gaily among the branches—some of them gazing at her in mute surprise, as if they had discovered some new species of gigantic acorn.

She arose with alacrity, her face flushed with abounding health, and her eyes dancing with a gush of youthful hope. But memory stepped in, and the thought of her sad mission caused a sudden collapse. The collapse, however, did not last long. Her eyes chanced to fall on the bundle of dried meat. Appetite immediately supervened. Falling-to, she made a hearty breakfast, and then, looking cautiously round to see that no danger was near, she slipped down from her perch, took up the bow and quiver and bundle of food, threw her blanket, or striped piece of Phoenician cloth, over her shoulder, and resumed her journey.

It was soon after this that Branwen found out the misfortune of ignorance and want of experience. Ere long she began to feel the cravings of thirst, and discovered that she had forgotten to take with her a bottle, or any other sort of receptacle for water. About noon her thirst became so great that she half repented having undertaken the mission. Then it became so intolerable that she felt inclined to sit down and cry. But such an act was so foreign to her nature that she felt ashamed; pursed her lips; contracted her brows; grasped her bow and strode bravely on.

She was rewarded. The tinkling of water broke upon her senses like celestial music. Running forward she came to a little spring, at which she fell on her knees, put her lips to the pool, and drank with thankfulness in her heart. Arising refreshed, she glanced upward, and observed a bird of the pheasant species gazing fixedly down.

"How fortunate!" exclaimed the maiden, fitting an arrow to her bow.

It was not fortunate for the pheasant, evidently, whatever Branwen may have meant, for next moment the bird fell dead—transfixed with an arrow.

Being high noon by that time, the demands of nature made our huntress think of a mid-day meal. And now it was that she became aware of another omission—the result, partly, of inexperience. Having plucked and cleaned the bird, she prepared to roast it, when a sudden indescribable gaze overspread her pretty face. For a moment she stood as if petrified. Then she suddenly laughed, but the laugh was not gleeful, for it is trying to human nature to possess a good appetite and a good dinner without the means of cooking! She had forgotten to take with her materials for producing fire. She knew, indeed, that sticks and friction and fungus were the things required, but she knew not what sort of sticks, or where to find the right kind of fungus, or tinder. Moreover, she had never tried her hand at such work before, and knew not how to begin.

Laying the bird on a bank, therefore, she dined off the dried meat—not, however, so heartily as before, owing to certain vague thoughts about supply and demand—the rudimentary ideas of what now forms part of the science of Political Economy. The first fittings of a careworn expression across her smooth brow, showed, at all events, that domestic economy had begun to trouble her spirit.

"For," she thought to herself, "the dried meat won't last long, and I can't eat raw things—disgusting!—and I've a long, long way to go."

Even at this early period of her mission, her character was beginning to develop a little and to strengthen.

For several days she continued her journey through the great solitudes lying to the north-west of King Hudibras' town, keeping carefully out of the way of open places, lest wandering hunters should find her, and sleeping in the forked branches of trees at night. Of course the necessity of thus keeping to the dense woods, and making her way through thorny thickets, rendered her journey very fatiguing;

but Branwen was unusually strong and healthy, though the grace of her slender frame gave her a rather fragile appearance, and she did not find herself exhausted even at the end of a long day's march; while her dressed-deerskin skirt and leggings bid defiance to thorns. So did the rude but serviceable shoes which her friend Beniah had constructed for her out of raw hide.

One thing that troubled the poor girl much was the fact that she had not yet discovered the trail of Bladud. In reality, she had crossed it more than once, but, not being possessed of the keen eye of the hunter, she had not observed it, until she came to a muddy swamp, on the edge of which there was an unmistakable track—a trail which a semi-blind man could hardly have missed. Stopping for a few minutes to take particular note of it, she afterwards went on with renewed hope and energy.

But this state of things did not last, for the trail became to her indistinguishable the moment the swamp was passed, and at last, during a very dark wet day, she lost herself as well as the trail. At evening of the same day she climbed into a tree. Opening out her bundle of dried meat, she began to eat and bemoan her fate. Tears were in her eyes, and there was a slight tendency to sob in her voice, as she muttered to herself—

"I—I wouldn't mind being lost so much, if I only knew what to do or where to go. And this meat won't hold out another week at the rate I've been eating. But I could hardly help it— I have been *so* hungry. Indeed, I'm hungry *now*, but I must not eat so much. Let me see. I shall divide it into two parts. That will last me twelve days or so, by which time I should be there—if I'm still going in the right direction. And now, divide the half into six—there—each of these will do for— Oh! but I forgot, that's only enough for breakfast. It will need two portions for each day, as it will be impossible to do without supper. I must just eat half of to-night's portion, and see how it feels."

With this complicated end in view, she dried her eyes and began supper, and when she had finished it she seemed to "see" that it didn't "feel" enough, for, after much earnest consideration, she quietly began to eat the second portion, and consumed it.

She was putting away the remnants, and feeling altogether in a more satisfactory state of mind, when her eyes fell upon an object which caused her heart to bound with alarm, and drove all the colour from her cheeks.

At the foot of the tree, looking up at her in blank amazement—open-eyed and mouthed—stood a man; a big, rough-looking man, in hairy garments and with a hairy face, which was topped by a head of hair that rendered a cap needless. He stood with his feet apart and an arrow across his bow, like one who sees a lovely bird which he is about to bring down.

"Oh! don't shoot!" she cried, becoming suddenly and alarmingly aware of the action—"don't shoot! It's me! I—I'm a girl—not a beast!"

To make quite sure that the man understood her, Branwen jumped to the ground quickly and stood before him.

Recovering himself, the man lowered his bow and said something in a dialect so uncouth, that the poor girl did not understand him. Indeed, she perceived, to her horror, that he was half-witted, and could articulate with difficulty.

"I don't know what you say, good man, but I am lost in this

forest, and belong to King Hudibras' town. I am on my way to visit the hunter of the Hot Swamp, and I would think it so very, *very* kind if you would guide me to his hut."

The idiot—for such he was—evidently understood the maiden, though she did not understand him, for he threw back his head, and gave vent to a prolonged gurgling laugh.

Branwen felt that her only chance was to put a bold face on matters. She, therefore, by a violent effort, subdued her emotion and continued.

"You know King Hudibras?"

The man nodded and grinned.

"Then I am quite sure that if you behave well, and show me the way to the Hot Swamp, he will reward you in a way that will make your heart dance with joy. Come, guide me. We have a good deal of the day still before us."

Thus speaking, she put her hand quietly within that of the idiot, and in a voice of authority said—"lead on!"

Regarding the girl with a look of mute surprise, the man obeyed, but, instead of leading her to the region named, he conducted her over a neighbouring ridge, into what appeared to her to be a robber's den. There was nothing for it now but to carry out the *role* which she had laid down. The desperate nature of the case seemed to strengthen her to play her part, for, as she was led into the circle of light caused by a camp-fire, round which a band of wild-looking men were standing, a spirit of calm determination seemed to take possession of her soul.

"What strange sort of animal is this you have caught, lad?"

demanded one of the band.

Before an answer could be given, a tall, fierce-looking woman came out of a booth, or temporary hut, close to the camp-fire, pushed her way through the crowd of men, who fell back respectfully, and, going up to Branwen, grasped her by the wrist.

"Never ye mind what animal she is," cried the woman, shaking her fist at the man who had spoken, "she is my property." Then, turning to her captive as she led her into the hut, she said:

"Don't be afraid, my dear. Black-hearted though some of them are, not one will dare to touch you as long as you are under my protection."

R. M. Ballantyne

CHAPTER SEVENTEEN

BRANWEN IN IMMINENT DANGER

It is a wonderful, but at the same time, we think, a universal and important fact, that love permeates the universe. Even a female snail, if we could only put the question, would undoubtedly admit that it loves its little ones.

At least we have the strongest presumption from analogy that the idea is correct, for do we not find lions and tigers, apes and gorillas, engaged in lovingly licking—we don't mean whipping—and otherwise fondling their offspring? Even in Hades we find the lost rich man praying for the deliverance of his brethren from torment, and that, surely, was love in the form of pity. At all events, whatever name we may give it, there can be no doubt it was unselfish. And even selfishness is love misapplied.

Yes, let us be thankful that in one form or another love permeates the universe, and there is no place, however unfavourable, and no person, however unlikely, that can altogether escape from its benign influence.

We have been led to these reflections by the contemplation of that rugged, hard-featured, square-shouldered, angry old woman who so opportunely took Branwen under her protection.

Why she did so was a complete mystery to the poor girl, for the woman seemed to have no amiable traits of character about her, and she spoke so harshly to every one—even to her timid captive—that Branwen could not help suspecting she was actuated by some sinister motive in protecting her.

And Branwen was right. She had indeed a sinister end in view—but love was at the bottom even of that. The woman, whose name was Ortrud, had a son who was to the full as ugly and unamiable as herself, and she loved that son, although he treated her shamefully, abused her, and sometimes even threatened to beat her. To do him justice, he never carried the threat into execution. And, strange to say, this unamiable blackguard also loved his mother—not very demonstratively, it is true, except in the abusive manner above mentioned.

This rugged creature had a strong objection to the wild, lawless life her son was leading, for instead of sticking to the tribe to which he belonged, and pillaging, fighting with, and generally maltreating every other tribe that was not at peace with his, this mistaken young man had associated himself with a band of like-minded desperadoes—who made him their chief—and took to pillaging the members of every tribe that misfortune cast in his way. Now, it occurred to Ortrud that the best way to wean her son from his evil ways would be to get him married to some gentle, pretty, affectionate girl, whose influence would be exerted in favour of universal peace instead of war, and the moment she set eyes on Branwen, she became convinced that her ambition was on the point of attainment. Hence her unexpected and sudden display of interest in the fair captive, whom she meant to guard till the return of her son from a special marauding expedition, in which he was engaged at the time with a few picked men.

Whatever opinion the reader may have by this time formed of Branwen, we wish it to be understood that she had "a way with her" of insinuating herself into the good graces of all sorts and conditions of men—including women and children. She was particularly successful with people of disagreeable and hardened character. It is not possible to explain why, but, such being the case, it is not surprising that she soon wormed herself into the confidence of the old woman, to such an extent, that the latter was ere long tempted to make her more or less of a confidant.

One day, about a week after the arrival of our heroine in the camp, old Ortrud asked her how she would like to live always in the green woods. The look of uncertainty with which she put the question convinced the captive that it was a leading one.

"I should like it well," she replied, "if I had pleasant company to live with."

"Of course, of course, my dear, you would need that—and what company could be more pleasant than that of a good stout man who could keep you in meat and skins and firewood?"

Any one with a quarter of Branwen's intelligence would have guessed at once that the woman referred to her absent son, about whose good qualities she had been descanting at various times for several days past. The poor girl shuddered as the light broke in on her, and a feeling of dismay at her helpless condition, and being entirely in the power of these savages, almost overcame her, but her power of self-restraint did not fail her. She laughed, blushed in spite of herself, and said she was too young to look at the matter in *that* light!

"Not a bit; not a bit!" rejoined Ortrud. "I was younger than you when my husband ran away with me."

"Ran away with you, Ortrud?" cried Branwen, laughing outright.

"Ay; I was better-looking then than I am now, and not nigh so heavy. He wouldn't find it so easy," said the woman, with a sarcastic snort, "to run away with me now."

"No, and he wouldn't be so much inclined to do so, I should think," thought Branwen, but she had the sense not to say so.

"That's a very, very nice hunting shirt you are making," remarked Branwen, anxious to change the subject.

The woman was pleased with the compliment. She was making a coat at the time, of a dressed deer-skin, using a fish-bone needle, with a sinew for a thread.

"Yes, it is a pretty one," she replied. "I'm making it for my younger son, who is away with his brother, though he's only a boy yet."

"Do you expect him back soon?" asked the captive, with a recurrence of the sinking heart.

"In a few days, I hope. Yes, you are right, my dear; the coat is a pretty one, and he is a pretty lad that shall wear it—not very handsome in the face, to be sure; but what does that matter so long as he's stout and strong and kind? I am sure his elder brother, Addedomar, will be kind to you though he *is* a bit rough to me sometimes."

Poor Branwen felt inclined to die on the spot at this cool assumption that she was to become a bandit's wife; but she succeeded in repressing all appearance of feeling as she rose, and, stretching up her arms, gave vent to a careless yawn.

"I must go and have a ramble now," she said. "I'm tired of sitting so long."

"Don't be long, my dear," cried the old woman, as the captive left the hut, "for the ribs must be nigh roasted by this time."

Branwen walked quickly till she gained the thick woods; then she ran, and, finally sitting down on a bank, burst into a passion of tears. But it was not her nature to remain in a state of inactive woe. Having partially relieved her feelings she dried her tears and began to think. Her thinking was seldom or never barren of results. To escape somehow, anyhow, everyhow, was so urgent that she felt it to be essential to the very existence of the universe—her universe at least—that she should lift herself out of the Impossible into the Stick-at-nothing. The thing *must* be done—by miracle if not otherwise.

And she succeeded—not by miracle but by natural means—as the reader shall find out all in good time.

CHAPTER EIGHTEEN

THE PRINCE UNDERTAKES STRANGE WORK

When Prince Bladud entered upon what he really believed would be his last journey, he naturally encountered very different experiences, being neither so ignorant, so helpless, nor so improvident as his helpless follower.

After a good many days of unflagging perseverance, therefore, he reached the neighbourhood of the Hot Swamp, in good spirits and in much better health than when he set out. He was, indeed, almost restored to his usual vigour of body, for the fever by which he had been greatly weakened had passed away, and the constant walking and sleeping in fresh air had proved extremely beneficial. We know not for certain whether the leprosy by which he had been attacked was identical in all respects with the fatal disease known in the East, or whether it was something akin to it, or the same in a modified form. The only light which is thrown by our meagre records on this point is that it began with fever and then, after a period of what seemed convalescence, or inaction, it continued to progress slowly but surely. Of course the manner in which it had been caught was more than presumptive evidence that it was at least of the nature of the fatal plague of the East.

R. M. Ballantyne

Although his immunity from present suffering tended naturally to raise the spirits of the prince, it did not imbue him with much, if any, hope, for he knew well he might linger for months—even for years—before the disease should sap all his strength and finally dry up the springs of life.

This assurance was so strong upon him that, as we have said, he once—indeed more than once—thought of taking his own life. But the temptation passed quickly. He was too conscientious and too brave to do that; and had none of that moral cowardice which seeks escape from the inevitable in hoped-for oblivion. Whether his life was the gift of many gods or of one God, he held that it was a sacred trust which he was bound in honour to guard. Therefore he fought manfully against depression of spirits, as one of the destroyers of life, and even encouraged hope, frequently looking at the fatal white spot on his shoulder, and trying to persuade himself that it was not spreading.

In this state of mind Bladud arrived one day at the abode of the hunter of the Hot Swamp. It was not, indeed, close to the springs which caused the swamp, but stood in a narrow sequestered gully quite five miles distant from it. The spot had been chosen as one which was not likely to be discovered by wanderers, and could be easily defended if it should be found. Moreover, its owner, as Bladud had been warned, was a fierce, morose man, who loved solitude and resented interference of any kind, and this was so well known in the thinly-peopled neighbourhood that every one kept carefully out of his way.

Sometimes this eccentric hunter appeared at the nearest village—twenty miles distant from his home—with some pigs to barter for the few commodities which he wanted from time to time; but he and his horse, cow, and dogs ate up all the remaining produce of his small farm—if such it might be called.

It was a beautiful evening when the prince walked up to the door of the little hut, in front of which its owner was standing, eyeing him with a forbidding scowl as he approached.

He was in truth a strange and formidable man, such as one would rather not meet with in a lonely place. There appear to have been giants in those days; for this hunter of the Hot Swamp was nearly, if not quite, as tall as Bladud himself, and to all appearance fully as strong of limb. A mass of black hair covered his head and chin; a skin hunting-shirt his body, and a hairy boar-skin was thrown across his broad shoulders. Altogether, he seemed to his visitor the very personification of ferocity. A huge bow, ready strung, leaned against his hut. As Bladud advanced with his own bow unstrung, the man apparently scorned to take it up, but he grasped and leaned upon a staff proportioned to his size.

Anxious to propitiate this mysterious being, the prince approached with steady, unaffected ease of manner, and a look of goodwill which might have conciliated almost any one; but it had no effect on the hunter.

"What want ye here?" he demanded, when his visitor was near enough.

"To enter your service."

"*My* service!" exclaimed the man with a look of surprise that for a moment banished the scowl. "I want no servant. I can serve myself well enough. And, truly, it seems to me that a man like you should be ashamed to talk of service. You are more fitted for a master than a servant. I trow you must have some bad motive for seeking service with a man like me. Have you murdered any one, that you flee from the face of your fellows and seek to hide you here?"

"No, I am not a murderer."

"What then? Are you desirous of becoming one, and making me your victim?" asked the hunter, with a look of contempt; "for you will find that no easy job, stout though you be. I have a good mind to crack your crown for coming here to disturb my solitude!"

"Two can play at that game," replied Bladud, with a seraphic smile. "But I am truly a man of peace. I merely want to look after your cattle for occupation; I will gladly live in the woods, away from your dwelling, if you will let me serve you—my sole desire being, like your own, to live—and, if need be, to die—alone."

For a few moments there was a softened expression on the hunter's face as he asked, in a tone that had something almost of sympathy in it—

"Is there a woman at the bottom of this?"

"No. Woman has nothing to do with it—at least, not exactly—not directly," returned Bladud.

"Hah!" exclaimed the man, paying no regard to the modification implied in the answer; and advancing a step, with eager look, "did she tempt you on and then deceive you; and scorn you, and forsake you for another man?"

"You mistake me. The poor woman I was thinking of was an old one, labouring under a deadly disease."

On hearing this the hunter's softened look vanished, and his former scowl returned.

"Go!" he said, sternly; "I can take care of the cattle myself, without help. But stay, a man of your peaceful nature and humility may, perchance, not be too proud to take charge of pigs."

Bladud flushed—not so much because of the proposal as the tone of contempt in which it was uttered; but, remembering his condition and his object, he mastered his feelings.

"I am willing to take charge of your pigs," he said, in a quiet tone; "where do they feed?"

"A goodish bit from here. Not far from the Hot Swamp, that lies on the other side of the hill."

The man pointed to a high ridge, just visible beyond the gully in which his hut lay concealed, which was clothed from base to summit with dense forest.

"There are plenty of pigs there," he continued in a milder tone. "How many I don't know, and don't care. I brought the old ones here, and they have multiplied. If you choose to keep them together, you are welcome. I want only a few of them now and then. When I do, I hunt them together and drive them with my dogs. You may kill and eat of them as you please; but don't come nigh my hut, mind you, else will I put an arrow in your heart."

"Good, I will take care," returned the prince gravely. "And if you come nigh *my* dwelling, is it understood that I am to put an arrow in *your* heart? I could easily do it, for I am a fair marksman."

Something approaching almost to a smile crossed the hunter's swart visage at this reply. It did not last, however.

"Go!" he said. "Keep your jesting for the pigs, if they have a mind to listen."

"I will try them. Mayhap they are more sociable than their owner. And now, master, might I ask for the loan of one of your dogs? It might be useful in herding."

"None of them would follow you. Yet—yes, the pup might do so. It has not yet come to care for me much."

So saying, the man went to the rear of his hut, and, from the kennel there, fetched a young but full-grown dog, somewhat resembling a retriever, which gambolled joyously at the prospect of being let out for a run.

"There, take him. He comes of a good breed. Keep the leash on his neck till you have given him his first feed; he'll follow you after that."

"What is his name?" asked the prince.

"No name. Like his master in that!"

Taking the leash in his hand, Bladud said farewell, and went away into the woods, while the hunter of the Swamp, turning round, stooped as he entered his hut, and shut the door behind him.

It may seem strange that the prince should thus voluntarily seek for menial occupation, but, in truth, he shrank from the idea of living absolutely to himself alone, and felt a strong desire to have some sort of responsibility in connection with a human being, however short his life on earth might be, or however uncouth the individual with whom he might have to do—for man is intensely social, as only those who have dwelt in absolute solitude can thoroughly understand.

CHAPTER NINETEEN

PRINCE BLADUD TAKES POSSESSION OF HIS ESTATE AND BEGINS BUSINESS

Pondering over the circumstances of the strange being from whom he had just parted, Bladud proceeded to the summit of the hill, or ridge of high land, on the other side of which lay the region in which he had made up his mind to end his days.

It took him full two hours to make his way through the dense underwood to the top; but when this point was reached, the magnificent panorama of land and water which met his view was a feast to his eyes, which for a time caused him to forget his forlorn condition.

In all directions, wherever he gazed, ridges and knolls, covered with dense woods and richest vegetation, were seen extending from his elevated outlook to the distant horizon. Cliffs, precipices, dells, and bright green open spaces varied the landscape; and in the bottom of the great valley which lay immediately beneath his feet there meandered a broad river, in whose waters were reflected here and there the overhanging trees, or green patches of its flower-bespangled banks, or the rich browns and yellows of spots where these banks had been broken away by floods; while, elsewhere, were seen glittering patches of the blue sky.

Far away in the extreme distance a soft cloud of thin transparent vapour hung steadily over a partially open space, which he rightly conjectured to be the Hot Swamp, of which he had often heard wondrous stories in his boyhood, but which he had not been permitted to visit, owing to the tribes living near the springs having been at war with his father. During his absence in the East, King Hudibras had attacked and almost exterminated the tribes in question, so that the Hot Swamp region, just at the time when the prince arrived, was a land of desolation.

Though desolate, however, it was, as we have tried to show, exceeding lovely, so that our wanderer was ravished with the prospect, and seated himself on a bank near the top of the ridge to contemplate its beauties in detail.

His canine companion sat down beside him, and looked up inquiringly in his face.

During the first part of the journey the pup had strained a good deal at the leash, and had displayed a strong desire to return to its former master, as well as a powerful objection to follow its new one. It had also, with that perversity of spirit not uncommon in youth, exhibited a proneness to advance on the other side of bushes and trees from its companion, thus necessitating frequent halts and numerous disentanglements. On all of these occasions Bladud had remonstrated in tones so soft, and had rectified the error so gently, that the pup was evidently impressed. Possibly it was an observant pup, and appreciated the advantages of human kindness. Perhaps it was a sagacious pup, and already recognised the difference between the old master and the new.

Be this as it may, Bladud had not been long seated there in a state of dreamy abstraction, when he became conscious of the inquiring look. Returning it with interest, but without speaking, he gazed steadily into the soft brown eyes that were turned up to his. At last the prince opened his lips, and the dog, turning his head slightly to one side with a look of expectancy, cocked his ears.

"Browneyes," he said, "you'll grow to be a fine dog if you live."

There was the slightest possible tremor in the pup's tail. Of course there might have been more than a tremor if the caudal appendage had been at liberty instead of being sat upon. It was enough, however, to indicate a tendency to goodwill.

"Come here, Browneyes," said Bladud, holding out his hand.

But the pup was hardly prepared for such a complete and sudden concession as the invitation implied. He repeated the tremor, however, and turned his head to the other side, by way of a change, but sat still.

A happy thought occurred to the prince—justifying the remark of Solomon that there is nothing new under the sun. He opened his wallet, took out a small piece of meat, and held it out.

"Here, Brownie, have a bit." Another justification of Solomon, for the natural abbreviation of names is not new!

The pup advanced with confidence, ate the morsel, and looked inquiringly for more, at the same time wagging its tail with unqualified satisfaction.

"Yes, Brownie, you shall have more."

The second morsel was bestowed; the tail wagged effusively;

the name of Brownie became irrevocably associated with food, and a loving look and tone with favours to come. Thus a title and a friendship were established which endured through life and was terminated only by death. So trivial sometimes are the incidents on which the great events of life are hinged!

We pause here to deprecate the idea that this fine animal's affection was gained through its stomach. Many a time had its old master thrown it savoury junks and bones of food; but a scowl and sometimes a growl, had often been thrown into the mess, thereby robbing the gift of all grace, and checking the outflow of affection. Bladud's character similarly, was as clearly perceived by the manner of his gifts. Indeed, it would have been a poor compliment to the intelligence of Brownie—or of any dog, young or old—to suppose it capable of misunderstanding the gentle tone, the kindly glance, and the patting hand of Bladud. At all events, the result was that Brownie, with an expressive wag and bark, vowed fidelity from that date to the prince, and, in the same act, renounced allegiance to the hunter of the Hot Swamp.

From that date, too, the master and the dog entered upon, and kept up at frequent though brief intervals, a species of conversation or mental intercourse which, if not profound, was equal to much that passes for intercourse among men, and was, at all events, a source of eminent satisfaction to both.

Removing the leash, Bladud descended the hill, with Brownie gambolling delightedly round him.

That night they slept together under the spreading branches of a magnificent oak.

There was no need to keep watch against wild beasts, for

R. M. Ballantyne

Brownie slept, as it were, with one eye open, and the slightest symptom of curiosity among the wild fraternity was met by a growl so significant that the would-be intruder sheered off.

The sun was high when the prince awoke and arose from his bed of leaves. The pup, although awake long before, had dutifully lain still, abiding his master's time. It now arose and shook itself, yawned, and looked up with an expression of "what next?"

Having lighted a fire, Bladud set up the carcase of a wild duck to roast. He had shot it the day before on his way to the valley of the Swamp. As this was a proceeding in which the pup had a prospective interest, he sat by attentively.

"Ah! Brownie," said his master, sitting down to wait for the cooking of the bird, "you little know what a sad life awaits you. No companionship but that of a doomed man, and I fear you will be a poor nurse when the end comes, though assuredly you will not be an unsympathetic one. But it may be long before the end. That's the worst of it. Come, have a bit."

He threw him a leg as he spoke, and the two breakfasted peacefully together on the banks of the shining river, slaking their thirst, after it was finished, at the same pure stream.

While doing so the prince observed with satisfaction that large trout were rising freely, and that several flocks of wild ducks and other aquatic birds passed both up and down the river.

"Now, Brownie," he said, when the meal was concluded, "you and I must search for a convenient spot on which to build our hut."

Before starting off, however, he uncovered his shoulder and looked anxiously at the white spot. It was as obvious as ever, but did not seem to him increased since he left home. A very slight matter will sometimes give hope to a despairing man. Under the influence of this negative comfort, Bladud took up his weapons and sallied forth, closely followed by the pup.

In the haste of departure and the depressed state of his mind he had, as has been said, forgotten his sword, or deliberately left it behind him. The only weapon he now possessed, besides the bow and arrows given to him by the Hebrew, was a small bronze hatchet, which was, however, of little use for anything except cutting down small trees and branches for firewood. He carried a little knife, also, in his girdle, but it was much too small to serve the purpose of an offensive weapon, though it was well suited to skin wild animals and cut up his food. As for his staff, or club—it might be of use in a contest with men, but would be of little service against bears or wolves. Casting it aside, therefore, he cut for himself a ponderous oaken staff about five feet long, at one end of which there was a heavy knotted mass that gave it great weight. The other end he sharpened to a fine point. This formidable weapon he purposed to wield with both hands when using it as a club, while, if need should arise, he might also use it as a spear.

"I was foolish, Brownie," he remarked, while rounding off the head of this club, "to leave my good sword behind me, for though I have no desire to kill men, there may arise a need-be to kill bears. However, it cannot be helped, and, verily, this little thing will be a pretty fair substitute."

He twirled the little thing round his head with one hand, in a way that would have rejoiced the heart of a modern Irishman, had he been there to see, and induced the pup to jump aside in surprise with his tail between his legs.

R. M. Ballantyne

A few minutes later, and he was striding over the beautiful land in all directions, examining and taking possession, as it were, of his fair domain.

In passing over a knoll which was crowned by several magnificent oaks, they came suddenly on a family of black pigs, which were luxuriating on the acorns that covered the ground.

"My future care!" muttered the prince, with a grim smile, for he hardly believed in the truth of all he was going through, and almost expected to awake and find it was a dream.

The pigs, headed by a huge old boar, caught sight of the intruders at the same time, and stood for a moment or two grunting in stolid astonishment.

With all the gaiety of inexperience, the pup went at them single-handed, causing the whole herd to turn and fly with ear-splitting screams—the old boar bringing up the rear, and looking round, out of the corner of his little eyes, with wicked intent.

Bladud, knowing the danger, sprang after them, shouting to the pup to come back. But Brownie's war-spirit had been aroused, and his training in obedience had only just begun. In a moment he was alongside the boar, which turned its head and gave him a savage rip with a gleaming tusk. Fortunately it just barely reached the pup's flank, which it cut slightly, but quite enough to cause him to howl with anger and pain.

Before the boar could repeat the operation, Bladud sent his club whizzing in advance of him. It was well aimed. The heavy head alighted just above the root of the boar's curly tail. Instantly, as if anticipating the inventions of the future, fifty steam whistles seemed to burst into full cry. The other pigs, in sympathetic alarm, joined in chorus, and thus, yelling inconceivably, they plunged into a thicket and disappeared.

Bladud almost fell to the ground with laughing, while Brownie, in no laughing mood, came humbly forward to claim and receive consolation. But he received more than consolation, for, while the prince was engaged in binding up the wound, he poured upon him such a flood of solemn remonstrance, in a tone of such injured feeling, that the pup was evidently cut to the heart—his self-condemned, appealing looks proving beyond a doubt that the meaning of what was said was plain to him, though the language might be obscure.

On continuing the march, Brownie limped behind his master—a sadder and a wiser dog. They had not gone far when they came on another family of pigs, which fled as before. A little further on, another herd was discovered, wallowing in a marshy spot. It seemed to Bladud that there was no good feeding in that place, and that the creatures were dirtying themselves with no obvious end in view, so, with the pup's rather unwilling assistance, he drove them to more favourable ground, where the acorns were abundant.

At this point he reached a secluded part of the valley, or, rather, an off-shoot from it, where a low precipice rose on one side, and thick flowering shrubs protected the other. The spot was considerably elevated above the level of the low ground, and from an opening in the shrubbery at the further extremity could be seen the larger valley with all its wealth of forest and meadow, its knolls, and slopes, and wooded uplands, with the river winding like a silver thread throughout its whole extent.

R. M. Ballantyne

Here the prince resolved to fix his abode, and, not a little pleased with the successful way in which he had commenced his amateur pig-herding, he set vigorously and patiently to work with the little bronze hatchet, to fell such trees as would be required in the construction of his future home.

CHAPTER TWENTY

A STRANGE ABODE AND A WILD VISITOR

Bladud's idea of a palace worthy of a prince was not extravagant. He erected it in three days without assistance or tools, except the bronze axe and knife—Brownie acting the part of superintendent of the works. Until it was finished, he slept with the forest trees for a shelter and the sky for a canopy.

The edifice was nothing better than a small hut, or booth, constructed of long branches bent in the shape of semi-hoops, the ends of which were thrust into the ground. The whole was thatched with dried grass and bound down with ropes made of the same material. It was further secured against the possible influence of high winds, by heavy branches being laid across it and weighted with stones. Dried grass also formed the carpeting on the floor.

Of course it was not so high that its architect could stand up in it, but he could sit in it erect, and could lie down at full length without showing his heels outside. There was no door, but one end was left unfinished as a substitute. Neither was there a fireplace, the space in front sufficing for a kitchen.

While engaged in its erection, Bladud was too busy to

indulge in gloomy thoughts, but as soon as it was finished and he had lain down to rest under its shade, the terrible, almost incredible, nature of his position rushed upon him in full force. The opening of the hut had been so arranged as to present a view of the wide-spreading valley, and he gazed upon scenes of surpassing loveliness, in which all the sights that met the eye breathed of beauty and repose, while the sounds that broke upon the ear were suggestive of bird and beast revelling in the enjoyment of the gifts and sunshine of a bountiful Creator. But such sights and sounds only enhanced the misery of the poor man, and he started up, after a few minutes' contemplation, and rushed outside in the vain hope of escaping from his misery by energetic action.

"This will drive me mad," he thought, as he paused and stood for a few minutes irresolute. "Better far to return to the East where tyrants reign and people dare not call body and soul their own, and die fighting in the front rank for liberty— but—but—who would let me join them, knowing my disease? 'Unclean!' I may not even come within touch of my kind—"

His head sank on his breast and he tried to banish thought altogether. At the same moment his eyes met the meek, patient look of Brownie.

"Ah, pup," he exclaimed, stooping to fondle the soft brown head as he muttered to himself, "you teach me a lesson and put me to shame, despite your want of speech. You are awaiting my commands, ready to give unquestioning obedience—whether to go to the right, or left, or to lie down. And here am I, not only a prince, but supposed to be a reasoning man, rebelling against the decree of my Maker— my Spirit-Father! Surely there must be One who called my spirit into being—else had I never been, for I could not create myself, and it must be His will that I am smitten—and for a *good* end, else He were not good!"

For a few minutes longer he continued to meditate in silence. Then he turned quickly and picked up the axe which lay at the entrance of the hut.

"Come, pup," he cried, cheerfully, "you and I must build another house. You see, we shall have plenty of game and venison soon to guard from the wolves, and it would be disagreeable to keep it in the palace along with ourselves— wouldn't it? So, come along, Brownie."

Thus appealed to, the pup gave its assent by some violent tail activities, and, in a few minutes, had resumed its former post as superintendent of the works, while its master toiled like a second Samson in the hope of driving mental distress away through the pores of his skin.

He was not indeed altogether unsuccessful, for so intimate is the mysterious connection between spirit and matter that he felt comparative relief—even to the extent of cheerfulness— when the muscles were in violent action and the perspiration was streaming down his brow; but when the second hut, or larder, was completed his depression returned in greater power than before.

Then he took to hunting with tremendous energy, a plan which was highly approved of by his canine companion. He also devoted himself to his specific duties as swine-herd; collected the animals from all quarters into several large herds, counted them as well as he could, and drove them to suitable feeding-grounds. On retiring each day from this work, into which he threw all his power, he felt so fatigued as to be quite ready for supper and bed.

Gradually he became accustomed to the life, and at length,

R. M. Ballantyne

after a considerable time of it, a feeling of resignation to his fate began to tell upon him.

The effect of prolonged solitude also began even to numb the powers of his mind. He was fully aware of this, and tried to shake it off, for he shuddered more at the thought of mental than of physical decay. Among other things, he took to talking more frequently to Brownie, but although the pup was, in many respects, a most valuable and sympathetic companion, he could not prevent the conversation from being rather one-sided.

By degrees the summer merged into autumn; the foliage assumed the tints of green and gold. Then it became russet, and finally the cold bleak winds of a northern winter shrieked through the valley and swept the leaves away.

During all this time no human being had gone near that region, or paid the forlorn prince a visit, except once when the hunter of the Hot Swamp made his appearance.

The rebellious tribes retained too vivid a recollection of the slaughter that had taken place during and after the fight with King Hudibras, to risk a second encounter with that monarch, so that the place was at that time absolutely deserted by human beings—though it was sufficiently peopled by the lower animals. On the occasion when the hunter unexpectedly appeared, he demanded of Bladud an account of his stewardship. The report was so satisfactory that the hunter became, for him, quite amiable; commended his swine-herd and drove off a number of the pigs to market. On his return, laden with the few household goods for which he had bartered them, he paid the prince another visit, and even condescended to accept an invitation to enter his hut and partake of a roast of venison which was at the time being prepared for the mid-day meal. He was still, however, very brusque and taciturn.

"No one has been near me during the whole summer or autumn but yourself," observed Bladud with an involuntary sigh.

"You must be pleased at that," returned the hunter, sharply; "you said you came here for solitude."

"Truly I did; but I had not thought it would be so hard to bear."

"Why do you seek it, then, if you don't like it?" asked the hunter in the same brusque, impatient manner which characterised all his words and actions.

"I am forced to seek it by a Power which may not be resisted with impunity."

"There is no such power!" exclaimed the hunter with a wild, demoniac laugh. "I can resist any power—all powers. There is nothing that I cannot resist and overcome."

The gigantic man, with his dishevelled locks and shaggy beard, looked so fierce and powerful, as he sat on the opposite side of the fire glaring at his host, that Bladud became impressed with a hope that the maniac—for such he evidently was—would not attempt to prove his resistless power there and then. In order to avert such a catastrophe, he assumed an air of the most perfect ease and indifference to the boast, and asked him with a bland smile if he would have another slice of venison.

The hunter seemed to be disconcerted by the question, but, being a hungry man and a ravenous eater, he accepted the offer and began to eat the slice in moody silence.

"Your good pup has been a real blessing to me," resumed the prince a few minutes later, during which time he had devoted himself to his own portion of food, "not only in the way of helping me to hunt and drive the pigs, but as a companion who can do all but speak."

"He could speak if you would let him," returned the hunter. "I speak to my dogs continually, and they always answer— not with their tongues, for that is not dog-language, but with their eyes—and I know every word they speak. You would wonder how clever they are, and what droll things they say sometimes."

He burst into a wild hilarious laugh at this point, as if the thought of the canine pleasantries were too much for him; then suddenly became grave, and scowled furtively at his host, as if he felt that he had committed himself.

"You are right," replied Bladud, affecting not to observe the scowl. "My pup often speaks to me with his eyes, but I am not so good at understanding the language as you appear to be. No doubt I shall acquire it in time."

"Then you don't like being alone?" said the hunter, after a pause, during which Bladud saw that he was eyeing him keenly, though he pretended not to observe this.

"No, I don't like it at all, but it can't be helped."

"Well, it might have been helped, for I could have sent them to you."

"Sent whom?"

"A man and a boy. They were not together, but came to my hut at different times inquiring for you, but, knowing your desire for solitude, I turned them away on the wrong scent."

"I'm glad you did," returned the prince, "for I want to be troubled by neither man nor boy. Yet I wonder who they could be. Did they say why they wanted to find me?"

"No, they did not say, and I would not ask; what cared I about their reasons?"

"Yet you care enough for me, it appears, to say you would have sent them to me if you knew I had been lonely. What was the appearance of the man?"

"He was old, but very strong, though not so big as me—or you. His hair was long and white; so was his beard. He wore a long dark robe, and carried a very big staff."

Bladud had no difficulty in recognising the description of his friend the Hebrew.

"And the boy; what was he like?"

"Like all boys, active and impudent."

"I am afraid," returned the prince with a slight smile, "that your acquaintance with boys cannot have been extensive—they are not all active and impudent."

"Most of those that have crossed my path are so. At all events, this one was, for when I pointed out the direction you had gone—which was just the opposite way from here—he said, 'I don't believe you!' and when I leaped on him to give him his deserts, he dodged me, and fled into the woods like a squirrel. It was as well, for I should have killed him."

"I am not sorry he escaped you, then," said Bladud, with a

laugh, "though I scarcely think you would have killed the poor lad even if you had caught him."

"Oh yes, I would. And I'll kill *you* if you venture to doubt my word."

As he said this the hunter sprang to his feet, and, drawing his knife, seemed about to leap upon his host, who, however, sat perfectly still.

"I should be sorry that you should die," said Bladud in a calm voice, while he kept his eyes steadily fixed on those of the maniac. "*You* have heard, have you not, of that terrible disease of the East, called leprosy?"

"Yes—the ship-captains have often spoken of it," said the madman, whose mind, like that of a child, could be easily turned into new channels.

"Look! I have got that disease. The Power which you profess to despise has sent it to me. If you so much as touch me, your doom is fixed."

He uncovered his shoulder as he spoke and displayed the white spot.

Bladud felt quite uncertain how this would be received by the madman, but he was scarcely prepared for what followed. No sooner did the hunter see the spot and realise what it meant, than without a word he turned, caught up his bundle, uttered a yell of terror, and fled from the spot, closely followed by his dogs, which howled as if in sympathy.

CHAPTER TWENTY ONE

A STRANGE ENCOUNTER
AND A FRIEND IN NEED

About a week after the events narrated in the last chapter, an incident occurred which, trifling in itself, was nevertheless the cause of momentous issues in the life of our hero.

He was returning one evening from a long ramble with his dog, when the screams of a pig in evident distress attracted his attention. Hastening to the place he found that a small member of his charge had fallen over a cliff into a crevice in the rock, where it stuck fast and was unable to extricate itself. The violent nature of the porcine family is well known. Although very little hurt, this little pig felt its position so unbearable that it immediately filled the woods with agonising shrieks until Bladud dragged it out of the cleft, and carried it in his arms to the foot of the precipice, where he set it free. Then the whirlwind of its outcry came to a sudden stop, thereby proving beyond a doubt that passion, not pain, was the cause of its demonstrations.

From that date many of the pigs became affected by a cutaneous disease, which gradually spread among all the herds. It was some time before Bladud observed this; but when he did notice it, he jumped at once to the conclusion that he must have communicated leprosy to his unfortunate herds while rescuing the little pig. Whether or not he was right in this conjecture, we cannot say; but the probability of his mere touch being so contaminating was sufficient to increase greatly the depression of spirits which had been stealing over him—a condition which was not a little aggravated by the fact that the white spot on his arm was slowly but surely spreading. Still the disease had not, so far, affected his general health or strength in any serious degree.

About that time there set in a long period of fine sunny weather, during which Bladud busied himself in hunting and drying meat, as well as fish, which he stored in his larder for future use. He also cut a large quantity of firewood, and built another booth in which to protect it from the weather, and otherwise made preparation for the winter when it should arrive.

One day he had wandered a considerable way into the forest, and was about to turn to retrace his steps homeward, when he was surprised to hear some creature crashing through the woods towards him. It could not have been startled by himself, else it would have run away from him. Stepping behind a tree, he strung his bow, called Brownie close to his heel, and waited. A few seconds later a deer dashed close past him, but, as his belt was already hung round with game, and home was still far distant, he did not shoot. Besides, he was curious to know what had startled the deer. A few minutes revealed that, for suddenly the sound of footsteps was heard; then the bushes opposite were parted, and a boy, or youth just emerging from boyhood, ran past him at full speed, with an arrow sticking through his left sleeve. He was unarmed, and gasped like one who runs for his life. Catching sight of the prince as he passed the tree that had concealed him, the boy doubled like a hare, ran up to Bladud, and, grasping one of his hands, cried—"O! save me!—save me!—

from robbers!" in the most agonising tones.

"That will I, poor lad, if I can."

He had barely time to make this reply when a man burst from the shrubbery on the other side of the tree, and almost plunged into his arms. So close was he, and so unexpected the meeting, that the prince had not time or space to use his bow, but saluted the man's forehead with such an Olympic crack from his fist, that he fell prone upon the ground and remained there. Bladud had dropped his bow in the act, but his club leant handily against the tree. Catching it up, he wheeled round just in time to face three tall and strong men, with bows in their hands. Seeing their leader on the ground, they simultaneously discharged three arrows, which were well aimed, and struck the prince full on the chest; but they did not penetrate far, for, in anticipation of some such possible encounter with foes, he had covered his chest with a breastplate of thick double-ply hide, which effectually checked them.

Before they could draw other arrows Bladud rushed at them with a terrific shout, hurling his mighty club in advance. The weapon caught the nearest robber full in the chest and laid him flat on the grass. The other two, dropping their bows, turned and fled.

"Guard them, Brownie!" cried Bladud, as he followed.

The dog obediently took up a position between the two fallen men, and eyed them in a way and with an ominous growl, that meant mischief if they dared to stir.

Bladud easily overtook the other two, grasped them by their necks, and, using their heads as battering-rams, rapped them together. They sank half-stunned upon their knees, and begged for mercy.

"You shall have it," said Bladud, "on the condition that you go and tell your comrades that if they ever come within twenty miles of the Swamp, they shall find a man in the woods who will turn them inside out, and roast them all alive! Away!"

They went precipitately, as may be readily believed, and, as the prince had intended, spread a report that gave to him thenceforth the rank of a sorcerer, and secured him from future annoyance.

Returning to the tree, Bladud found the fallen robbers beginning to recover consciousness—the one being held in submission by the fugitive youth, who stood, bow in hand, pointing an arrow at his throat; the other by Brownie, who merely curled his nose, displayed his magnificent teeth, and uttered a low growl of remonstrance.

"Get up!" he said to the one he had knocked down with his fist.

But as the order was not obeyed with sufficient promptitude, he lifted the man up by the collar, like a kitten, and sent him staggering against the tree with a violence that astounded him. Calling off the dog, he gave a similar order to the second robber, who displayed much greater agility in his movements.

Repeating the little threat with which he had dismissed their comrades, Bladud ordered them to be off. The second robber thankfully turned and took to his heels; but the first stooped to pick up his bow, whereupon Bladud wrenched it from his grasp, broke it over his head, and belaboured him with the wreck for a couple of hundred yards through the woods, while the robber ran as if he thought the evil spirit was at his heels.

Returning somewhat blown from this unusual exercise, he found the youth in a state of great amusement and satisfaction.

"Hah! you may laugh, my lad; but I can assure you it would have been no laughing matter if these scoundrels had caught you."

"You speak but the sober truth," returned the boy, still smiling; "for well assured am I that it would have cost me my life if they had caught me. But, believe me, I am not only pleased to see such villains get a little of what they deserve, but am exceedingly grateful to you for so kindly and effectually coming to my aid."

"As to that, I would aid any one in distress—especially if pursued by robbers. But, come, sit down and tell me how you fell into their power. This bout has winded me a little. I will sit down on this bank; do you sit on the bank opposite to me."

"The explanation is simple and short," replied the boy; "I wanted to have my own way, like most other boys, so I left home without leave, or saying farewell."

"That was bad," said the prince, shaking his head. He was on the point of advancing some profitable reflections on this head, but the memory of his own boyhood checked him.

"I know it was bad, and assuredly I have been well punished," returned the boy, "for these robbers caught me and have kept me with them for a long time, so long that I have quite lost count of the days now."

R. M. Ballantyne

"Does your father live far from here?"

"Yes, very, very far, and I know not where to go or what to do," answered the boy, with a pitiful look.

"Never mind, you are safe at present, and no doubt I shall find means of having you sent safe home—though I see not the way just yet."

"Is that blood on your coat?" asked the lad anxiously, as he pointed to the prince's breast.

"It is. The arrow-heads must have gone through the breastplate and scratched the skin. I will look to it."

"Let me help you," said the boy, rising and approaching.

"Back! you know not what you do," said the prince sternly. "You must not touch me. You have done so once to-day. It may cost you your life. Ask not why, but obey my orders."

Not less surprised at the nature of these remarks than at the severe tone in which they were uttered, the boy re-seated himself in silence, while Bladud removed the breastplate and examined his wounds.

They were deeper than he had imagined, the three arrow-heads being half imbedded in his flesh.

"Nothing serious," he said, drawing out the heads and stanching the flow of blood with a little moss. "Come, now, I will show you my home, and give you something to eat before you tell me more of your history. You shall have a couch in one of my outhouses. Have a care as you walk with me that you do not come against me, or touch me even with a finger. My reasons you may not know, but—remember what I say."

Bladud spoke the last words with the severity that he had assumed before; then, dismissing the subject, he commented on the beauty of the landscape, the wickedness of robbers, the liveliness of animated nature and things in general with the cheerful air that had been habitual to him before he was compelled to flee the face of man. The pleasure he had felt in his brief intercourse with the gruff hunter of the Swamp had remained a bright spot in his lonely life. He naturally enjoyed with much greater zest the company of the lively boy who had thus unexpectedly crossed his path, but when he retired for the night—having told the lad to make for himself a couch in the fire-wood hut—the utter desolation of his life became, if possible, more deeply impressed on him.

During the night his wounds inflamed and became much more painful, and in the morning—whether from this cause or not, we cannot say—he found himself in a high fever.

His new friend, like most healthy boys, was a profound sleeper, and when the time for breakfast arrived he found it necessary to get up and awake him.

"Ho! lad, rise," he cried at the entrance to the firewood hut, "you slumber soundly. Come out and help me to get ready our morning meal."

The lad obeyed at once.

"What is your name?" he asked, as the lad appeared.

"Cormac," he replied.

"Well, Cormac, do you roast the meat this morning. Truly, it seems that you have come just in the nick of time, for I feel so ill that my head seems like a lump of stone, and my skin is burning. It is not often that I have had to ask the aid of man in such matters. Will you get me a draught of water from the spring hard by? I will lie down again for a little."

Cormac willingly ran to a neighbouring spring and filled thereat a cup made of the bark of the birch tree, with which he returned to Bladud's hut.

"Just put it inside the door where I can reach it," shouted the prince. "Do not enter on any account."

Lifting a corner of the skin that covered the entrance, the lad placed the cup inside, and then, sitting down by the fire outside, proceeded to prepare breakfast.

When it was ready he called to Bladud to say whether he would have some, at the same time thrusting a savoury rib underneath the curtain; but the prince declined it.

"I cannot eat," he said; "let me lie and rest if possible. My poor boy, this is inhospitable treatment. Yet I cannot help it."

"Never mind me," returned Cormac, lightly. "I like to nurse the sick, and I'll keep you well supplied with water, and cook venison or birds too if you want them. I can even shoot them if required."

"No need for that," returned Bladud, "there is plenty of food laid up for winter. But don't come inside my hut, remember. It will be death if you do!"

All that day the lad sat by the fire or went to the well for water, of which his patient drank continuously. During the night the prince was very restless, and groaned a good deal, so the boy resolved to sit up and watch by the fire. Next morning Bladud was delirious, and as he could not rise even to fetch from the door the water for which he thirsted, Cormac resolved to disobey orders and risk the consequences. Entering the hut, therefore, and sitting down beside the patient, he tended him for many days and nights—taking what rest he could obtain by snatches beside the camp-fire.

R. M. Ballantyne

CHAPTER TWENTY TWO

THE PIGS' CURE

It was not long before our hero recovered from his delirium. Leading, as he had been doing, an abstemious and healthy life, ordinary disease could not long maintain its grasp of him. His superabundant life seemed to cast it off with the ease with which his physical frame was able to cast aside human foes. But he could not thus shake off the leprosy.

One of the first things he did on recovering consciousness was to uncover his arm. The fatal spot had increased considerably in size. With something of a shudder he looked round his little hut, endeavouring to remember where he was and to recall recent events. He was alone at the time, and he fancied the fight with the robbers and rescue of the boy must have been all a dream. The name Cormac, however, puzzled him not a little. Many a time before that had he dreamed of vivid scenes and thrilling incidents, but never in his recollection had he dreamt a name!

Being thoughtfully disposed, he lay meditating listlessly on this point in that tranquil frame of mind which often accompanies convalescence, and had almost fallen asleep when a slight noise outside awoke him. The curtain-door was lifted, and Cormac, entering, sat quietly down on a block of wood beside him.

Bladud became suddenly aware that he had not been dreaming, but he did not move. Through his slightly opened eyelids he watched the lad while he mixed some berries in a cup of water. As he lay thus silently observant, he was deeply impressed with the handsome countenance of his nurse and the graceful movements of his slight figure.

Presently the thought of his disease recurred to him—it was seldom, indeed, absent from his mind—and the strict injunctions which he had given to his young companion.

"Boy!—boy!" he cried suddenly, with a vigour that caused the boy to start off his seat and almost capsize the cup, "did I not forbid you to enter my hut or to touch me?"

At first Cormac looked alarmed, but, seeing that a decided change for the better had taken place in his patient, his brow smoothed and he laughed softly.

"How dared you to disobey me?" exclaimed Bladud again in stern tones.

"I dared because I saw you were unable to prevent me," returned the lad, with a quiet smile. "Besides, you were too ill to feed yourself, so, of course, I had to do it for you. Do you suppose I am so ungrateful to the man who saved my life as to stand aside and let him die for want of a helping hand? Come, now, be reasonable and let me give you this drink." He approached as he spoke.

"Keep off!—keep off, I say," shouted the prince in a voice so resolute that Cormac was fain to obey. "It is bad enough to come into my hut, but you *must not* touch me!"

"Why not?—I have touched you already."

"How! when?"

"I have lifted your head many a time to enable you to drink when you could not lift it yourself."

A groan escaped Bladud.

"Then it is too late! Look at this," he cried, suddenly uncovering his arm.

"What is that?" asked the boy, with a look of curiosity.

"It is—leprosy!"

"I am not afraid of leprosy!"

"Not afraid of it!" exclaimed the prince, "that may well be, for you have the air of one who fears nothing; but it will kill you for all that, unless the Maker of all defends you, for it is a dread—a terrible—disease that no strength can resist or youth throw off. It undermines the health and eats the flesh off the bones, renders those whom it attacks horrible to look at, and in the end it kills them. But it is possible that you may not yet have caught the infection, poor lad, so you must keep away from me now, and let not a finger touch me henceforth. Your life, I say, may depend on it."

"I will obey you as to that," replied Cormac, "now that you are beginning to recover, but I must still continue to put food and water within your reach."

"Be it so," rejoined the prince, turning away with a slight groan, for his excitement not less than the conversation had exhausted him. In a few minutes more he was asleep with an expression of profound anxiety stereotyped on his countenance.

It was not long after the fever left him that returning strength enabled Bladud to crawl out of his hut, and soon after that he was able to ramble through the woods in company with Cormac, and with Brownie—that faithful friend who had lain by his master's side during all his illness. The sparkling river gladdened the eyes, and the bracing air and sunshine strengthened the frame of the prince, so that with the cheerful conversation of Cormac and the gambols of his canine friend he was sometimes led to forget for a time the dark cloud that hung over him.

One day he was struck by something in the appearance of his dog, and, sitting down on a bank, he called it to him. After a few minutes' careful examination he turned to Cormac with a look of deep anxiety.

"My boy," he said, "I verily believe that the hound is smitten with my own complaint. In his faithful kindness he has kept by me until I have infected him."

"That cannot be," returned Cormac, "for, during my rambles alone, when you were too ill to move, I saw that a great many of the pigs were affected by a skin disease something like that on the dog, and, you know, you could not have infected the pigs, for you have never touched them."

Bladud's anxiety was not removed but deepened when he heard this, for he called to remembrance the occasion when he had rescued one of the little pigs and carried it for some distance in his arms.

"And, do you know," continued the lad, "I have observed a strange thing. I have seen that many of the pigs, affected

R. M. Ballantyne

with this complaint, have gone down to the place where the hot waters rise, and, after bathing there, have returned all covered with mud, and these pigs seem to have got better of the disease, while many of those which did not go down to the swamp have died."

"That is strange indeed," returned the prince; "I must see to this, for if these waters cure the pigs, why not the dog?"

"Ay," rejoined Cormac, "and why not the man?"

"Because my disease is well known to be incurable."

"Are you sure?"

"We can hardly be sure of anything, not even of killing our mid-day meal," rejoined the prince. "See, there goes a bird that is big enough to do for both of us. Try your hand."

"That will be but losing an opportunity, for, as you know, I am not a good marksman," returned the youth, fitting an arrow quickly to his bow nevertheless, and discharging it. Although the bird in question was large and not far off, the arrow missed the mark, but startled the bird so that it took wing. Before it had risen a yard from the ground, however, an arrow from Bladud's bow transfixed it.

That night, after the bird had been eaten, when Brownie was busy with the scraps, and Cormac had retired to his couch in the firewood booth, Bladud lay in his hut unable to sleep because of what he had heard and seen that day. "Hope springs eternal in the human breast"—not less in the olden time than now. At all events it welled up in the breast of the royal outcast with unusual power as he waited anxiously for the first dawn of day.

Up to this time, although living within a few miles of it, the prince had not paid more than one or two visits to the Hot Swamp, because birds and other game did not seem to inhabit the place, and the ground was difficult to traverse. He had, of course, speculated a good deal as to the cause of the springs, but had not come to any conclusions more satisfactory than have been arrived at by the scientific minds of modern days. That heat of some sort was the cause applied in one fashion or another to the water so as to make it almost boil he had no manner of doubt, but what caused the heat he could not imagine, and it certainly did not occur to him that the interior of the earth was a lake of fire—the lovely world of vision being a mere crust. At least, if it did, he was never heard to say so.

But now he went down to the swamp with a renewed feeling of hope that gave fresh impulse to his heart and elasticity to his tread.

Arrived at the place, he observed that numbers of his porcine family were there before him. On seeing him they retreated with indignant grunts—their hasty retreat being accelerated by a few remarks from Brownie.

Making his way to what he believed to be the main fountain of the spring, the prince and the dog stood contemplating it for some time. Then the former dipped his hand in, but instantly withdrew it, for he found the water to be unbearably hot. Following its course, however, and testing it as he went along, he soon came to a spot where the temperature was sufficiently cool to render it agreeable. Here, finding a convenient hole big enough to hold him, he stripped and bathed. Brownie, who seemed much interested and enlivened by his master's proceedings, joined him on invitation, and appeared to enjoy himself greatly. Thereafter they returned home to breakfast and found Cormac already up and roasting venison ribs before the fire.

"I thought you were still sound asleep in your hut," he said in surprise, as they came up, "and I have been doing my best to make little noise, for fear of awaking you. Have you been bathing at the springs? I see the hound's coat is muddy."

"Thanks for your care, Cormac. Ay, we have indeed had a bath—Brownie and I. You see I have taken your advice, and am trying the pigs' cure."

"Right, Bladud. Wiser men have learned lessons from pigs."

"Are you not presumptuous, my lad, to suggest that there may be a wiser man than I?"

"Truly, no, for taking the advice of a mere stripling like me, is not a sign of wisdom in a man."

"In the present case you are perhaps right, but there are some striplings whose wisdom is sufficient to guide men. However, I will hope that even you, with all your presumption, may be right this time."

"That encourages me to offer additional advice," retorted the lad with a laugh, "namely, that you should devote your attention to these ribs, for you will find them excellent, and even a full-grown man can hardly fail to know that without food no cure can be effected."

"You are right, my boy. Sit down and set me an example, for youth, not less than age, must be supported."

Without more words they set to work, first throwing a bone to the hound, in order, as Bladud remarked, that they might all start on equal terms.

From that day the health of the prince began to mend—slowly but steadily the spot on his arm also began to diminish and to assume a more healthy aspect. Brownie also became convalescent, and much to the joy of Bladud, Cormac showed no symptoms of having caught the disease. Still, as a precaution, they kept studiously apart, and the prince observed—and twitted the boy with the fact—that the more he gained in health, and the less danger there was of infection, the more anxious did he seem to be to keep away from him!

Things were in this state when, one evening, they received a visit—which claims a new chapter to itself.

CHAPTER TWENTY THREE

IN WHICH VERY PERPLEXING EVENTS OCCUR

The visitor referred to in the last chapter was a tall, broad-shouldered old man with a snowy head of hair and a flowing white beard, a long, loose black garment, and a stout staff about six feet long.

Cormac had gone to a spring for water at the time he arrived, and Bladud was lying on his back inside his hut.

"Is any one within?" demanded the stranger, lifting a corner of the curtain.

"Enter not here, whoever you are!" replied the prince quickly, springing up—"stay—I will come out to you."

"You are wonderfully inhospitable," returned the stranger, as the prince issued from the hut and stood up with an inquiring look which suddenly changed to one of astonishment.

"Beniah!" he exclaimed.

"Even so," replied the Hebrew, holding out his hand, but Bladud drew back.

"What! will you neither permit me to enter your house nor shake your hand? I was not so churlish when you visited my dwelling."

"You know well, old man, that I do not grudge hospitality, but fear to infect you."

"Yes, I know it well," rejoined the Hebrew, smiling, "and knowing that you were here, I turned aside on my journey to inquire as to your welfare."

"I have much to say about my welfare and strange things to tell you, but first let me know what has brought you to this part of the land—for if you have turned aside to see me— seeing me has not been your main object."

"You are right. Yet it pleases me well to use this opportunity, and to see by your looks and bearing, that the disease seems to have been arrested."

"Yes, thanks be to the All-seeing One, I am well, or nearly so. But proceed to explain the reason of your journey."

"The cause of it is the unaccountable disappearance of the girl named Branwen."

"What! she who is the bosom friend of my sister Hafrydda?"

"The same. She had fled, you may remember, from your father's court for fear of being compelled to wed with Gunrig, the chief whose crown you cracked so deftly on the day of your arrival. She, poor thing, took refuge at first with me. I hid her for some time—"

"Then," interrupted the prince, "she must have been hidden in your hut at the time of my visit!"

R. M. Ballantyne

"She was. But that was no business of yours."

"Surely it was, old man, for my father's business is my business."

"Yea, but it was not my business to enlighten you, or the king either, while I had reason to know that he meant unduly to coerce the maiden. However, there she was hidden, as I tell you. Now, you are aware that Branwen's father Gadarn is a great chief, whose people live far away in the northern part of Albion. I bade Branwen remain close in my hut, in a secret chamber, while I should go and acquaint her father with her position, and fetch him down with a strong band of his retainers to rescue her. You should have seen the visage of Gadarn, when I told him the news. A wild boar of the woods could scarce have shown his tusks more fiercely. He not only ordered an armed band to get ready, instantly, but he roused the whole country around, and started off that same day with all his followers armed to the teeth. Of course I led them. In due course we arrived at my hut, when—lo! I found that the bird was flown!"

"I could see by the appearance of things," continued the Hebrew, "that the foolish girl had left of her own will, for there was no evidence of violence anywhere—which would doubtless have been the case if robbers had found her and carried her away, for they would certainly have carried off some of my goods along with her. The rage of her father on making this discovery was terrible. He threatened at once to cut off my old head, and even drew his sword with intent to act the part of executioner. But I reminded him that if he did so, he would cut off the only head that knew anything about his daughter, and that I had still some knowledge regarding her with which he was not acquainted.

"This arrested his hand just in time, for I actually fancied that

I had begun to feel the edge of his sword slicing into my spinal marrow. When he had calmed himself enough to listen, I told him that Branwen had spoken about paying a visit to the Hot Springs—that I knew she was bent on going there, for some reason that I could not understand, and that I thought it more than likely she had gone. 'Axe-men, to the front! Form long line! hooroo!' yelled the chief—(or something of that sort, for I'm a man of peace, and don't understand warlike orders), and away went the whole host at a run, winding through the forest like a great snake; Gadarn and I leading them, except when the thickets became impenetrable, and then the axe-men were ordered to the front and soon broke them down. And so, in course of time, we came within a few miles of the Hot Swamp, and—and, as I have said, I have been permitted to turn aside to visit you."

"Truly a strange tale," remarked the prince. "And is the armed host of Gadarn actually within a few miles of us?"

"It is; and, to say truth, I have come out to search for you chiefly to inquire whether you have seen any young woman at all resembling Branwen during your wanderings in this region?"

The Hebrew looked keenly at the prince as he put this question.

"You forget I have never seen this girl, and, therefore, could not know her even if I had met her. But, in truth, I have not seen any woman, young or old, since I came here. Nor have I seen any human being save my mad master, Konar, and a poor youth whom I rescued some time ago from the hands of robbers. He has nursed me through a severe illness, and is even now with me. But what makes you think that Branwen intended to come to the Swamp?"

R. M. Ballantyne

"Because—because, she had reasons of her own. I do not profess to understand the workings of a young girl's mind," answered the Hebrew.

"And what will you do," said Bladud, "now that you find she has not been here? Methinks that when Gadarn hears of your failure to find her at the Swamp, your spinal marrow and his sword will still stand a good chance of becoming acquainted."

The Hebrew looked perplexed, but, before he could answer, Brownie came bounding gaily round the corner of the hut. Seeing a stranger, he stopped suddenly, displayed his teeth and growled.

"Down, pup! He is not accustomed to visitors, you see," said his master apologetically.

At that moment Cormac turned the corner of the hut, bearing an earthen jar of water on his shoulder. His eyes opened wide with surprise, so did those of the Hebrew, and the jar dropped to the ground, where it broke, and Brownie, quick to see and seize his opportunity, began to lap its contents. The prince—also wide-eyed—gazed from one to the other. It was a grand *tableau vivant*!

The first to recover himself and break the spell was Cormac. Leaping forward, he grasped the old man by the hand, and turning so as to present his back to Bladud, gave the Hebrew a look so powerfully significant that that son of Israel was quite disconcerted.

"My old, kind friend—is it—can it—be really yourself? So far from home—so unexpected! It makes me so glad to see you," said the youth. Then, turning to Bladud, "A very old friend of mine, who helped me once in a time of great distress. I am so rejoiced, for now he will guide me back to my own home. You know I have sometimes talked of leaving you lately, Bladud."

"You say truth, my young friend. Frequently of late, since I have been getting well, you have hinted at a wish to go home, though you have not yet made it clear to me where that home is; and sad will be the day when you quit me. I verily believe that I should have died outright, Beniah, but for the kind care of this amiable lad. But it is selfish of me to wish you to stay—especially now that you have found a friend who, it would seem, is both able and willing to guard you through the woods in safety. Yet, now I think, my complaint is so nearly cured that I might venture to do that myself."

"Not so," returned the lad, quickly. "You are far from cured yet. To give up using the waters at this stage of the cure would be fatal. It would perhaps let the disease come back as bad as before."

"Nay, but the difficulty lies here," returned the prince, smiling at the boy's eagerness. "This good old man is at present engaged as guide to an army, and dare not leave his post. A foolish girl named Branwen fled some time ago from my father's house, intending, it is supposed, to go to some friends living not far from the Hot Swamp. They have been searching for her in all directions, and at last her father, with a host at his heels, has been led to within a few miles of this place, but the girl has not yet been discovered; so the search will doubtless be continued."

"Is that so?" asked Cormac of the Hebrew, pointedly.

"It is so."

R. M. Ballantyne

"What is the name of the chief whose daughter has been *so foolish* as to run away from her friends?"

"Gadarn," answered Beniah.

"Oh! I know him!" exclaimed Cormac in some excitement, "and I know many of his people. I lived with them once, long, long ago. How far off is the camp, did you say?"

"An hour's walk or so."

"In *that* direction?" asked Cormac, pointing.

"Yes, in that direction."

"Then I will go and see them," said the lad, picking up his bow and arrows. "You can wait here till I come back, Beniah, and keep Bladud company—for he is accustomed to company now! Who knows but I may pick up this *foolish* girl on my way to the camp!"

The lad hurried into the woods without waiting a reply; but he had not gone a hundred yards when he turned and shouted, "Hi, Beniah!" at the same time beckoning with his hand.

The Hebrew hurried towards him.

"Beniah," said the lad impressively, as he drew near, "go back and examine Bladud's arm, and let me know when we meet again what you think of it."

"But how—why—wherefore came you—?" exclaimed the Hebrew, pausing in perplexity.

"Ask no questions, old man," returned the youth with a

laugh. "There is no time to explain—. He will suspect—robbers—old mother—bad son—escape—boy's dress—fill up that story if you can! More hereafter. But—observe, if you say one word about *me to anybody*, Gadarn's sword is sharp and his arm strong! You promise?"

"I promise."

"Solemnly—on your word as a Hebrew?"

"Solemnly—on my word as a Hebrew. But—?"

With another laugh the boy interrupted him, turned, and disappeared in the woods.

"A strange, though a good and affectionate boy," remarked Bladud when the Hebrew returned. "What said he?"

"He bade me examine your arm, and tell him what I think of it on his return."

"That is of a piece with all the dear boy's conduct," returned the prince. "You have no idea what a kind nurse he has been to me, at a time when I was helpless with fever. Indeed, if I had not been helpless and delirious, I would not have allowed him to come near me. You have known him before, it seems?"

"Yes; I have known him for some time."

From this point the prince pushed the Hebrew with questions, which the latter—bearing in remembrance the sharpness of Gadarn's sword, and the solemnity of his promise—did his best to evade, and eventually succeeded in turning the conversation by questioning Bladud as to his intercourse with the hunter of the Swamp, and his mode of life since his arrival in that region. Then he proceeded to examine the arm critically.

"It is a wonderful cure," he said, after a minute inspection. "Almost miraculous."

"Cure!" exclaimed the prince. "Do you, then, think me cured?"

"Indeed I do—at least, very nearly so. I have had some experience of your complaint in the East, and it seems to me that a perfect cure is at most certain—if it has not been already effected."

CHAPTER TWENTY FOUR

DESCRIBES AN ARDENT SEARCH

While the prince and the Hebrew were thus conversing, Cormac was speeding towards the camp of Gadarn. He quickly arrived, and was immediately arrested by one of the sentinels. Taken before one of the chief officers, he was asked who he was, and where he came from.

"That I will tell only to your chief," said the lad.

"*I* am a chief," replied the officer proudly.

"That may be so; but I want to speak with *your* chief, and I must see him alone."

"Assuredly thou art a saucy knave, and might be improved by a switching."

"Possibly; but instead of wasting our time in useless talk, it would be well to convey my message to Gadarn, for my news is urgent; and I would not give much for your head if you delay."

The officer laughed; but there was that in the boy's tone and manner that induced him to obey.

R. M. Ballantyne

Gadarn, the chief, was seated on a tree-stump inside of a booth of boughs, leaves, and birch-bark, that had been hastily constructed for his accommodation. He was a great, rugged, north-country man, of immense physical power—as most chiefs were in those days. He seemed to be brooding over his sorrows at the time his officer entered.

"A prisoner waits without," said the officer. "He is a stripling; and says he has urgent business to communicate to you alone."

"Send him hither, and let every one get out of ear-shot!" said Gadarn gruffly.

A minute later Cormac appeared, and looked wistfully at the chief, who looked up with a frown.

"Are you the pris—"

He stopped suddenly, and, springing to his feet, advanced a step with glaring eyes and fast-coming breath, as he held out both hands.

With a cry of joy, Cormac sprang forward and threw his arms round Gadarn's neck, exclaiming—

"Father!—*dear* father!"

For a few moments there was silence, and a sight was seen which had not been witnessed for many a day—two or three gigantic tears rolled down the warrior's rugged cheeks, one of them trickling to the end of his weather-beaten nose and dropping on his iron-grey beard.

"My child," he said at length, "where—how came you— why, this—"

"Yes, yes, father," interrupted the lad, with a tearful laugh. "I'll tell you all about it in good time; but I've got other things to speak of which are more interesting to both of us. Sit down and let me sit on your knee, as I used to do long ago."

Gadarn meekly obeyed.

"Now listen," said Cormac, putting his mouth to his father's ear and whispering.

The chief listened, and the first effect of the whispering was to produce a frown. This gradually and slowly faded, and gave place to an expression of doubt.

"Are you sure, child?—sure that you—"

"Quite—quite sure," interrupted Cormac with emphasis. "But that is not all—listen!"

Gadarn listened again; and, as the whispering continued, there came the wrinkles of humour over his rugged face; then a snort that caused Cormac to laugh ere he resumed his whispering.

"And he knows it?" cried Gadarn, interrupting and suppressing a laugh.

"Yes; knows all about it."

"And the other doesn't?"

"Has not the remotest idea!"

"Thinks that you're a—"

Here the chief broke off, got up, placed his hands on both his sides and roared with laughter, until the anxious sentinels outside believed that he had gone mad.

With the energy of a strong nature he checked himself and became suddenly grave.

"Listen!" he said; "you have made me listen a good deal to you. It is my turn now. Before the sun stands there (pointing), you will be on your way to the court of King Hudibras, while I remain, and make this Hebrew lead me all over the country in search of—ha! ha!—my daughter. We must search and search every hole and corner of the land; for we must—we must find her—or perish!"

Again the chief exploded, but subdued himself immediately; and, going to the entrance of the booth, summoned his lieutenant, who started forward with the promptitude of an apparition, and with an expression of some curiosity on his countenance, for he also had heard the laughter.

"Get ready forty men," said the chief; "to convey this lad in safety to the court of King Hudibras. He is well known there. Say not that I sent you, but that, in ranging the country, you found him lost in the woods, and, understanding him to belong to the household of the king, you brought him in."

Without a word the lieutenant withdrew, and the plotters looked at each other with that peculiarly significant expression which has been the characteristic of intriguers in all ages.

"Thou wilt know how to act, my little one," said the chief.

"Yes, better even than you imagine, my big one," replied Cormac.

"What! is there something beyond my ken simmering in thy noddle, thou pert squirrel?"

"Perchance there is, father dear."

A sound at the root of Gadarn's nose betrayed suppressed laughter, as he turned away.

Quarter of an hour later a band of foot-soldiers defiled out of the camp, with Cormac in their midst, mounted on a small pony, and Gadarn, calling another of his lieutenants, told him to let it be known throughout the camp, that if any officer or man should allow his tongue to wag with reference to the lad who had just left the camp, his tongue would be silenced for all future time, and an oak limb be decorated with an acorn that never grew on it.

"You know, and they know, that I'm a man of my word— away!" said the chief, returning to the privacy of his booth.

While these events were happening at the camp, Bladud and Beniah were discussing many subjects—religion among others, for they were both philosophical as well as seriously-minded. But neither their philosophy nor their religion were profound enough at that time to remove anxiety about the youth who had just left them.

"I wish that I were clear of the whole business," remarked the Hebrew uneasily, almost petulantly.

"Why, do you fear that any evil can happen to the boy?" asked Bladud anxiously.

"Oh! I fear not for him. It is not that. He will be among friends at the camp—but—but I know not how Gadarn may take it."

R. M. Ballantyne

"Take what?" demanded the prince in surprise.

"Take—take my failure to find his daughter."

"Ha! to be sure; he may be ill-pleased at that. But if I thought there was any chance of evil befalling Cormac in the camp, by all the gods of the east, west, north, and south," cried the prince, carried away by the strength of his feelings into improper and even boastful language, "I would go and demand his liberation, or fight the whole tribe single-handed."

"A pretty boast for a man in present safety," remarked the Hebrew, with a remonstrative shake of the head.

"Most true," returned the prince, flushing; "I spoke in haste, yet it was not altogether a boast, for I could challenge Gadarn to single combat, and no right-minded chief could well refuse to let the issue of the matter rest on that."

"Verily he would not refuse, for although not so tall as you are, he is quite as stout, and it is a saying among his people that he fears not the face of any man—something like his daughter in that."

"Is she so bold, then?"

"Nay, not bold, but—courageous."

"Humph! that is a distinction, no doubt, but the soft and gentle qualities in women commend themselves more to me than those which ought chiefly to characterise man. However, be this as it may, if Cormac does not return soon after daybreak to-morrow, I will hie me to the camp to see how it fares with him."

As next morning brought no Cormac, or any news of him,

Bladud started for the camp, accompanied by the anxious Hebrew.

They found the chief at a late breakfast. He looked up without rising when they were announced.

"Ha! my worthy Hebrew—is it thou? What news of my child? Have you heard of her whereabouts?"

"Not yet, sir," answered Beniah with a look of intense perplexity. "But I had thought that—that is, by this time—"

"What! no news?" cried the chief, springing up in fierce ire, and dropping the chop with which he had been engaged. "Did you not say that you felt sure you would hear of her from your friend? Is this the friend that you spoke of?"

He turned a keen look of inquiry, with not a little admiration in it, on Bladud.

"This is indeed he," answered Beniah, "and I have—but, but did not a lad—a fair youth—visit your camp yesterday?"

"No—no lad came near the camp yesterday," answered the chief gruffly.

Here was cause for wonder, both for the Hebrew and the prince.

"Forgive me, sir," said the latter, with a deferential air that greatly pleased the warrior, "forgive me if I venture to intrude my own troubles on one whose anxiety must needs be greater, but this youth left my hut yesterday to visit you, saying that he knew you well, and if he has not arrived some evil must have befallen him, for the distance he had to traverse was very short."

"That is sad," returned the chief in a tone of sympathy, "for he must either have been caught by robbers, or come by an accident on the way. Did you not follow his footsteps as you came along?"

"We never thought of following them—the distance being so short," returned the prince with increasing anxiety.

"Are you, then, so fond of this lad?" asked the chief.

"Ay, that am I, and with good reason, for he has tended me with self-denying care during illness, and in circumstances which few men would have faced. In truth, I feel indebted to him for my life."

"Say you so?" cried the chief with sudden energy; "then shall we search for *him* as well as for my daughter. And you, Hebrew, shall help us. Doubtless, young man, you will aid us by your knowledge of the district. I have secured the services of the hunter of the Swamp, so we can divide into three bands, and scour the whole country round. We cannot fail to find them, for neither of them can have got far away, whether they be lost or stolen. Ho! there. Assemble the force, instantly. Divide it into three bands. My lieutenant shall head one. You, Bladud, shall lead another, and I myself will head the third, guided by Beniah. Away!"

With a wave of both hands Gadarn dismissed those around him, and retired to his booth to arm himself, and prepare for the pending search.

The Hebrew was sorely tempted just then to speak out, but his solemn promise to Branwen sealed his lips. The fact also that the girl seemed really to have disappeared, filled him with alarm as well as surprise, and made him anxious to participate in the search. In a perplexed state of mind, and unenviable temper, he went away with Bladud to the place where the force was being marshalled.

"Strange that fate should send us on a double search of this kind," remarked the prince as they hurried along.

"Whether fate sent us, or some mischievous sprite, I know not," growled the Hebrew, "but there is no need for more than one search."

"How!" exclaimed Bladud sternly. "Think you that my poor lad's fate is not of as much interest to me as that of Gadarn's daughter is to him?"

"Nay, verily, I presume not to gauge the interest of princes and chiefs," returned Beniah, with an exasperated air. "All I know is, that if we find the lad, we are full sure to find the lass not far off."

"How? You speak in riddles to-day."

"Ay, and there are like to be more riddles tomorrow, for what the upshot of it will be is more than I can tell. See you not that, as the two were lost about the same time, and near the same place, they will probably be found together?"

"Your wits seem to be shaken to-day, old man," rejoined Bladud, smiling, "for these two were not lost about the same place or time."

Fortunately for the Hebrew's peace of mind, an officer accosted them at that moment, and, directing the one to head a band just ready to march, led the other to the force which was to be commanded by the chief in person.

In a few minutes the three bands were in motion, the main

R. M. Ballantyne

bodies marching north, south, and east, while strong parties were sent out from each to skirmish in all directions.

"Think you we shall find them, Hebrew?" asked the chief, who seemed to be in a curiously impulsive state of mind.

"I trust we may. It seems to me almost certain."

"I hope so, for your sake as well as my own, old man; for, if we do not, I will surely cut your head off for bringing me here for nothing."

"Does it not seem unjust to punish a man for doing his best?" asked Beniah.

"It may seem so to you men of the east, but to the men of the west justice is not held of much account."

Proceeding round by the Hot Springs, the party led by Gadarn made a careful inspection of every cavern, defile, glade, and thicket, returning at evening towards the camp from which they set out, it having been arranged that they were all to meet there and start again to renew the search, in a wider circle, on the following morning.

"No success," remarked Gadarn sternly, unbuckling his sword and flinging it violently on the ground.

"Not yet, but we may have better fortune tomorrow," said Beniah.

"Don't you think the small footprints we saw near the Springs were those of the boy?"

"They may have been."

"And those that we saw further on, but lost sight of in the rocky ground—did they not look like those of a girl?"

"They certainly did."

"And yet strangely like to each other," said the chief.

"Marvellously," returned Beniah.

A slight sound in Gadarn's nose caused the Hebrew to look up quickly, but the chief was gazing with stern gravity out at the opening of his booth, where the men of his force could be seen busily at work felling trees, kindling fires, and otherwise preparing for the evening meal.

CHAPTER TWENTY FIVE

MORE SECRETS AND SURPRISES

All went well with the party that conducted Branwen to King Hudibras' town until they reached the hut of Beniah the Hebrew, when the lad suggested to the leader of the escort that they should put up there, as it was too late to think of intruding on the king that night.

As the lieutenant had been told to pay particular regard to the wishes of his charge, he at once agreed. Indeed, during the journey, Cormac (as we may here continue to call the girl) had expressed his wishes with such a quiet, matter-of-course air of authority that the officer in charge had come to the conclusion that the youth must be the son of some person of importance—perhaps even of King Hudibras himself. He therefore accorded him implicit obedience and deference.

"The hut is too small for all of us," said Cormac; "the greater number of your men must sleep outside; but that does not matter on so fine a night."

"True, it matters nothing," replied the officer. "We will all of us sup and sleep round the campfires."

"Nay, you and your lieutenant will sup with me. Afterwards

you can join the men. By-the-by, there is an old woman here, who takes charge—or ought to take charge—of the Hebrew's dwelling during his absence."

"I have not seen her," said the officer.

"True—but she will no doubt make her appearance soon. Let her come and go as she pleases without hindrance. It is not safe to thwart her, for her temper is none of the sweetest, and she is apt to scratch."

Supper was soon over, for the party had travelled all day, and were weary. When it was finished Cormac again cautioned the officers not to interfere with the old woman, for she was dangerous.

"I will have a care," said the officer, laughing, as he and his subaltern rose, bade their charge good-night, and took their leave.

The instant they were gone Branwen pushed the plank-bridge across the chasm, and disappeared in the secret cave.

Half an hour later the two officers were seated with some of the men at the camp-fire nearest the hut, making preparations for going to rest, when they were startled by the creaking of the hut door. To their intense surprise it opened wide enough to let a little old woman step out. She was much bent, wore an old grey shawl over her head, and leaned on a staff. For some moments she looked from side to side as if in search of something.

"See! the old woman!" murmured the officer in a low whisper.

"True, but we did not see her enter the hut," replied the sub with a solemn look.

In those days witchcraft was implicitly believed in, so, when they saw the old creature hobble towards them, they experienced feelings of alarm that had never yet affected their manly bosoms in danger or in war. Their faces paled a little, but their courage stood the test, for they sat still till she came close enough to let her piercing dark eyes be seen peering at them like those of a basilisk from out the folds of the shawl that enveloped her.

"Y-you are the—the old woman, I suppose?" said the officer in a deferential tone.

"Yes, I am the old woman, young man, and you will be an old woman too when you reach my time of life," she replied, in a deep metallic voice.

"I hope not," returned the officer, sincerely.

"At all events you'll be a dead man before long if you don't attend to what I say," continued the woman. "Your young master in the hut there told me to tell you that he is tired and wants a good long rest, so you are not to disturb him in the morning till he calls you. D'you hear?"

"I hear, and will obey."

"Eh? What? Speak out. I'm deaf."

"I hear, and will attend to your wishes."

"Humph! it will be worse for you if you don't," muttered the old hag, as she turned away, hobbled into the woods, and slowly disappeared.

It need scarcely be said that the lieutenant and his sub did not sleep much that night. They discussed the subject of witches, their powers and propensities, and the bad luck likely to attend those who actually had the misfortune to see them, until the hair on their heads betrayed a tendency to rise, and the grey dawn began to appear. Then they lay down and indulged in some fitful slumber. But the discomforts of the night were as nothing to the anxieties of the morning, for the lazy Cormac seemed to have gone in for an extent of slumber that was out of all reason, considering his circumstances. The ordinary breakfast hour arrived, but there was no intimation of his having awoke. Hours passed, but there was no call from the hut, and the officer, with ever-increasing anxiety, bade his men to kick up a row—or words to that effect. No command they ever received was more easy of fulfilment. They laughed and talked; they cut down trees and cleaned their breakfast utensils with overwhelming demonstration; they shouted, they even sang and roared in chorus, but without effect. Noon arrived and passed, still Cormac slept on. It was worse than perplexing—it was becoming desperate!

The officer commanding the party was a brave man; so was the sub. Their native courage overcame their superstitious fears.

"I'll be battle-axed!" exclaimed the first, using a very objectionable old British oath, "if I don't rouse him, though all the witches in Albion should withstand me."

"And I'll back you up," said the sub with a frown that spoke volumes—perhaps, considering the times, we should have written—rolls of papyrus.

Accordingly the two went towards the hut, with pluck and misgiving contending for the mastery.

R. M. Ballantyne

"Perchance the witch may have returned while we slept," said the sub in a low voice.

"Or she may have re-entered the hut invisibly—as she did at first," replied the other.

The door was found to be on the latch. The lieutenant opened it a little and peeped in.

"Ho! Cormac!" he shouted; "hi! ho! hooroo hooh!" but he shouted in vain.

Becoming accustomed to the dim light, he perceived that there was no one within to answer to the call, so he suddenly sprang in, followed by the sub and a few of the more daring spirits among the men.

A hasty search revealed the fact that the lad was not to be seen. A more minute and thorough inspection showed clearly that no one was there. They did not, of course, discover the cave, for the plank had been removed, but they gazed solemnly into the depths of the dark chasm and wondered if poor Cormac had committed suicide there, or if the witch had murdered him and thrown him in. Having neither rope nor ladder, and the chasm appearing to be bottomless, they had no means of settling the question.

But now a point of far greater moment pressed on their consideration. What was to be said to King Hudibras about the disappearance of the lad? Would he believe them? It was not likely. And, on the other hand, what would Gadarn say? Would *he* believe them? He might, indeed, for he knew them to be faithful, but that would not mitigate his wrath, and when he was roused by neglected duty they knew too well that their lives would hang on a thread. What was to be done? To go forward or backward seemed to involve death!

One only resource was left, namely, for the whole band to go off on its own account and take to the woods as independent robbers—or hunters—or both combined.

In an unenviable frame of mind the lieutenant and his sub sat down to the discussion of these knotty points and their mid-day meal.

Meanwhile the witch, who had been the occasion of all this distress, having got out of sight in the woods, assumed a very upright gait and stepped out with a degree of bounding elasticity that would have done credit to a girl of nineteen.

The sun was just rising in a flood of glorious light when she entered the suburbs of King Hudibras' town—having previously resumed her stoop and hobbling gait.

The king was lazy. He was still a-bed snoring. But the household was up and at breakfast, when the witch—passing the guards who looked upon her as too contemptible to question—knocked at the palace door. It was the back-door, for even at that time palaces had such convenient apertures, for purposes, no doubt, of undignified retreat. A menial answered the knock—after wearisome delay.

"Is the Princess Hafrydda within?"

"She is," answered the menial, with a supercilious look, "but she is at breakfast, and does not see poor people at such an hour."

"Would she see rich people if they were to call at such an hour?" demanded the witch, sharply.

"Per—perhaps she would," replied the menial with some hesitation.

R. M. Ballantyne

"Then I'll wait here till she has finished breakfast. Is the king up?"

"N-no. He still slumbers."

"Hah! Like him! He was always lazy in the mornings. Go fetch me a stool."

The manner of the old woman with her magnificent dark eyes and deep metallic voice, and her evident knowledge of the king's habits, were too much for the menial—a chord of superstition had been touched; it vibrated, and he was quelled. Humbly but quickly he fetched a stool.

"Won't you step in?" he said.

"No, I'll stop out!" she replied, and sat herself doggedly down, with the air of one who had resolved never more to go away.

Meanwhile, in the breakfast room of the palace, which was on the ground floor—indeed, all the rooms of the palace were on the ground floor, for there was no upper one—the queen and her fair daughter Hafrydda were entertaining a stranger who had arrived the day before.

He was an exceedingly handsome man of about six-and-twenty; moderately tall and strong, but with an air of graceful activity in all his movements that gave people, somehow, the belief that whatever he chose to attempt he could do. Both his olive complexion and his tongue betokened him a foreigner, for although the language he spoke was Albionic, it was what we now style broken—very much broken indeed. With a small head, short curly black hair, a very young beard, and small pointed moustache, fine intellectual features, and an expression of imperturbable good-humour, he presented an appearance which might have claimed the regard of any woman. At all events the queen had formed a very high opinion of him—and she was a woman of much experience, having seen many men in her day. Hafrydda, though, of course, not so experienced, fully equalled her mother, if she did not excel her, in her estimate of the young stranger.

As we should be unintelligible if we gave the youth's words in the broken dialect, we must render his speech in fair English.

"I cannot tell how deeply I am grieved to hear this dreadful news of my dear friend," he said, with a look of profound sorrow that went home to the mother's heart.

"And did you really come to this land for the sole purpose of seeing my dear boy?" asked the queen.

"I did. You cannot imagine how much we loved each other. We were thrown together daily—almost hourly. We studied together; we competed when I was preparing for the Olympic games; we travelled in Egypt and hunted together. Indeed, if it had not been for my dear old mother, we should have travelled to this land in the same ship."

"Your mother did not wish you to leave her, I suppose?"

"Nay, it was I who would not leave *her*. Her unselfish nature would have induced her to make any sacrifice to please me. It was only when she died that my heart turned with unusual longing to my old companion Bladud, and I made up my mind to quit home and traverse the great sea in search of him."

A grateful look shot from Hafrydda's blue eyes, but it was

lost on the youth, who sat gazing at the floor as if engrossed with his great disappointment.

"I cannot understand," he continued, in an almost reproachful tone, "how you could ever make up your minds to banish him, no matter how deadly the disease that had smitten him."

The princess's fair face flushed deeply, and she shook back her golden curls—her eyes flashing as she replied—

"We did not 'make up our minds to banish him.' The warriors and people would have compelled us to do it whether we liked or not, for they have heard, alas! of the terrible nature of the disease. But the dear boy, knowing this, went off in the night unknown to us, and without even saying farewell. We have sent out parties to search for him several times, but without success."

The youth was evidently affected by this burst of feeling.

"Ah," he returned, with a look of admiration at the princess, "that was like him—like his noble, self-denying nature. But I will find him out, you may depend on it, for I shall search the land in all directions till I discover his retreat. If King Hudibras will grant me a few men to help me—well. If not, I will do it by myself."

"Thank you, good Dromas, for your purpose and your sympathy," said the queen. "The king will be only too glad to help you—but here he comes to speak for himself."

The curtain door was tossed aside at the moment, and Hudibras strode into the room with a beaming smile and a rolling gait that told of redundant health, and showed that the cares of state sat lightly on him.

"Welcome, good Dromas, to our board. I was too sleepy to see much of you after your arrival last night. Mine eyes blinked like those of an owl. Kiss me, wife and daughter," he added, giving the ladies a salute that resounded through the room. "Have they told you yet about our poor son Bladud?"

The visitor had not time to reply, when a domestic appeared and said there was an old woman at the door who would not go away.

"Give her some cakes and send her off!" cried the king with a frown.

"But she will not go till she has had converse with the princess."

"I will go to her," said Hafrydda, rising.

"Ay, go, my girl, and if thy sweet tongue fails to prevail, stuff her mouth with meat and drink till she is too stout to walk. Come, my queen, what have we this morning for breakfast? The very talking of meat makes me hungry."

At this juncture several dogs burst into the room and gambolled with their royal master, as with one who is a familiar friend.

When the princess reached the outer door she found the woman standing, and evidently in a rage.

"Is this the way King Hudibras teaches his varlets to behave to poor people who are better than themselves?"

"Forgive them, granny," said the princess, who was inclined to laugh, but strove to keep her gravity, "they are but stupid rogues at worst."

R. M. Ballantyne

"Nay, but they are sly rogues at best!" retorted the old woman. "The first that came, took me for a witch, and was moderately civil, but the second took away my stool and threatened to set the dogs at me."

"If this be so, I will have him cow-hided; but tell me—what would you with me? Can I help you? Is it food that you want, or rest?"

"Truly it is both food and rest that I want, at the proper times, but what I want with you now, is to take me to your own room, and let me talk to you."

"That is a curious desire," returned Hafrydda, smiling, "but I will not deny you. Come this way. Have you anything secret to tell me?" she asked, when they were alone.

"Ay, that have I," answered the woman in her natural voice, throwing off her shawl and standing erect.

The princess remained speechless, for her friend Branwen stood before her.

"Before I utter a word of explanation," she said, "let me say that your brother is found, and safe, and well—or nearly so. This is the main thing, but I will not tell you anything more, unless you give me your solemn promise not to tell a word of it all to any one, till I give you leave. Do you promise?"

Hafrydda was so taken aback that she could do nothing for some time but gaze in the girl's face. Then she laughed in an imbecile sort of way. Then she burst into tears of joy, threw her arms round her friend's neck, hugged her tight, and promised anything—everything—that she chose to demand.

When, an hour later, the Princess Hafrydda returned to the

breakfast room, she informed the king and queen that the old woman was not a beggar; that she had kept her listening to a long story about lost men and women and robbers; that she was a thorough deceiver; that some of the servants believed her to be a witch, and that she had sent her away.

"With an invitation to come back again, I'll be bound," cried the king, interrupting. "It's always your way, my girl,—any one can impose on you."

"Well, father, she *did* impose on me, and I *did* ask her to come back again."

"I knew it," returned the king, with a loud laugh, "and she'll come, for certain."

"She will, you may be quite sure of that," rejoined the princess with a gleeful laugh, as she left the room.

About the same time, the little old woman left the palace and returned to the hut of the Hebrew.

Here, as she expected, she found that her escort had flown, and, a brief inspection of their footprints showed that, instead of proceeding towards the town, they had returned the way they came.

R. M. Ballantyne

CHAPTER TWENTY SIX

FURTHER SEARCHINGS AND PERPLEXITIES

While these events were taking place at court, the bold chief Gadarn was ranging the country far and wide in search of his daughter Branwen.

There was something in his manner which puzzled his followers not a little, for he seemed to have changed his character—at least to have added to it a strange, wild hilarity which suggested the idea that he enjoyed the hunt and was in no hurry that it should come to an end. Those who knew him best began at last to fear that anxiety had unsettled his reason, and Bladud, who liked the man's gay, reckless disposition and hearty good-humour, intermingled with occasional bursts of fierce passion, was not only puzzled but distressed by the wild inconsistency of his proceedings. The Hebrew, knowing to some extent the cause of what he did, and feeling bound by his promise to conceal his knowledge, was reduced to a state of mind that is not describable.

On the one hand there was the mystery of Cormac's total disappearance in a short walk of three miles. On the other hand, there was the utter uselessness of searching for Branwen, yet the urgent need of searching diligently for Cormac. Then there was the fear of consequences when the fiery Gadarn should come to find out how he had been deceived, or rather, what moderns might style humbugged; add to which he was debarred the solace of talking the subject over with Bladud, besides being, in consequence of his candid disposition, in danger of blurting out words that might necessitate a revelation. One consequence was that, for the time at least, the grave and amiable Hebrew became an abrupt, unsociable, taciturn man.

"What ails you just now, Beniah?" asked Bladud, one evening as they walked together to Gadarn's booth, having been invited to supper. "You seem out of condition mentally, if not bodily, as if some one had rubbed you the wrong way."

"Do I?" answered Beniah, with a frown and something between a grin and a laugh. "Well, it is not easy to understand one's mental complaints, much less to explain them."

Fortunately their arrival at the booth put a timely end to the conversation.

"Ha! my long-legged prince and stalwart Hebrew!" cried the jovial chief in a loud voice, "I began to fear that you had got lost—as folk seem prone to do in this region—or had forgotten all about us! Come in and sit ye down. Ho! varlet, set down the victuals. After all, you are just in the nick of time. Well, Beniah, what think you of our search to-day? Has it been close? Is it likely that we have missed any of the caves or cliffs where robbers might be hiding?"

"I think not. It seems to me that we have ransacked every hole and corner in which there is a chance that the lad could be found."

"The *lad*!" exclaimed Gadarn.

"I—I mean—your daughter," returned the Hebrew, quickly.

"Why don't you say what you mean, then? One expects a man of your years to talk without confusion—or is it that you are really more anxious about finding the boy than my girl?"

"Nay, that be far from me," answered the Hebrew. "To say truth, I am to the full as anxious to find the one as the other, for it matters not which you—"

"Matters not!" repeated Gadarn, fiercely.

"Well, of course, I mean that my friendship for you and Bladud makes me wish to see you each satisfied by finding both the boy and the girl."

"For my part," said Bladud, quietly, "I sincerely hope that we may find them both, for we are equally anxious to do so."

"Equally!" exclaimed Gadarn, with a look of lofty surprise. "Dost mean to compare your regard for your young friend with a father's love for his only child!"

The prince did not easily take offence, but he could not refrain from a flush and a frown as he replied, sharply—

"I make no useless comparisons, chief. It is sufficient that we are both full of anxiety, and are engaged in the same quest."

"Ay, the same quest—undoubtedly," observed the Hebrew in a grumbling, abstracted manner.

"If it were possible," returned Gadarn, sternly, "to give up the search for your boy and confine it entirely to my girl, I would do so. But as they went astray about the same place, we are compelled, however little we like it, to hunt together."

"Not compelled, chief," cried Bladud, with a look and a flash in his blue eye which presaged a sudden rupture of friendly relations. "We can each go our own way and hunt on our own account."

"Scarcely," replied the chief, "for if you found my daughter, you would be bound in honour to deliver her up; and if I found your boy, I should feel myself bound to do the same."

"It matters not a straw which is found," cried the Hebrew, exasperated at the prospect of a quarrel between the two at such an inopportune moment. "Surely, as an old man, I have the right to remonstrate with you for encouraging anything like disagreement when our success in finding the boy,—I—I mean the girl,—depends—"

A burst of laughter from the chief cut him short.

"You don't seem to be quite sure of what you mean," he cried, "or to be able to say it. Come, come, prince, if the Hebrew claims a right to remonstrate because he is twenty years or so older than I am, surely I may claim the same right, for I am full twenty years older than you. Is it seemly to let your hot young blood boil over at every trifle? Here, let me replenish your platter, for it is ill hunting after man, woman, or beast without a stomach full of victuals."

There was no resisting the impulsive chief.

Both his guests cleared their brows and laughed—though there was still a touch of exasperation in the Hebrew's tone.

While the search was being thus diligently though needlessly prosecuted in the neighbourhood of the Hot Swamp by Gadarn, who was dearly fond of a practical joke, another chief, who was in no joking humour, paid a visit one evening

R. M. Ballantyne

to his mother. Perhaps it is unnecessary to say that this chief was Gunrig.

"From all that I see and hear, mother," he said, walking up and down the room, as was his habit, with his hands behind him, "it is clear that if I do not go about it myself, the king will let the matter drop; for he is convinced that the girl has run off with some fellow, and will easily make her way home."

"Don't you think he may be right, my son?"

"No, I don't, my much-too-wise mother. I know the girl better than that. It is enough to look in her face to know that she could not run away with any fellow!"

"H'm!" remarked the woman significantly.

"What say you?" demanded the chief, sharply.

"I scarcely know what to say. Perhaps the best thing to do would be to take a band of our own men and go off in search of the girl yourself."

"That's just what I've made up my mind to do; but I wanted to see if Hudibras would get up a band to join mine, for I dare not take many away from the town when that scoundrel Addedomar is threatening to make a raid upon us."

"My son," said the woman anxiously, "what threatened raid do you speak of?"

"Did you not hear? Since the last time we gave that robber a drubbing at the Hot Swamp, he has taken to the woods and gathered together a large band of rascals like himself. We would not have minded that—for honest men are always numerous enough to keep villains in order—but two chiefs who have long been anxious to take possession of the land round the Swamp have agreed to join with him, so that they form a formidable body of warriors—too large to be treated with contempt."

"This is bad news, Gunrig. How does the king take it?"

"In his usual way. He does not believe in danger or mischief till it has overtaken him, and it is almost too late for action. There is one hope, however, that he will be induced to move in time. A young fellow has come from the far East, who was a great friend of that long-legged fellow Bladud, and he is bent on finding out where his friend has gone. Of course the king is willing to let him have as many men as he wants, though he sternly refuses to let Bladud return home; and I hope to induce this youth—Dromas, they call him—to join me, so that we may search together; for, of course, the search for the man may result in finding the girl. My only objection is that if we do find Bladud, I shall have to fight and kill him—unless the leprosy has happily killed him already. So, now, I will away and see what can be done about this hunt. My object in coming was to get my men, and to warn those left in charge of the town to keep a keen look-out for Addedomar, for he is a dangerous foe. Farewell, mother."

The woman was not addicted to the melting mood. She merely nodded as her son went out.

In pursuance of this plan, a band of about two hundred warriors was raised, armed, and provisioned for a long journey. Gunrig put himself at the head of a hundred and fifty of these, and Dromas, being a skilled warrior, was given command of the remaining fifty, with Captain Arkal, who begged to be allowed to go as his lieutenant, and little Maikar as one of his fighting men.

The orders were, that they should start off in the direction of the Hot Swamp, searching the country as they went, making diligent inquiries at the few villages they might pass, and questioning all travellers whom they might chance to meet with by the way. If Branwen should be found, she was to be sent back escorted by a detachment of a hundred men. If the retreat of Bladud should be discovered, news of the fact was to be sent to the king, and the prince was to be left there in peace with any of the men who might volunteer to live with him. But on no account were they or Bladud to return to Hudibras' town as long as there was the least danger of infection.

"Is he *never* to return?" asked the queen, whimpering, when she heard these orders given.

"No, *never*!" answered the king in that awful tone which the poor queen knew too well meant something like a decree of Fate.

"Oh, father!" remonstrated Hafrydda—and Dromas loved her for the remonstrance—"not even if he is cured?"

"Well, of course, if he is cured, my child, that alters the case. But how am I to know that he is cured?—who is to judge? Our court doctor knows as much about it as a sucking pig— perhaps less!"

"Perhaps the Hebrew knows," suggested Hafrydda—and Dromas loved her for the suggestion!

"Ah, to be sure! I forgot the Hebrew. You may call at his hut in passing and take him with you, if he has come home yet. He's an amiable old man, and may consent to go. If not— make him. Away! and cease to worry me. That's the way to get rid of business, my queen; isn't it?"

"Certainly—it is one way," answered the queen, turning to the two commanders. "Go, and my blessing go with you!"

"Success attend you!" murmured the princess, glancing timidly at Dromas—and as Dromas gazed upon her fair face, and golden curls, and modest mien, he felt that he loved her for herself!

Success did not, however, attend them at first, for on reaching the Hebrew's hut they found it empty, and no amount of shouting availed to call Beniah from the "vasty deep" of the chasm, or the dark recesses of the secret chamber.

Pursuing their way, therefore, the small army was soon lost to view in the forest.

R. M. Ballantyne

CHAPTER TWENTY SEVEN

CROSS PURPOSES AND COMPLICATIONS

We turn now to another scene in the wild-woods, not far distant from the Hot Swamp.

It is a thickly-wooded hollow on the eastern slopes of the high ridge that bounds one side of the valley of the Springs. Sturdy oaks, tall poplars, lordly elms and beeches, cast a deep shade over the spot which was rendered almost impenetrable by dense underwood. Even in brightest sunshine light entered it with difficulty, and in gloomy weather a sort of twilight constantly prevailed, while at night the place became the very abode of thick darkness.

In this retreat was assembled, one gloomy afternoon, a large body of armed men, not connected with the searching parties which had been ransacking the region in the vain duplex search which we have tried to describe. It was a war-party under the command of Addedomar the outlaw—if we may thus characterise a man in a land where there was little or no law of any kind, save that of might.

It was a strong band, numbering nearly four hundred warriors, all of whom were animated with the supposed-to-be noble desire to commit theft on a very large scale. It is true, they called it "conquest," which word in those days, as in modern times even among civilised people, meant killing many of the natives of a place and taking possession of their lands. Then—as now—this was sometimes styled "right of conquest," and many people thought then, as some think even now, that by putting this word "right" before "conquest" they made it all right! and had somehow succeeded in abrogating the laws, "Thou shalt not steal," and "Do to others as thou wouldest have others do to thee," laws which were written by God in the human understanding long before Moses descended with the decalogue from Sinai.

However, as we have said, there was little or no law in the land of old Albion at the time of which we write, so that we can scarcely wonder at the aspirations of the band under Addedomar—aspirations which were to the full as strong—perhaps even as noble—as those of Alexander the Great or the first Napoleon.

It had been ascertained by some stray hunter of Addedomar's party that considerable bands of men were ranging the valley of the Springs and its neighbourhood in search of something or some one, and that they went about usually in small detached parties. The stray hunter, with an eye, doubtless, to his personal interest, conveyed the news to the robber chief, who, having made secret and extensive preparations, happened at the time to be on his way to raid the territories of King Hudibras, intending to take the town of Gunrig as a piece of by-play in passing.

Here, however, was an opportunity of striking a splendid blow without travelling so far. By keeping his force united, and sending a number of scouts in advance, he could attack and overwhelm the scattered detachments in succession. He, therefore, in the meantime, abandoned his original plan, and turned aside to the neighbourhood of the Hot Swamp. There he remained in the sequestered hollow, which has been described, awaiting the return of his scouts. There was no difficulty in feeding an army in those days, for the forests of Albion abounded with game, and the silent bow, unlike the noisy fire-arm, could be used effectively without betraying the presence of the hunter.

The eyes of Addedomar opened wider and wider as his scouts dropped in one by one, and his heart beat high with glee and hope at the news they brought, for it opened up a speedy conquest in detail of more foes than he had counted on meeting with, and left the prospect of his afterwards carrying into execution his original plan.

The first scout brought the intelligence that it was not the men of King Hudibras who were in the neighbourhood, but those of Gadarn, the great chief of the far north, who had come there with an armed force in search of his daughter— she having gone lost, stolen, or strayed in the wilderness.

"Is the band a large one?" demanded Addedomar.

"It is; but not so large as ours, and it is weakened every day by being sent into the woods in different directions and in three detachments."

"Excellent! Ha! we will join Gadarn in this search, not only for his daughter, but for himself, and we will double the number of his detachments when we meet them, by slicing each man in two."

A loud laugh greeted this pleasantry, for robbers were easily tickled in those days.

"I also discovered," continued the scout, "that there is search being made at the same time for some boy or lad, who seems to have disappeared, or run away, or been caught by robbers."

Again there was a laugh at the idea that there were other robbers about besides themselves, but the chief checked them.

"Did you find out anything else about this lad?" he asked.

"Only that he seemed from his dress to be a hunter."

Addedomar frowned and looked at the ground for some moments in meditation.

"I'm convinced," he said at last, "that this lad is none other than the girl who escaped in the hunting dress of my young brother, just the day before I returned to camp. Mother was not as careful as she might have been at that time, and lost me a pretty wife. Good! Things are turning out well to-day. We will rout Gadarn, find his daughter and this so-called lad, and then I shall have two wives instead of one."

The robber chief had just come to this satisfactory conclusion, when another scout arrived.

"How now, varlet? Do you bring good news?"

"That depends on what you consider good," answered the scout, panting. "I have just learned that a large body of King Hudibras' men—about two hundred, I believe—is on its way to the Swamp to search for his son Bladud—"

"What! the giant whom we have heard tell of—who gave Gunrig such a drubbing?"

"The same. It seems that he has been smitten with leprosy,

has been banished from court, and has taken up his abode somewhere near the Swamp."

"But if he has been banished, why do they send out to search for him, I wonder?" said the robber chief.

"It is said," returned the scout, "that a friend of Bladud from the far East wants to find him."

"Good! This is rare good luck. We, too, will search for Bladud and slay him. It is not every day that a man has the chance to kill a giant with leprosy, and a king's son into the bargain."

"I also learned," continued the scout, "that some lady of the court has fled, and the army is to search of her too."

"What! more women? Why, it seems as if these woods here must be swarming with them. I should not wonder, too, if it was Hudibras' own daughter that has run away. Not unlikely, for the king is well known to be a tyrannical old fellow. H'm! we will search for her also. If we find them all, I shall have more than enough of wives—the king's daughter, and Gadarn's daughter, and this run-away-lad, whoever she may be! Learned you anything more?"

"Nothing more, except that Gadarn intends to make an early start to-morrow morning."

"It is well. We, also, will make an early—an even earlier— start to-morrow morning. To your food, now, my men, and then—to rest!"

While the robber chief was thus conversing with his scouts, two men were advancing through the forest, one of whom was destined to interfere with the plans which were so well conceived by Addedomar. These were our friends Arkal and Maikar.

Filled with a sort of wild romance, which neither the waves of the sea nor the dangers of the land could abate, these two shipmates marched through the woods all unconscious, of course, of the important part they were destined to play in that era of the world's history. The two sailors were alone, having obtained leave to range right and left in advance of the column to which they were attached, for the purpose of hunting.

"We are not much to boast of in the way of shooting," remarked Arkal; "but the troops don't know that, and good luck may prevent them finding it out."

"Just so," returned Maikar, "good luck may also bring us within arrow-shot of a wolf. I have set my heart on taking home a wolf-skin to that little woman with the black eyes that I've spoken to you about sometimes."

"Quite right, young man," said the captain, in an approving tone. "Nothing pleases folk so much as to find that they have been remembered by you when far away. Moreover, I think you stand a good chance, for I saw two wolves the other day when I was rambling about, but they were out of range."

Chance or luck—whichever it was—did not bring a wolf within range that day, but it brought what was more important and dangerous—namely, a large brown bear. The animal was seated under a willow tree, with its head on one side as if in meditation, when the men came upon it. An intervening cliff had prevented the bear from hearing the footsteps of the men, and both parties, being taken by surprise, stared at each other for a moment in silence.

No word was spoken, but next instant the bear ran at them, and stood up on its hind legs, according to bear-nature, to attack. At the same moment both men discharged arrows at it with all their force. One arrow stuck in the animal's throat, the other in his chest. But bears are proverbially hard to kill, and no vital part had been reached. Dropping their bows, the men turned and made for the nearest trees. They separated in doing so, and the bear lost a moment or two in making up its mind which to follow. Fortunately it decided in favour of Maikar. Had it followed Arkal, it would have caught him, for the captain, not being as agile as might be wished, missed his first spring up his tree, and slid back to the bottom.

Maikar, on the other hand, went up like a squirrel. Now, the little seaman had been told that some kinds of bears can climb while others cannot. Remembering the fact, he glanced anxiously down, as he went up. To his horror he saw that this bear could climb! and that his only chance would be to climb so high, that the branches which would bear his weight would not support the bear. It was a forlorn hope, but he resolved to try it.

Arkal, in the meantime, had recovered breath and self-possession. Seeing the danger of his comrade, he boldly dropped to the ground, picked up his bow, ran under the other tree, and sent an arrow deep into the bear's flank. With a savage growl, the animal looked round, saw the captain getting ready a second arrow, and immediately began to descend. This rather disconcerted Arkal, who discharged his arrow hastily and missed.

Dropping his bow a second time he ran for dear life to his own tree and scrambled up. But he need not have been in such haste, for although some bears can ascend trees easily, they are clumsy and slow in descending. Consequently the captain was high up before his enemy began to climb. That was of little advantage, however, for in a few moments the bear would have been up with him, had not Maikar, moved by the consideration no doubt, that one good turn deserves another, dropped quickly to the ground, picked up his bow and repeated the captain's operation, with even more telling effect, for his arrow made the bear so furious, that he turned round to bite it. In doing so he lost his hold, and fell to the ground with such a thud, that he drove the arrow further into him, and a vicious squeal out of him.

At this point little Maikar resolved to vary the plan of action. He stood his ground manfully, and, when the bear arose with a somewhat confused expression, he planted another arrow up to the feathers in its chest. Still the creature was unsubdued. It made a rush, but the sailor sprang lightly behind a tree, getting ready an arrow as he did so. When the animal rushed at him again, it received the shaft deep in the left shoulder, so that, with blood pouring from its many wounds, it stumbled and fell at its next rush.

Seeing how things were going, you may be sure that Arkal did not remain an idle spectator. He dropped again from the outer end of the bough he had reached, and when the bear rose once more to its feet, it found a foe on either side of it.

"Don't shoot together," panted Maikar, for all this violent action was beginning to tell on him. "Do you shoot first."

This was said while the bear was in a state of indecision.

The captain obeyed and put another arrow in its neck. The bear turned savagely on him, thus exposing its side to Maikar, who took swift advantage of the chance, and, sending an arrow straight to its heart, turned it over dead!

It must be remarked here, that all this shooting was done at such close range that, although the two seamen were, as we have said, rather poor shots, they had little difficulty in hitting so large an object.

"Now, then, out with your knife and off with the claws for the little woman at home with the black eyes," said Arkal, wiping the perspiration from his brow, "and be quick about it, so as to have it done before the troops come up."

The little man was not long in accomplishing the job, and he had just put the claws in his pouch, and was standing up to wipe his knife, when the captain suddenly grasped his arm and drew him behind the trunk of a tree, from which point of vantage he cautiously gazed with an anxious expression and a dark frown.

CHAPTER TWENTY EIGHT

ENEMIES, FRIENDS, SCOUTS, SKIRMISHES, AND COUNCILS OF WAR

Arkal's attention had been arrested by the figure of a man who suddenly appeared from behind a cliff not four hundred yards distant from the scene of their recent exploit. The stealthy manner in which the man moved among the bushes, and the earnest gaze which he directed from time to time in one particular direction, showed clearly that he was watching the movements of something—it might be a deer or an enemy.

"Evidently he has not seen us," whispered Maikar.

"Clear enough that, for he is not looking this way," returned Arkal. "He presents his back to us in a careless way, which he would hardly do if he knew that two crack bowmen were a hundred yards astern of him."

"Shall I shoot him?" whispered Maikar, preparing his weapons.

"He may be a friend," returned the captain. "But, see! yonder comes what interests him so much. Look!"

He pointed to a distant ridge, over the brow of which the head of Gunrig's column of men was just appearing.

"He is a scout!" exclaimed Maikar.

"Ay, and you may be sure that an enemy is not far off ahead of our column—unless, perchance, he may be the scout of some tribe friendly to the king. Hold your hand, Maikar. You are ever too ready to fight. Listen, now; yonder is a convenient hollow where I may get into the thick wood unseen by this scout, and run back to warn our friends. Ahead, yonder, is a narrow pass which leads, no doubt, into the next valley. Run you, as fast as your legs can wag, get through that pass, and see what you can see. In the nature of things the scout is almost sure to return through it, if he intends to carry the news of our approach to his people, who are probably there. You must hide and do the best you can to prevent him from doing this—either by killing him or knocking him down. Be off, we have no time to lose."

"But how if he should be a friend?" asked Maikar with a smile. "How am I to find out?"

Arkal paused and was perplexed.

"You must just exercise your wisdom," he replied. "If the fellow has an ill-looking countenance, kill him. If he looks a sensible sort of man, stretch him out somehow. I would offer to go instead of you, being more of a match for him, but I could not match his legs or yours, so it might well chance that he would reach the pass before me."

"Pooh, captain," retorted Maikar, with a look of scorn. "Ye think too much of yourself, and are unwarrantably puffed up about the advantage of size."

Without a reply—save a grin—Arkal turned, and, jumping into the bushes, was immediately out of sight. His comrade, before starting off to carry out his part of the programme, took a good look at the scout whom he was bound to circumvent.

He was evidently a tall, powerful man, armed with a bow, a short sword, and a stout staff somewhat longer than himself. That he was also a brave and cool man seemed probable, from the fact that, instead of hurrying off hastily to warn his friends that troops were in sight, he stood calmly leaning on his staff as if for the purpose of ascertaining the exact number of the strangers before reporting them.

He was still engaged in this inspection when Maikar started off and fled on the wings of hope and excitement toward the pass. Arrived there, his first glance revealed to him the troops of Addedomar busy with their evening meal in the valley below.

"The question is, are they friends or foes?" thought the little seaman. "H'm! it's an awkward thing for a poor fellow not to be quite sure whether to prepare for calms or squalls. Such a misfortune never could befall one at sea. Well, I must just take them to be foes till they prove themselves to be friends. And this scout, what in the world am I to do about *him*? I have no heart to hide in the bushes and shoot him dead as he passes."

The little man had probably forgotten his readiness to shoot the scout in the back only a few minutes before—but is not mankind at large prone to inconsistency at times?

"I know what I'll do," he muttered, pursuing his thoughts, and nodding his head, as he stepped aside into the shrubbery that clothed the slopes of the pass.

R. M. Ballantyne

Cutting down a suitable branch from a tree, he quickly stripped off the smaller branches and reduced it to a staff about six feet in length. Then, hiding himself behind a part of the cliff which abutted close on the footpath that had been worn through the pass by men and wild animals, he laid his bow and quiver at his feet and awaited the coming of the scout.

He had not to wait long, for that worthy, having ascertained the size of the invading band, came down the pass at a swinging trot. Just as he passed the jutting rock his practised eye caught sight of Maikar in time to avoid the blow of the pole or staff, which was aimed at his head, but not to escape the dig in the ribs with which the little man followed it up.

Instantly the scout's right hand flew to his quiver, but before he could fix an arrow another blow from the staff broke the bow in his left hand.

Blazing with astonishment and wrath at such rough treatment from so small a man, he stepped back, drew his sword and glared at his opponent.

Maikar also stepped back a pace or two and held up his hand as if for a truce.

"I too have a sword," he said, pointing to the weapon, "and can use it, but I have no desire to slay you till I know whether you are friend or foe."

"Slay me! thou insignificant rat!" cried the scout in savage fury. "Even if we were friends I would have to pay thee for that dig in the ribs and the broken bow. But I scorn to take advantage of such a squirrel. Have at thee with my staff!"

Running at him as he spoke, the scout delivered a blow that

would have acted like the hammer of Thor had it taken effect, but the seaman deftly dipped his head and the blow fell on a neighbouring birch, and a foot or so of the staff snapped off. What remained, however, was still a formidable weapon, but before the scout could use it he received another dig in the ribs which called forth a yell of indignation rather than of pain.

The appropriateness of the name squirrel now became apparent, for Maikar even excelled that agile creature in the rapidity with which he waltzed round the sturdy scout and delivered his stinging little blows. To do the scout justice, he played his part like a brave and active warrior, so that it seemed to rain blows and digs in all directions, and, once or twice, as by a miracle, Maikar escaped what threatened to be little, if at all, short of extermination. As in running, so in fighting, it is the pace that kills. After five minutes or so both combatants were winded. They separated, as if by mutual consent, and, leaning on their staves, panted vehemently.

Then at it they went again.

"Thou little scrap of a pig's snout, come on," shouted the scout in huge disdain.

"Thou big skinful of pride! look out!" cried Maikar, rendering the adoption of his own advice impossible by thrusting the butt of his staff against the scout's nose, and thereby filling his eyes with water. At the next moment he rendered him still more helpless by bestowing a whack on his crown which laid him flat on the footpath.

A cheer behind him at that moment caused the little man to look round, when he found that the head of Gunrig's column, led by Arkal, had come up just in time to witness the final blow.

They were still crowding round the fallen man, and asking hurried questions about him, when a voice from the heights above hailed them. Instantly a score or two of arrows were pointed in that direction.

"Hold your hands, men!" shouted Gunrig. "I know that voice—ay, and the face too. Is it not the white beard of our friend the Hebrew that I see?"

A few minutes more proved that he was right, for the well-known figure of Beniah descended the sides of the pass.

The news he brought proved to be both surprising and perplexing, for up to that moment Gunrig had been utterly ignorant of the recent arrival of Gadarn from the far north in search of his lost daughter, though of course he was well aware of the various unsuccessful efforts that had been made by King Hudibras in that direction. Moreover, he chanced to be not on the best of terms with Gadarn just at that time. Then the fact that Bladud had recovered his health and was actively engaged in the search—not, indeed, so much for Branwen as for a youth named Cormac—was also surprising as well as disagreeable news to Gunrig.

"And who is this Cormac in whom the prince seems to be so interested?" he asked.

Here poor Beniah, held fast by his solemn promise, was compelled to give an evasive answer.

"All that I can tell about him," he replied, "is that he is a kind young fellow to whose attention and nursing the prince thinks himself indebted for his life. But had we not better question this young man?" he added, turning to the scout. "I have heard rumours about robbers lurking somewhere hereabouts—hence my coming out alone to scout the country round, little dreaming that I should find the men of King Hudibras so near."

"If robbers are said to be hereabouts," broke in Maikar at this point, "I can tell you where to find them, I think, for I saw a band of men in the hollow just beyond this pass."

"Say you so?" exclaimed Gunrig; "fetch the prisoner here."

The scout, who had recovered his senses by that time, was led forward, but doggedly refused to give any information.

"Kindle a fire, men; we will roast him alive, and perhaps that will teach him to speak."

It was by no means unusual for men in those days to use torture for the purpose of extracting information from obstinate prisoners. At first the man maintained his resolution, but when he saw that his captors were in earnest, and about to light the fire, his courage failed him. He confessed that he was a scout, and that Addedomar was there with several other well-known chiefs and a body of four hundred men.

Thereupon the man was bound and put in the safe keeping of several men, whose lives were to be forfeited if he should escape. Then Gunrig, Dromas, Beniah, Arkal, Maikar, and several other chief men retired under a tree to hold a council of war. Their deliberations resulted in the following conclusions.

First, that the number of warriors at their disposal, counting those of King Hudibras and those under Gadarn, amounted to a sufficient force wherewith to meet the invaders in open fight; second, that a junction between their forces must be effected that night, for, according to usual custom in such circumstances, the enemy would be pretty sure to attack before daybreak in the morning; and, third, that what was to be done must be set about as soon as darkness favoured their operations.

"You can guide us in the dark, I suppose," said Gunrig, turning to Beniah.

"Ay, as well almost as in the light," replied the Hebrew.

"Let the men feed, then, and be ready for the signal to start," said the chief to his officers, "and see that no louder noise be heard than the crunching of their jaws."

The night was favourable to their enterprise. The moon was indeed risen, but clouds entirely hid it, yet allowed a soft light to pass through which rendered objects close at hand quite visible. Before midnight they started on the march in profound silence, and, led by Beniah, made a wide *detour* which brought them to the encampment of Gadarn. As may easily be understood, that chief was well pleased at the turn events had taken, for, to say truth, his little joke of trotting Beniah about the land and keeping him in perplexity, had begun to pall, and he had for some days past been hunting about for a plausible excuse for abandoning the search and going to visit King Hudibras.

His difficulty in this matter was increased by his unwillingness to reveal the true state of matters to Bladud, yet he knew that unless he did so the prince would utterly refuse to abandon the search for Cormac. Another thing that perplexed the chief greatly was—how the Hebrew, knowing Branwen as he did, had failed to recognise her in the lad Cormac, for of course he knew nothing of the promise that held the Hebrew's lips tied; his daughter—who was as fond of a joke as himself—having taken care not to reveal *all* the complications that had arisen in regard to herself.

The sudden appearance, therefore, of foes with whom he could fight proved to be a sort of fortunate safety-valve, and, besides, he had the comfort of thinking that he would fight in a good cause, for the region of the Hot Swamp belonged to his friend Hudibras, and this robber Addedomar was a notorious rascal who required extirpating, while the chiefs who had joined him were little better.

The council of war that was hastily called included Bladud, who was sent for, being asleep in his own booth when the party arrived. The council chamber was under an old oak tree.

When Bladud came forward he was suddenly struck motionless and glared as if he had seen a ghost. For the first time in his life he felt an emotion of supernatural fear—for there, in the flesh apparently, stood his friend Dromas.

A smile from the latter reassured him. Leaping forward he seized his friend's hand, but the impulsive Greek was not to be put off thus. He threw an arm round the prince's neck and kissed his cheek.

"Dromas!" cried Bladud, "can it be? Am I dreaming?"

"This is all very well," interrupted the impatient Gadarn, "and I have no doubt you are excellent friends though somewhat demonstrative, but we are holding a council of war—not of affection—and as the enemy may be close at hand it behoves us to be smart. Shake hands, Gunrig; you and I must be friends when we fight on the same side. Now, let us to work. Who is to have the chief command?"

By universal desire the council appointed Gadarn.

R. M. Ballantyne

"Well, then," said the commander-in-chief, "this is my view: Addedomar will come expecting to find us all asleep. He will find us all very wide awake. There is a slope in front of this camp leading down to the Swamp. At the bottom is a nice level piece of flat land, bordering on the Swamp, that seems just made for a battlefield. We will drive him and his men down the slope on to that flat, from which, after giving them the toothache, we will drive them into the Swamp, and as close up to the spring-head as we can, so that they may be half boiled alive, if possible. Those who escape the Swamp will find men ambushed on the other side who will drive them into the river. Those who escape the river may go home and take my blessing along with them."

"Then do you intend to divide our troops into two bodies?" asked Bladud.

"Of course I do. We can't have an ambush without dividing, can we?"

"Division means weakness," observed Gunrig.

"You were ever obstinate, Gunrig," said Gadarn, sharply.

"Division sometimes means strength," said Dromas in a conciliatory tone, for he was anxious at least to prevent division in the council. "As Addedomar is ignorant of the strength of our force, his being attacked unexpectedly, and in the dark, by two or three bands at once, from different quarters, will do much to demoralise his men and throw them into confusion."

"Right, my young friend," rejoined Gadarn; "though you do speak in the tones of one who has been born under other stars, there is sense in your head. That is the very thing I mean to do. We will divide into four bands. I will keep the biggest at the camp to drive them down the slope and begin the fight. Prince Bladud will take one detachment round through the woods to the river and fall upon them from that side. Gunrig, who I know loves the post of danger, will go down between the two mounds and meet the enemy right in the teeth when they are being driven out upon the flat land, and Dromas, as he seems to be a knowing man, might take the ambush on the other side of the Swamp."

"Nay, if I may choose, I would rather fight under my friend Bladud."

"Be it so. Settle that among yourselves. Only I must have Konar with me, for he knows the Swamp well and can roar splendidly. All the enemy below a certain point of courage will turn and split off when they hear his yell. I'm going to make him keep it for them as a little treat at the last. The Hebrew will also keep by me. Now marshal your men and take them off at once. We shan't have to wait long, for Addedomar is an active villain."

CHAPTER TWENTY NINE

THE BATTLE OF THE SPRINGS

Gadarn was right. The robber chief was very early astir that morning, and marched with his host so silently through the forest, that the very birds on the boughs gave them, as they passed underneath, but a sleepy wink of one eye and thrust their beaks again under their wings.

Not knowing the country thoroughly, however, Addedomar met some slight obstructions, which, necessitating occasional detours from the straight path, delayed him a little, so that it was very near dawn when he reached the neighbourhood of Gadarn's camp. Hesitation in the circumstances he knew would be ruinous; he therefore neglected the precaution of feeling his way by sending scouts in advance, and made straight for the enemy's camp. Scouts previously sent out had ascertained its exact position, so that he had no doubt of effecting a complete surprise.

Many noted battles have been fought and described in this world, but few, if any, we should think, will compare with the famous battle of the Springs in the completeness of the victory.

Coming out upon the flat which Gadarn had determined

should be the battle-field, and to the left of which the hot springs that caused the swamp were flowing, Addedomar marshalled his men for the final assault. Before reaching the flat they had passed almost within bow-shot of the spot where Gunrig and his men lay in ambush, and that chief might easily have fallen upon and killed many of them, had he not been restrained by the strict orders of Gadarn to let them pass on to the camp unmolested. It is true Gunrig found it very hard to hold his hand, but as Gadarn had been constituted commander-in-chief without a dissentient voice, in virtue of his superior intelligence and indomitable resolution, he felt bound to obey.

Bladud and his friend Dromas, with their contingent, being at the lower end of the flat and far out of bow-shot, were not thus tempted to disobey orders. The ambuscade on the other side of the Swamp had been put under the command of Captain Arkal, with Maikar for his lieutenant. Being entirely ignorant of what was going on, the men of this contingent lay close, abiding their time.

Inaction, during the development of some critical manoeuvre, while awaiting the signal to be up and doing, is hard to bear. Arkal and his men whiled away the time in whispered conversations, which related more or less to the part they were expected to play.

"If any of the robbers reach this side of the swamp alive," remarked Arkal, "there will be no need to kill them."

"What then? would you let them escape?" asked Maikar in surprise.

"Not on this side of the river," returned the captain. "But we might drive them into it, and as it is in roaring flood just now, most of them will probably be drowned. The few who escape will do us service by telling the tale of their defeat to their friends."

He ceased to whisper, for just then the dawning light showed them the dusky forms of the enemy stealing noiselessly but swiftly over the flat.

At their head strode Addedomar and a few of his stoutest men. Reaching the slope that led to the camp the four hundred men rushed up, still, however, in perfect silence, expecting to take their victims by surprise. But before they gained the summit a body of men burst out from the woods on either side of the track, and leaped upon them with a prolonged roar that must have been the rudimentary form of a British cheer.

The effect on the robbers was tremendous. On beholding the huge forms of Gadarn, Konar, and Beniah coming on in front they turned and fled like autumn leaves before a gale, without waiting even to discharge a single arrow. The courageous Addedomar was overwhelmed by the panic and carried away in the rush. Gadarn, supposing that the attack would have been made earlier and in the dark, had left the bows of his force behind, intending to depend entirely on swords and clubs. But he found that the robbers were swift of foot and that terror lent wings, for they did not overtake them at once. Down the slope went the robbers, and down went the roaring northmen, until both parties swept out upon the flat below.

They did not scatter, however. Addedomar's men had been trained to keep together even in flight, and they now made for the gully between the mounds, their chief intending to face about there and show fight on the slopes of the pass. But the flying host had barely entered it, when they were assaulted and driven back by the forces under Gunrig, who went at them with a shout that told of previous severe restraint. The fugitives could not stand it. The arrows, which even during flight were being got ready for Gadarn's host, were suddenly discharged at the men in the gully; but the aim was wild, and the only shaft which took serious effect found its billet in the breast of Gunrig himself. He plucked it savagely out and continued the charge at the head of his men.

Turning sharp to the left, the robbers then made for the lower end of the flat, still followed closely by Gadarn's band, now swelled by that of Gunrig. As had been anticipated, they almost ran into the arms of Bladud's contingent, which met them with a yell of rage, and the yell was answered by a shriek of terror.

Their retreat being thus cut off in nearly all directions, the panic-stricken crew doubled to the left again, and sprang into the swamp, closely followed by their ever-increasing foes. At first and at some distance from the fountain-head the water felt warm and grateful to the lower limbs of the fugitives, but as they plunged in deeper and nearer to the springs, it became uncomfortably hot, and they began to scatter all over the place, in the hope of finding cool water. Some who knew the locality were successful. Others, who did not know it, rushed from hot to hotter, while some, who were blindly struggling toward the source of the evil, at last began to yell with pain, and no wonder, for the temperature of the springs then—as it has been ever since, and is at the present day—was 120 degrees of Fahrenheit—a degree of heat, in water, which man is not fitted to bear with equanimity.

"Now, Konar, give them a tune from *your* pipe," said Gadarn, whose eyes were blazing with excitement.

The hunter of the Swamp obeyed, and it seemed as though a mammoth bull of Bashan had been suddenly let loose on the fugitives.

To add to the turmoil a large herd of Bladud's pigs, disturbed from their lair, were driven into the hot water, where they swam about in a frantic state, filling the whole region with horrid yells, which, mingling with those of the human sufferers, and the incessant barking of Brownie, rendered confusion worse confounded, and caused the wild animals far and near to flee from the region as if it had become Pandemonium!

The pigs, however, unlike the men, knew how to find the cooler parts of the swamp.

Perceiving his error when he stood knee-deep in the swamp, Gadarn now sought to rectify it by sending a detachment of swift runners back for his bows and arrows. But this manoeuvre took time, and before it could be carried out the half-boiled host had gained the other side of the Swamp, and were massing themselves together preparatory to a retreat into the thick woods.

"Now is *our* time," said Arkal, rising up and drawing his sword. Then, with a nautical shout, and almost in the words of a late warrior of note, he cried, "Up, men, and at them!"

And the men obeyed with such alacrity and such inconceivable violence, that the stricken enemy did not await the onset. They incontinently sloped at an angle of forty-five degrees with mother earth, and scooted towards the river, into which they all plunged without a moment's consideration.

Arkal and his men paused on the brink to watch the result; but the seaman was wrong about the probable fate of the vanquished, for every man of the robber band could swim like an otter, besides being in a fit condition to enjoy the cooler stream. They all reached the opposite bank in safety. Scrambling out, they took to the woods without once looking back, and finally disappeared.

During the remainder of that day Gadarn could do little else than chuckle or laugh.

Bladud's comment was that it had been "most successful."

"A bloodless victory!" remarked Beniah.

"And didn't they yell?" said Arkal.

"And splutter?" added Maikar.

"And the pigs! oh! the pigs!" cried Gadarn, going off into another explosion which brought the tears to his eyes, "it would have been nothing without the pigs!"

The gentle reader must make allowance for the feelings of men fresh from the excitement of such a scene, existing as they did in times so very remote. But, after all, when we take into consideration the circumstances; the nature of the weapons used; the cause of the war, and the objects gained, and compare it all with the circumstances, weapons, causes, and objects of modern warfare, we are constrained to admit that it was a "most glorious victory"—this Battle of the Springs.

R. M. Ballantyne

CHAPTER THIRTY

SMALL BEGINNINGS OF FUTURE GREAT THINGS

There was one thing, however, which threw a cloud over the rejoicing with which the conquerors hailed this memorable victory.

Gunrig's wound turned out to be a very severe one—much more so than had been at first supposed—for the arrow had penetrated one of his lungs, and, breaking off, had left the head in it.

As Bladud was the only one of the host who possessed any knowledge of how to treat complicated wounds, he was "called in," much against the wish of the wounded man; but when the prince had seen and spoken to him, in his peculiarly soft voice, and with his gentle manner, besides affording him considerable relief, the chief became reconciled to his new doctor.

"I thought you a savage monster," said the invalid, on the occasion of the amateur doctor's third visit; "but I find you to be almost as tender as a woman. Yet your hand was heavy enough when it felled me at the games!"

"Let not your mind dwell on that, Gunrig; and, truth to tell, if it had not been for that lucky—or, if you choose, unlucky—blow, I might have found you more than my match."

The chief held out his hand, which the doctor grasped.

"I thought to kill you, Bladud; but when I get well, we shall be friends."

Poor Gunrig, however, did not from that day show much evidence of getting well. His case was far beyond the skill of his amateur doctor. It was, therefore, resolved, a day or two later, to send him home under an escort led by Beniah.

"I will follow you ere long," said Gadarn, as he grasped the hand of the invalid at parting, "for I have business at the court of King Hudibras."

Gunrig raised himself in the litter in which he was borne by four men, and looked the northern chief earnestly in the face.

"You have not yet found your daughter?" he asked.

"Well—no. At least not exactly."

"Not exactly!" repeated Gunrig in surprise.

"No; not exactly. That's all I can say at present. All ready in front there? Move on! My greetings to the king, and say I shall see him soon. What, ho! Konar, come hither! Know you where I can find Prince Bladud?"

"In his booth," replied the hunter.

"Send him to me. I would have speech with him."

When the prince entered the booth of the commander-in-chief, he found that worthy with his hands on his sides, a tear or two in his eyes, and very red in the face. He frowned suddenly, however, and became very grave on observing Bladud.

"I sent for you," he said, "to let you know my intended movements, and to ask what you mean to do. To-morrow I shall start for your father's town with all my men."

"What! and leave your daughter undiscovered?"

"Ay. Of what use is it to search any longer? There is not a hole or corner of the land that we have not ransacked. I am certain that she is not here, wherever she may be; so I must go and seek elsewhere. Wilt go with me?"

"That will not I," returned Bladud decisively.

"Wherefore? The Hebrew tells me you are cured; and your father will be glad to have you back."

"It matters not. I leave not this region until I have made a more thorough search for and found the lad Cormac, or at least ascertained his fate."

"Why so anxious about the boy? is he of kin to you?" said Gadarn in a tone that seemed to convey the slightest possible evidence of contempt.

"Ay, he is of kin," returned Bladud, warmly; "for it seems to me sometimes that friendship is a closer tie than blood. At all events, I owe my life to him. Moreover, if he has been captured by robbers, I feel assured that he will escape before long and return to me."

"Indeed! Are you, then, so sure of his affection? Has he ever dared to say that he—he is fond of you?"

"Truly, he never has; for we men of the southern parts of Albion are not prone to speak of our feelings, whatever you of the north may be. But surely you must know, chief, that the eyes, the tones, and the actions, have a language of their own which one can well understand though the tongue be silent. Besides, I do not see it to be a very daring act for one man to tell another that he is fond of him. And you would not wonder at my regard, if you only knew what a pure-minded, noble fellow this Cormac is,—so thoughtful, so self-sacrificing, for, you know, it must have cost him—it would cost any one—a terrible effort of self-denial to dwell in such a solitude as this for the sole purpose of nursing a stranger, and that stranger a doomed leper, as I thought at first, though God has seen fit to restore me."

"Nevertheless, I counsel you to come with me, prince, for I have no intention of giving up the search for my child, though I mean to carry it on in a more likely region; and who knows but we may find Cormac—ha!" (here there was a peculiar catch in Gadarn's throat which he sought to conceal with a violent sneeze)—"ha! find Cormac in the same region!"

"That is not likely. I see no reason why two people who were lost at different times, and not, as far as we know, in exactly the same place, should be found"—(here the chief had another fit of sneezing)—"be found together. At any rate, I remain here, for a time at least. My old friend Dromas will remain with me, and some of my father's men."

As Gadarn could not induce the prince to alter his decision, and, for reasons of his own, did not choose to enlighten him, they parted there—the chief setting off with his troops in the direction of Hudibras' town, and the prince returning to his booth, accompanied by Captain Arkal, little Maikar, the hunter of the Hot Swamp, and about thirty of his father's men, who had elected to stay with him.

"As I am now cured, good Konar," said Bladud to the hunter, while returning to the booth, "and as I have enough to do in searching for my lost friend, I fear that I must end my service with you, and make over the pigs to some other herd."

"As you please, prince," returned the eccentric hunter with the utmost coolness, "the pigs were well able to look after themselves before you came, and, doubtless, they will be not less able after you go."

Bladud laughed, and, putting his hand kindly on the man's shoulder, assured him that he would find for him a good successor to herd his pigs. He also asked him if he would agree to act as hunter to his party, as he intended to remain in that region and build a small town beside the springs, so that people afflicted with the disease from which he had suffered, or any similar disease, might come and be cured.

Konar agreed at once, for a new light burst upon him, and the idea of living to serve other people, and not merely to feed himself, seemed to put new life into him.

"Do you really mean to build a town here?" asked Dromas, when he heard his friend giving orders to his men to erect a large booth to shelter them all for some time to come.

"Indeed, I do. So thankful am I, Dromas, for this cure, that I feel impelled to induce others to come and share the blessing. I only wish I could hope that you would stay in Albion and aid me. But I suppose there is some fair one in Hellas who might object to that."

"No fair one that I know of," returned Dromas, with a laugh, "and as I have left neither kith nor kin at home, there is nothing to prevent my taking the proposal into consideration."

"That is good news indeed. So, then, I will ask you to come along with me just now, and mayhap you will make up your mind while we walk. I go to fix on a site for the new town, and to set the men to work."

That day the voices of toilers, and the sound of hatchets and the crash of falling trees, were heard in the neighbourhood of the Hot Swamp, while the prince and his friend examined the localities around in the immediate vicinity of the fountain-head.

On coming to the fountain itself, the young men paused to look at it, as it welled up from the earth. So hot was it that they could not endure to hold their hands in it, and in such volumes did it rise, that it overflowed its large natural basin continually, and converted a large tract of ground into a morass, while finding its way, by many rills and channels, into the adjacent river.

"What a singular work of Nature!" remarked Dromas.

"Why not say—a wonderful work of God?" replied the prince.

"Come now, my friend, let us not begin again our old discussions. What was suitable for the groves of Hellas is not appropriate to the swamps of Albion!"

"I agree not with that, Dromas."

"You were ever ready to disagree, Bladud."

R. M. Ballantyne

"Nay, not exactly to disagree, but to argue. However, I will fall in with your humour just now, and wait for what you may deem a more fitting time. But what, think you, can be the cause of this extraordinary hot spring?"

"Fire!" returned the Greek promptly.

"Truly that must be so," returned the prince, with a laugh. "You are unusually sharp this morning, my friend. But what originates the fire, and where is it, and why does it not set the whole world on fire, seeing that it must needs be under the earth?"

"It would be better to put such questions to the wise men of Egypt, next time you have the chance, than to me," returned Dromas, "for I am not deep enough in philosophy to answer you. Nevertheless, it does not seem presumptuous to make a guess. That there is abundance of fire beneath the ground on which we tread is clear from the burning mountains which you and I have seen on our way from Hellas. Probably there are many such mountains elsewhere, for if the fire did not find an escape in many places, it would assuredly burst our world asunder. What set the inside of the world on fire at the beginning is, of course, a puzzle; and why everything does not catch fire and blaze up is another puzzle—for it is plain that if you were to set fire to the inside of your booth, the outside would be shrivelled up immediately. Then," continued Dromas, knitting his brows and warming with his subject, "there must be a big lake under the earth somewhere, and quite close to the fire, which sets it a-boiling and makes it boil over—thus."

He pointed to the fountain as he spoke.

"There may be truth in what you say, Dromas. At all events your theory is plausible, and this, I know, that ever since I came here, there has not been the slightest diminution in the volume of hot water that has poured forth; from which I would conclude that it has been flowing thus from the beginning of time, and that it will go on flowing thus to the end."

We know not whether the reader will be inclined to class Bladud among the prophets, but there are some prophets who have less claim to the title, for it is a fact that in this year of grace, 1892, the output of hot water from the same fountain, in the town of Bath, is one million tons every year, while the quantity and the temperature never vary in any appreciable degree, summer or winter, from year to year!

Having discussed the philosophical aspect of the fountain, the two friends proceeded with the work then in hand.

Of course, as they gazed around at the richly wooded hills and attractive eminences, which were not only charming sites for the little town, but also well suited for fortresses to resist invasions they were naturally tempted to sacrifice the useful to the safe and beautiful. Fortunately wisdom prevailed, and it was that day decided that the site for Swamptown should be on a slope that rose gently from the river bank, passed close by the Hot Swamp, and was finally lost in the lovely wood-clad terraces beyond.

"We must, of course, confine the hot stream within banks, train it to the river, and drain the Swamp," observed Bladud, as he sat brooding over his plans that night at supper.

"Ay, and make a pond for sick folk to dip in," said Dromas.

"And another pond for the healthy folk," suggested Captain Arkal; "we like to give ourselves a wash now and then, and it would never do for the healthy to go spluttering about with the sick—would it?"

"Certainly not," interposed little Maikar, "but what about the women? They would need a pond for themselves, would they not? Assuredly they would keep us all in hot water if they didn't have one."

"I see," said Bladud, still in a meditative mood. "There would have to be a succession of ponds alongside of the hot stream, with leads to let the water in—"

"And other leads to let the overflow out," suggested the practical Arkal.

"Just so. And booths around the ponds for people to dry themselves and dress in. Ha!" exclaimed the prince, smiting his knee with his hand. "I see a great thing in this—a thing that will benefit mankind as long as disease shall afflict them—as long as the hot waters flow!"

He looked round on his friends with an air of combined solemnity and triumph. The solemnity without the triumph marked the faces of his friends as they returned the look in profound silence, for they all seemed to feel that the prince was in a state of exaltation, and that something approaching to the nature of a prophecy had been uttered.

For a few moments they continued to gaze at each other—then there was a general sigh, as if a matter of great importance had been finally settled, and the silence was at last broken by little Maikar solemnly demanding another rib of roast-beef.

CHAPTER THIRTY ONE

MORE PLOTS AND PLANS

Having laid the foundations of the new town, drawn out his plans and set his men to work, Bladud appointed Captain Arkal superintendent, and set out on his quest after his lost friend Cormac, taking Dromas and Maikar along with him and four of the men—one of them being Konar the hunter. Brownie was also an important member of the party, for his master hoped much from his power of scent.

Meanwhile Cormac—alias Branwen, *alias* the little old woman—forsook the refuge of the Hebrew's house, and, in her antique capacity, paid a visit one afternoon to the palace of Hudibras.

"Here comes that deaf old witch again," said the domestic who had formerly threatened to set the dogs at her.

"Yes," remarked the old woman when she came up to the door, "and the old witch has got her hearing again, my sweet-faced young man—got it back in a way, too, that, if you only heard how, would make your hair stand on end, your eyes turn round, and the very marrow in your spine shrivel up. Go and tell the princess I want to see her."

R. M. Ballantyne

"Oh!" replied the domestic with a faint effort at a sneer, for he was a bold man, though slightly superstitious.

"Oh!" echoed the old woman. "Yes, and tell her that if she keeps me waiting I'll bring the black cloud of the Boong-jee-gop over the palace, and that will bring you all to the condition of wishing that your grandmothers had never been born. Young man—go!"

This was too much for that domestic. The unheard-of horrors of the Boong-jee-gop, coupled with the tremendous energy of the final "go!" was more than he could stand. He went—meekly.

"Send her to me directly," said Hafrydda, and the humiliated servitor obeyed.

"Dearest Branwen!" exclaimed the princess, throwing back the old woman's shawl, straightening her up, and hugging her when they were alone, "how long you have been coming! Where have you been? Why have you forsaken me? And *I* have such quantities of news to tell you—but, what has become of your hair?"

"I cut it short after I fell into the hands of robbers—"

"Robbers!" exclaimed the princess.

"Yes—I shall tell you all about my adventures presently—and you have no idea what difficulty I had in cutting it, for the knife was so blunt that I had to cut and pull at it a whole afternoon. But it had to be done, for I meant to personate a boy—having stolen a boy's hunting dress for that purpose. Wasn't it fun to rob the robbers? And then—and then—I found your brother—"

"*You* found Bladud?"

"Yes, and—and—but I'll tell you all about that too presently. It is enough to say that he is alive and well—sickness almost, if not quite, gone. I *was* so sorry for him."

"Dear Branwen!" said the princess, with an emphatic oral demonstration.

Hafrydda was so loving and tender and effusive, and, withal, so very fair, that her friend could not help gazing at her in admiration.

"No wonder I love him," said Branwen.

"Why?" asked the princess, much amused at the straight-forward gravity with which this was said.

"Because he is as like you as your own image in a brazen shield—only far better-looking."

"Indeed, your manners don't seem to have been improved by a life in the woods, my Branwen."

"Perhaps not. I never heard of the woods being useful for that end. Ah, if you had gone through all that I have suffered—the—the—but what news have you got to tell me?"

"Well, first of all," replied the princess, with that comfortable, interested manner which some delightful people assume when about to make revelations, "sit down beside me and listen—and don't open your eyes too wide at first else there will be no room for further expansion at last."

Hereupon the princess entered on a minute account of various doings at the court, which, however interesting they were to Branwen, are not worthy of being recorded here. Among other things, she told her of a rumour that was going about to the effect that an old witch had been seen occasionally in the neighbourhood of Beniah's residence, and that all the people in the town were more or less afraid of going near the place either by day or night on that account.

Of course the girls had a hearty laugh over this. "Did they say what the witch was like?" asked Branwen.

"O yes. People have given various accounts of her—one being that she is inhumanly ugly, that fire comes out of her coal-black eyes, and that she has a long tail. But now I come to my most interesting piece of news—that will surprise you most, I think—your father Gadarn is here!"

Branwen received this piece of news with such quiet indifference that her friend was not only disappointed but amazed.

"My dear," she asked, "why do you not gasp, 'My father!' and lift your eyebrows to the roots of your hair?"

"Because I know that he is here."

"Know it!"

"Yes—know it. I have seen him, as well as your brother, and father knows that *I* am here."

"Oh! you deceiver! That accounts, then, for the mystery of his manner and the strange way he has got of going about chuckling when there is nothing funny being said or done—at least nothing that I can see!"

"He's an old goose," remarked her friend.

"Branwen," said the princess in a remonstrative tone, "is that the way to speak of your own father?"

"He's a dear old goose, then, if that will please you better— the very nicest old goose that I ever had to do with. Did he mention Bladud to you?"

"Yes, he said he had seen him, and been helped by him in a fight they seemed to have had at the Hot Swamp, but we could not gather much from him as to the dear boy's state of health, or where he lived, or what he meant to do. He told us, however, of a mysterious boy who had nursed him in sickness, and who had somehow been lost or captured, and that poor Bladud was so fond of the boy that he had remained behind to search for him. I now know," added the princess with a laugh, "who this dear boy is, but I am greatly puzzled still about some of his doings and intentions."

"Listen, then, Hafrydda, and I will tell you all." As we have already told the reader all, we will not tell it over again, but leap at once to that point where the princess asked, at the close of the narrative, what her friend intended to do.

"That," said Branwen with a perplexed look and a sigh, "is really more than I can tell you at present. You see, there are some things that I am sure of and some things that I am not quite so sure of, but that I must find out somehow. For instance, I am quite sure that I love your brother more than any man in the world. I am also quite sure that he is the bravest, handsomest, strongest, best, and most unselfish man that ever lived—much about the same as my father, except that, being younger, he is handsomer, though I have no doubt my father was as good-looking as he when he was as young. Then I am also quite sure that Bladud is very fond of the boy Cormac, but—I am not at all sure that he will love the girl Branwen when he sees her."

"But *I* am sure of it—quite sure," said the princess, demonstrating orally again.

At this there was a slight sound near the door of the apartment in which this confidential talk was held, which induced Branwen to spring up and fling it wide open, thus disclosing the lately humiliated servitor with the blush of guilt upon his brow.

"Enter!" cried the princess, in an imperious tone, looking up at the man, who was unusually tall and limp.

The servitor obeyed.

"Sit down," said the princess, with a view to get the tall man's head on a level with her blue indignant eyes. "Have you heard much?"

"Not much," answered the man, with intense humility. "I heard only a very little at the end, and that so imperfectly that I don't think I can remember it—I really don't."

"Now, listen," said the princess, with a look that was intended to scorch. "You know my father."

"Indeed I do,—have known him ever since I was a boy."

"Well, if you ever breathe a word of what you have seen or heard, or what you think you have seen or heard to-day, to any one, I will set my father at you, and that, as you know, will mean roasting alive over a slow fire at the very least."

"And," said Branwen, advancing and shaking her forefinger within an inch of the man's nose, "I will set *my* father at you, which will mean slow torture for hours. Moreover, I will set the Boong-jee-gop on your track, and that will mean—no, I won't say what. It is too horrible even to mention!"

"Now—go!" said the princess, pointing to the door.

The servitor went with an air of profound abasement, which changed into a look of complicated amusement when he got out of sight.

"He is quite safe," said the princess, "not that I count much on his fear, for he is as brave as a she-wolf with whelps, and fears nothing, but I know he likes me."

"I think he likes me too," said Branwen, thoughtfully. "Besides, I feel sure that the Boong-jee-gop has some influence over him. Yes, I think we are safe."

"Well, now," she continued, resuming the interrupted conversation, "it seems to me that the only course open to me is to appear to Bladud as a girl some day, and see if he recognises me. Yet I don't quite like it, for, now that it is all past and he is well again, I feel half ashamed of the part I have played—yet how could I help it when I saw the poor fellow going away to die—alone!"

"You could not help it, dear, and you should not wish it were otherwise. Now, never mind what you feel about it, but let us lay our heads together and consider what is to be done. You think, I suppose, that Bladud may go on for a long time searching for this youth Cormac?"

"Yes, for a very long time, and he'll *never* find him," replied Branwen with a merry laugh.

"Well, then, we must find some means of getting him home without letting him know why we want him," continued the princess.

"Just so, but that won't be easy," returned the other with a significant look, "for he is *very* fond of Cormac, and won't easily be made to give up looking for him."

"You conceited creature, you are too sure of him."

"Not at all. Only as Cormac. I wish I were sure of him as Branwen!"

"Perchance he might like you best as the little old woman in grey."

"It may be so. I think he liked me even as a witch, for he patted my shoulder once so kindly."

"I'll tell you what—I'll go and consult father," said the princess.

"No, you shan't, my dear, for he is not to know anything about it just yet. But I will go and consult *my* father. He will give me good advice, I know."

The result of Branwen's consultation with her father was that the Hebrew was summoned to his presence. An explanation took place, during which Gadarn attempted to look grave, and dignified, as became a noted northern chief, but frequently turned very red in the face and vented certain nasal sounds, which betrayed internal commotion.

"You will therefore start for the Hot Swamp to-morrow, Beniah," he finally remarked, "and let Bladud know that the king desires his return to court immediately. I have been told by the king to send him this message. But keep your own counsel, Hebrew, and be careful not to let the prince know what *you* know, else it will go ill with you! Tell him, from myself, that I have at last fallen on the tracks of the lad

Cormac, and that we are almost sure to find him in this neighbourhood. Away, and let not thy feet take root on the road."

R. M. Ballantyne

CHAPTER THIRTY TWO

BRANWEN VISITS GUNRIG

Before going off on his mission the Hebrew paid a visit to his own residence, where he found Branwen busy with culinary operations. Sitting down on a stool, he looked at her with an expression of mingled amusement and perplexity.

"Come hither, my girl," he said, "and sit beside me while I reveal the straits to which you have brought me. Verily, a short time ago I had deemed it impossible for any one to thrust me so near to the verge of falsehood as you have done!"

"I, Beniah?" exclaimed the maiden, with a look of surprise on her pretty face so ineffably innocent that it was obviously hypocritical—insomuch that Beniah laughed, and Branwen was constrained to join him.

"Yes—you and your father together, for the puzzling man has commissioned me to set out for the Hot Swamp, to tell Bladud that he is urgently wanted at home. And he would not even allow me to open my lips, when I was about to broach the subject of your disguises, although he almost certainly knows all about them—"

"What! my father knows?" interrupted Branwen, with raised eyebrows.

"Yes, and you know that he knows, and he knows that I know, and we all know that each other knows, and why there should be any objection that every one should know is more than I can—"

"Never mind, Beniah," interrupted the girl, with the slightest possible smile. "You are a dear, good old creature, and I know you won't betray me. Remember your solemn promise."

"Truly I shall not forget it soon," replied the Hebrew, "for the trouble it has cost me already to compose answers that should not be lies is beyond your light-hearted nature to understand."

"Ah! yes, indeed," rejoined Branwen, with a sigh of mock humility, "I was always very lighthearted by nature. The queen used frequently to tell me so—though she never said it was by 'nature,' and the king agreed with her—though by the way he used to laugh, I don't think he thought light-heartedness to be *very* naughty. But come, Beniah, I am longing to hear what my father commissioned you to say or do."

"Well, he was very particular in cautioning me *not* to tell what I know—"

"Ah! that knowledge, what a dreadful thing it is to have too much of it! Well, what more?"

"He told me what I have already told you, and bid me add from himself that he has fallen on the tracks of the lad Cormac, and that he is sure to be found in this neighbourhood."

"That, at least, will be no lie," suggested the maid.

"I'm not so sure of that, for the lad Cormac will never be found here or anywhere else, having no existence at all."

Branwen laughed at this and expressed surprise. "It seems to me," she said, "that age or recent worries must have touched your brain, Beniah, for if the lad Cormac has no existence at all, how is it possible that you could meet with him at the Hot Swamp, and even make a solemn promise to him."

Beniah did not reply to this question, but rose to make preparation for his journey. Then, as if suddenly recollecting something that had escaped him, he returned to his seat.

"My child," he said, "I have that to tell you which will make you sad—unless I greatly misunderstand your nature. Gunrig, your enemy, is dying."

That the Hebrew had not misunderstood Branwen's nature was evident, from the genuine look of sorrow and sympathy which instantly overspread her countenance.

"Call him not my enemy!" she exclaimed. "An enemy cannot love! But, tell me about him. I had heard the report that he was recovering."

"It was the report of a sanguine mother who will not believe that his end is so near; but she is mistaken. I saw him two days ago. The arrow-head is still rankling in his chest, and he knows himself to be dying."

"Is he much changed in appearance?" asked Branwen.

"Indeed he is. His great strength is gone, and he submits to be treated as a child—yet he is by no means childish. The manliness of his strong nature is left, but the boastfulness has departed, and he looks death in the face like a true warrior; though I cannot help thinking that if choice had been given him he would have preferred to fall by the sword of Bladud, or some doughty foe who could have given him a more summary dismissal from this earthly scene."

"Beniah, I will visit him," said Branwen, suddenly brushing back her hair with both hands, and looking earnestly into the Hebrew's face.

"That will be hard for you to do and still keep yourself concealed."

"Nothing will be easier," replied the girl, with some impatience; "you forget the old woman's dress. I will accompany you as far as his dwelling. It is only an easy day's journey on foot from here."

"But, my child, I go on horseback; and I am to be supplied with only one horse."

"Well, my father, that is no difficulty; for I will ride and you shall walk. You will bring the horse here instead of starting straight from the palace. Then we will set off together, and I will gallop on in advance. When you reach Gunrig's house in the evening, you will find the horse fed and rested, and ready for you to go on."

"But how will you return, child?"

"By using my legs, man! As an old witch I can travel anywhere at night in perfect safety."

According to this arrangement—to which the Hebrew was fain to agree—the pair started off a little after daybreak the following morning. Branwen galloped, as she had said, in advance, leaving her protector to make his slower way through the forest.

The sun was high when the domestics of Gunrig's establishment were thrown into a state of great surprise and no little alarm at sight of a little old woman in grey bestriding a goodly horse and galloping towards the house. Dashing into the courtyard at full speed, and scattering the onlookers right and left, she pulled up with some difficulty, just in time to prevent the steed going through the parchment window of the kitchen.

"Help me down!" she cried, looking full in the face of a lumpish lad, who stood gazing at her with open eyes and mouth. "Don't you see I am old and my joints are stiff? Be quick!"

There was a commanding tone in her shrill voice that brooked no delay. The lumpish lad shut his mouth, reduced his eyes, and, going shyly forward, held out his hand. The old woman seized it, and, almost before he had time to wink, stood beside him.

"Where is Gunrig's room?" she demanded.

All the observers pointed to a door at the end of a passage.

"Take good care of my horse! Rub him well down; feed him. *I* shall know if you don't!" she cried, as she entered the passage and knocked gently at the door.

It was opened by Gunrig's mother, whose swollen eyes and subdued voice told their own tale.

"May I come in and see him, mother?" said Branwen, in her

own soft voice.

"You are a strange visitor," said the poor woman, in some surprise. "Do you want much to see him? He is but a poor sight now."

"Yes—O yes!—I want very much to see him."

"Your voice is kindly, old woman. You may come in."

The sight that Branwen saw on entering was, indeed, one fitted to arouse the most sorrowful emotions of the heart; for there, on a rude couch of branches, lay the mere shadow of the once stalwart chief, the great bones of his shoulders showing their form through the garments which he had declined to take off; while his sunken cheeks, large glittering eyes, and labouring breath, told all too plainly that disease had almost completed the ruin of the body, and that death was standing by to liberate the soul.

"Who comes to disturb me at such a time, mother?" said the dying man, with a distressed look.

Branwen did not give her time to answer, but, hurrying forward, knelt beside the couch and whispered in his ear. As she did so there was a sudden rush of blood to the wan cheeks, and something like a blaze of the wonted fire in the sunken eyes.

"Mother," he said, with something of his old strength of voice, "leave us for a short while. This woman has somewhat to tell me."

"May I not stay to hear it, my son?"

"No. You shall hear all in a very short time. Just now—

R. M. Ballantyne

leave us!"

"Now, Branwen," said the chief, taking her hand in his, "what blessed chance has sent you here?"

The poor girl did not speak, for when she looked at the great, thin, transparent hand which held hers, and thought of the day when it swayed the heavy sword so deftly, she could not control herself, and burst into tears.

"Oh! poor, poor Gunrig! I'm so sorry to see you like this!—so very, very sorry!"

She could say no more, but covered her face with both hands and wept.

"Nay, take not your hand from me," said the dying man, again grasping the hand which she had withdrawn; "its soft grip sends a rush of joy to my sinking soul."

"Say not that you are sinking, Gunrig," returned the girl in pitying tones; "for it is in the power of the All-seeing One to restore you to health if it be His will."

"If He is All-seeing, then there is no chance of His restoring me to health; for He has seen that I have lived a wicked life. Ah! Branwen, you do not know what I have been. If there is a place of rewards and punishment, as some tell us there is, assuredly my place will be that of punishment, for my life has been one of wrong-doing. And there is something within me that I have felt before, but never so strong as now, which tells me that there *is* such a place, and that I am condemned to it."

"But I have heard from the Hebrew—who reads strange things marked on a roll of white cloth—that the All-seeing

One's nature is *love*, and that He has resolved Himself to come and save men from wrong-doing."

"That would be good news indeed, Branwen, if it were true."

"The Hebrew says it is true. He says he believes it, and the All-seeing One is a Redeemer who will save all men from wrong-doing."

"Would that I could find Him, Branwen, for that is what I wish. I know not whether there shall be a hereafter or not, but if there is I shall hope for deliverance from wrong-doing. A place of punishment I care not much about, for I never shrank from pain or feared death. What I do fear is a hereafter, in which I shall live over again the old bad life— and I am glad it is drawing to a close with your sweet voice sounding in my ears. I believe it was that voice which first shot into my heart the desire to do right, and the hatred of wrong."

"I am glad to hear that, Gunrig, though it never entered into my head, I confess, to do you such a good turn. And surely it must have been the All-seeing One who enabled me to influence you thus, and who now recalls to my mind what the Hebrew read to me—one of those sayings of the good men of his nation which are marked in the white roll I spoke of. It is this—'God is our refuge and strength, a very present help in trouble.'"

"That is a good word, if it be a true one," returned the chief, "and I hope it is. Now, my end is not far off. I am so glad and thankful that you have forgiven me before the end. Another thing that comforts me is that Bladud and I have been reconciled."

"Bladud!" exclaimed the girl.

"Ay, the prince with whom I fought at the games, you remember."

"Remember! ay, right well do I remember. It was a notable fight."

"It was," returned the chief, with a faint smile, "and from that day I hated him and resolved to kill him, till I met him at the Hot Swamp, where I got this fatal wound. He nursed me there, and did his best to save my life, but it was not to be. Yet I think that his tenderness, as well as your sweet voice, had something to do with turning my angry spirit round. I would see my mother now. The world is darkening, and the time is getting short."

The deathly pallor of the man's cheeks bore witness to the truth of his words. Yet he had strength to call his mother into the room.

On entering and beholding a beautiful girl kneeling, and in tears, where she had left a feeble old woman, she almost fell down with superstitious fear, deeming that an angel had been sent to comfort her son—and so indeed one had been sent, in a sense, though not such an one as superstition suggested.

A few minutes' talk with Gunrig, however, cleared up the mystery. But the unwonted excitement and exertion had caused the sands of life to run more rapidly than might otherwise have been the case. The chief's voice became suddenly much more feeble, and frequently he gasped for breath.

"Mother," he said, "Branwen wants to get home without any one knowing that she has been here. You will send our stoutest man with her to-night, to guard her through the woods as far as the Hebrew's cave. Let him not talk to her by the way, and bid him do whatever she commands."

"Yes, my dear, dear son, what else can I do to comfort you?"

"Come and sit beside me, mother, and let me lay my head on your knee. You were the first to comfort me in this life, and I want you to be the last. Speak with Branwen, mother, after I am gone. She will comfort you as no one else can. Give me your hand, mother; I would sleep now as in the days gone by."

The bronzed warrior laid his shaggy head on the lap where he had been so often fondled when he was a little child, and gently fell into that slumber from which he never more awoke.

CHAPTER THIRTY THREE

THE HEBREW'S MISSION

We turn now to Beniah the Hebrew. On arriving at the Hot Swamp he was amazed to find the change that had been made in the appearance of the locality in so short a time.

"United action, you see," said Captain Arkal, who did the honours of the new settlement in the absence of Bladud and his friends, these being still absent on their vain search for the lad Cormac, "united action, perseveringly continued, leads to amazing results."

He repeated this to himself, in a low tone, as if he were rather proud of having hit on a neat way of expressing a great truth which he believed was an original discovery of his own. "Yes," he continued, "I have got my men, you see, into splendid working order. They act from morning to night in concert—one consequence of which is that all is Harmony, and there is but one man at the helm, the consequence of which is, that all is Power. Harmony and Power! I have no faith, Beniah, in a divided command. My men work together and feed together and play together and sleep together, united in the one object of carrying out the grand designs of Prince Bladud, while I, as the superintendent of the work, see to it that the work is properly done. Nothing could be more simple or satisfactory."

"Or more amazing," added Beniah, as they walked by the margin of a hot rivulet. "I could scarcely have known the Swamp had I not recognised its beautiful surroundings."

"Just so; it is all, as I have said, the result of union, which I hold to be the very foundation of human power, for united action is strong," said the captain, with enthusiasm, as he originated the idea which, years afterwards, became the familiar proverb, "Union is Strength."

"Most true, O mariner," returned Beniah, "your wisdom reminds me of one of our kings who wrote many of our wisest sayings."

"Ah, wise sayings have their value, undoubtedly," returned Arkal, "but commend me to wise doings. Look here, now, at the clever way in which Bladud has utilised this bush-covered knoll. It is made to divide this rivulet in two, so that one branch, as you see, fills this pond, which is intended for the male population of the place, while the other branch fills another pond—not in sight at present—intended for the women. Then, you see that large pond away to the left, a considerable distance from the fountain-head—that is supplied by a very small stream of the hot water, so that it soon becomes quite cold, and branch rivulets from the cold pond to the hot ponds cool them down till they are bearable. It took six days to fill up the cold pond."

"We have not yet got the booths made for the women to dress in," continued the captain, "for we have no women yet in our settlement; but you see what convenient ones we have set up for the men."

"But surely," said the Hebrew, looking round with interest,

R. M. Ballantyne

"you have far more hot water than you require."

"Yes, much more."

"What, then, do you do with the surplus?"

"We just let it run into the swamp at present, as it has always done, but we are digging a big drain to carry it off into the river. Then, when the swamp is dry, we will plant eatable things in it, and perhaps set up more booths and huts and dig more baths. Thus, in course of time—who knows?—we may have a big town here, and King Hudibras himself may condescend to lave his royal limbs in our waters."

"That may well be," returned the Hebrew thoughtfully. "The Hot Spring is a good gift from the All-seeing One, and if it cures others as it has cured Prince Bladud, I should not wonder to see the people of the whole land streaming to the place before long. But have you given up all thought of returning to your native land, Arkal? Do you mean to settle here?"

"Nay, verily—that be far from me! Have I not a fair wife in Hellas, who is as the light of mine eyes; and a little son who is as the plague of my life? No, I shall return home once more to fetch my wife and child here—then I shall have done with salt water for ever, and devote myself to hot water in time to come."

"A wise resolve, no doubt," said Beniah, "and in keeping with all your other doings."

"See," interrupted Arkal, "there is the river and the women's bath, and the big drain that I spoke of."

He pointed to a wide ditch extending from the swamp

towards the river. It had been cut to within a few yards of the latter, and all the men of the place were busily engaged with primitive picks, spades, and shovels, in that harmonious unity of action of which the captain had expressed such a high opinion.

A few more yards of cutting, and the ditch, or drain, would be completed, when the waters of the swamp would be turned into it. Those waters had been banked up at the head of the drain and formed a lake of considerable size, which, when the neck of land separating it from the drain should be cut, would rush down the artificial channel and disappear in the river.

Engineering in those days, however, had not been studied—at least in Albion—to the extent which now prevails in England. The neck of land was not equal to the pressure brought to bear on it, and while the captain and his friend were looking at it, there appeared symptoms which caused the former some anxiety.

At that moment Konar the hunter came up. Although attached to the settlement as hunter, he had agreed to take his turn with the diggers, for the water accumulated in the lake so fast that the work had to be done rapidly, and every available man at the place was pressed into the service. The overseer himself, even, lent a hand occasionally.

"I don't like the look of the lower part of that neck," he remarked to the hunter.

Konar was a man of few words. By way of reply he laid aside his bow and descended the bank to examine the weak point. He was still engaged in the investigation and bending over a moist spot, when the entire mass of earth gave way and the waters burst into the drain with a gush and a roar quite indescribable. Konar was swept away instantly as if he had been a feather. Arkal and Beniah sprang down the bank to his assistance, and were themselves nearly swept into the flood which had swallowed up the hunter, but Konar was not quite gone. Another moment and his legs appeared above the flood, then his head turned up, and then the raging waters tossed him as if contemptuously on a projecting spit of bank, where he lay half in and half out of the torrent.

In a moment both Arkal and the Hebrew were at the spot, seized the hunter by an arm, the neck of his coat, and the hair of his head, and drew him out of danger; but no sign of life did the poor man exhibit as he lay there on the grass.

Meanwhile the energetic labourers at the lower end of the drain heard the turmoil and stood motionless with surprise, but were unable to see what caused it, owing to a thick bush which intervened. Another moment and they stood aghast, for, round the corner of the only bend in the drain, there appeared a raging head of foam, with mud, grass, sticks, stones, and rubbish on its crest, bearing down on them like a race-horse.

With a yell that was as fully united as their method of work, the men scrambled out of the drain and rushed up the bank, exhibiting a unity of purpose that must have gladdened the heart of Captain Arkal. And they were not a moment too soon, for the last man was caught by the flood, and would have been swept away but for the promptitude of his fellows.

"H'm! it has saved you some work, lads," observed the captain, with a touch of grave irony as he pointed to the portion of the bank on which they had been engaged. He was right. The flood had not only overleaped this, but had hollowed it out and swept it clean away into the river—thus accomplishing effectively in ten minutes what would have probably required the labour of several hours.

On carrying Konar up to the village of the Swamp—afterwards Swamptown, later Aquae Sulis, ultimately Bath—which had already begun to grow on the nearest height, they found that Bladud and his party had just arrived from the last of the searching expeditions.

"What! Beniah?" exclaimed the prince, when the Hebrew met him. "You have soon returned to us. Is all well at home?"

"All is well. I am sent on a mission to you, but that is not so urgent as the case of Konar."

As he spoke the young men laid the senseless form on the ground. Bladud, at once dismissing all other subjects from his mind, examined him carefully, while Brownie snuffed at him with sympathetic interest.

"He lives, and no bones are broken," said the prince, looking up after a few minutes; "here, some of you, go fetch hot water and pour it on him; then rub him dry; cover him up and let him rest. He has only been stunned. And let us have something to eat, Arkal. We are ravenous as wolves, having had scarce a bite since morning."

"You come in good time," replied the captain. "Our evening meal is just ready."

"Come along, then, let us to work. You will join us, Beniah, and tell me the object of your mission while we eat."

The men of old may not have been epicures, but there can be no question that they were tremendous eaters. No doubt, living as they did, constantly in fresh air, having no house drains or gas, and being blessed with superabundant exercise, their appetites were keen and their capacities great. For at least ten minutes after the evening meal began, Bladud, Arkal, Dromas, little Maikar, and the Hebrew, were as dumb and as busy as Brownie. They spake not a single word—except that once the prince took a turkey drumstick from between his teeth to look up and repeat, "All well at home, you say?" To which Beniah, checking the course of a great wooden spoon to his lips, replied, "All well."

There was roast venison at that feast, and roast turkey and roast hare, and plover and ducks of various kinds, all roasted, and nothing whatever boiled, except some sorts of green vegetables, the names of which have, unfortunately, not been handed down to us, though we have the strongest ground for believing that they were boiled in earthenware pots—for, in recent excavations in Bath, vessels of that description have been found among the traces of the most ancient civilisation.

"Now," said the prince, wiping his mouth with a bunch of grass when he came to the first pause, "what may be the nature of your mission, Beniah?"

"Let me ask, first," replied the Hebrew, also wiping his mouth with a similar pocket handkerchief, "have you found the lad Cormac yet?"

"No," answered the prince, gloomily, and with a slightly surprised look, for the expression of Beniah's countenance puzzled him. "Why do you ask?"

"Because that bears somewhat on my mission. I have to deliver a message from your father, the king. He bids me say that you are to return home immediately."

"Never!" cried Bladud, with that Medo-Persic decision of

tone and manner, which implies highly probable and early surrender, "never! until I find the boy—dead or alive."

"For," continued the Hebrew, slowly, "he has important matters to consider with you—matters that will not brook delay. Moreover, Gadarn bid me say that he has fallen on the tracks of the lad Cormac, and that we are almost sure to find him in the neighbourhood of your father's town."

"What say you?" exclaimed Bladud, dropping his drumstick —not the same one, but another which he had just begun— "repeat that."

Beniah repeated it.

"Arkal," said the prince, turning to the captain, "I will leave you in charge here, and start off by the first light to-morrow morning. See that poor Konar is well cared for. Maikar, you will accompany me, and I suppose, Dromas, that you also will go."

"Of course," said Dromas, with a meaning smile—so full of meaning, indeed, as to be quite beyond interpretation.

"By the way," continued Bladud,—who had resumed the drumstick,—"has that fellow Gadarn found his daughter Branwen?"

Beniah choked on a bone, or something, at that moment, and, looking at the prince with the strangest expression of face, and tears in his eyes, explained that he had not—at least not to his, Beniah's, absolutely certain knowledge.

"That is to say," he continued in some confusion, "if—if—he has found her—which seems to me highly probable—there must be some—some mystery about her, for—it is impossible that—"

Here the Hebrew choked again with some violence.

"Have a care, man!" cried the prince in some alarm. "However hungry a man may be, he should take time to swallow. You seem to be contradicting yourself, but I don't wonder, in the circumstances."

"Verily, I wonder at nothing, in the circumstances, for they are perplexing—even distressing," returned the Hebrew with a sigh, as he wiped his eyes with the sleeve of his coat.

"Better not speak with your mouth full, then. Ah! poor Gadarn," said Bladud, in an obviously indifferent tone of voice. "I'm sorry for him. Girls like his daughter, who are self-willed, and given to running away, are a heavy affliction to parents. And, truly, I ought to feel sympathy with him, for, although I am seeking for a youth of very different character, we are both so far engaged in similar work—search for the lost. And what of my father, mother, and sister?"

"All hale and hearty!" replied Beniah, with a sigh of relief, "and all anxious for your return, especially Hafrydda."

At this point Dromas looked at the speaker with deepened interest.

"She is a good girl, your sister," continued Beniah, "and greatly taken up just now with that old woman you met in my cave. Hafrydda has strange fancies."

"She might have worse fancies than being taken up with poor old women," returned the prince. "I'm rather fond of them myself, and was particularly attracted by the old woman referred to. She was—what! choking again, Beniah? Come, I think you have had enough for one meal. And so have we all, friends, therefore we had better away to roost if we are to be up betimes in the morning."

R. M. Ballantyne

CHAPTER THIRTY FOUR

BLADUD'S RETURN AND TRIALS

We need scarcely say that there was joy at the court of King Hudibras when Bladud returned home, cured of his terrible disease.

The first person whom the prince hurried off to visit, after seeing his father, and embracing his mother and sister, was the northern chief Gadarn. That jovial character was enjoying a siesta after the mid-day meal at the time, but willingly arose on the prince being announced.

"Glad to see you, Gadarn," said Bladud, entering the room that had been apportioned to the chief, and sitting down on a bench for visitors, which, according to custom, stood against the inner wall of the apartment. "I hope your head is clear and your arm strong."

"Both are as they should be," answered Gadarn, returning the salutation.

"I thank you," replied the prince, "my arm is indeed strong, but my head is not quite as clear as it might be."

"Love got anything to do with it?" asked Gadarn, with a

knowing look.

"Not the love of woman, if that is what you mean."

"Truly that is what I do mean—though, of course, I admit that one's horses and dogs have also a claim on our affections. What is it that troubles you, my son?"

The affectionate conclusion of this reply, and the chief's manner, drew the prince towards him, so that he became confidential.

"The truth is, Gadarn, that I am very anxious to know what news you have of Cormac—for the fate of that poor boy hangs heavy on my mind. Indeed, I should have refused to quit the Swamp, in spite of the king's commands and my mother's entreaties, if you had not sent that message by the Hebrew."

"Ah, Bladud, my young friend, that is an undutiful speech for a son to make about his parents," said the chief, holding up a remonstrative forefinger. "If that is the way you treat your natural parents, how can I expect that—that—I mean—"

Here the chief was seized with a fit of sneezing, so violent, that it made the prince quite concerned about the safety of his nose.

"Ha!" exclaimed Gadarn, as a final wind up to the last sneeze, "the air of that Swamp seems to have been too strong for me. I'm growing old, you see. Well—what was I saying?—never mind. You were referring to that poor lad Cormac. Yes, I have news of him."

"Good news, I hope?" said the prince, anxiously. "O yes— very good—excellent! That is to say—rather—somewhat

R. M. Ballantyne

indefinite news, for—for the person who saw him told me—in fact, it is difficult to explain, because people are often untrustworthy, and exaggerate reports, so that it is not easy to make out what is true and what is false, or whether both accounts may be true, or the whole thing false altogether. You see, Bladud, our poor brains," continued the chief, in an argumentative tone, "are so—so—queerly mixed up that one cannot tell—tell—why, there was once a fellow in my army, whose manner of reporting any event, no matter how simple, was so incomprehensible that it was impossible to—to—but let me tell you an anecdote about him. His name was—"

"Forgive my interrupting you, chief, but I am so anxious to hear something about my lost friend that—"

"Ha! Bladud, I fear that you are a selfish man, for you have not yet asked about my lost daughter."

"Indeed I am not by any means indifferent about her; but—but, you know, I have never seen her, and, to tell the plain truth, my anxiety about the boy drove her out of my mind for the moment. Have you found her?"

"Ay, that I have; as well and hearty as ever she was, though somewhat more beautiful and a trifle more mischievous. But I will introduce her to you to-morrow. There is to be a grand feast, is there not, at the palace?"

"Yes; something of the sort, I believe, in honour of my return," answered the prince, a good deal annoyed by the turn the conversation had taken.

"Well, then, you shall see her then; for she has only just arrived, and is too tired to see any one," continued Gadarn, with a suppressed yawn; "and you'll be sure to fall in love with her; but you had better not, for her affections are already engaged. I give you fair warning, so be on your guard."

The prince laughed, and assured his friend that there was no fear, as he had seen thousands of fair girls both in East and West, but his heart had never yet been touched by one of them.

At this the chief laughed loudly, and assured Bladud that his case had now reached a critical stage: for when young men made statements of that kind, they were always on the point of being conquered.

"But leave me now, Bladud," he continued, with a yawn so vast that the regions around the uvula were clearly visible; "I'm frightfully sleepy, and you know you have shortened my nap this afternoon."

The prince rose at once.

"At all events," he said, "I am to understand, before I go, that Cormac *has* been seen?"

"O yes! Certainly; no doubt about that!"

"And is well?"

"Quite well."

Fain to be content with this in the meantime, Bladud hurried to the apartment of his sister.

"Hafrydda!" he exclaimed, "has Gadarn gone out of his mind?"

"I believe not," she replied, sitting down beside her brother

R. M. Ballantyne

and taking his hand. "Why do you ask?"

"Because he talks—I say it with all respect—like an idiot."

Hafrydda laughed; and her brother thereupon gave her a full account of the recent interview.

"Now, my sister, you were always straightforward and wise. Give me a clear answer. Has Cormac been found?"

"No, he has not been found; but—"

"Then," interrupted Bladud, in a savage tone that was very foreign to his nature, "Gadarn is a liar!"

"Oh, brother! say not so."

"How can I help it? He gave me to understand that Cormac *has* been found—at least, well, no, not exactly found, but *seen* and heard of. I'm no better than the rest of you," continued Bladud, with a sarcastic laugh. "It seems as if there were something in the air just now which prevents us all from expressing ourselves plainly."

"Well, then, brother," said Hafrydda, with a smile, "if he told you that Cormac has been seen and heard of, and is well, surely that may relieve your mind till to-morrow, when I know that some one who knows all about the boy is to be at our festival. We begin it with games, as usual. Shall you be there?"

"I'd rather not," replied the prince almost testily; "but, of course, it would be ungracious not to appear. This, however, I do know, that I shall take no part in the sports."

"As you please, brother. We are only too glad to have you

home again, to care much about that. But, now, I have something of importance to tell you about myself."

Bladud was interested immediately; and for the moment forgot his own troubles as he gazed inquiringly into the fair countenance of the princess.

"I am going to wed, brother."

"Indeed! You do not surprise me, though you alarm me—I know not why. Who is the man?—not Gunrig, I hope."

"Alas! no. Poor Gunrig is dead."

"Dead! Ah, poor man! I am glad we met at the Swamp."

Bladud looked sad for a moment, but did not seem unduly oppressed by the news.

"The man who has asked me to wed is your friend Dromas."

"What!" exclaimed the prince, in blazing surprise, not unmingled with delight. "The man has been here only a few hours! He must have been very prompt!"

"It does not take many hours to ask a girl to wed; and I like a prompt man," returned the princess, looking pensively at the floor.

"But tell me, how came it all about? How did he manage it in so short a time?"

"Well, brother dear—but you'll never tell any one, will you?"

"Never—never!"

"Well, you must know, when we first met, we—we—"

"Fell in love. Poor helpless things!"

"Just so, brother; we fell, somehow in—whatever it was; and he told me with his eyes—and—and—I told him with mine. Then he went off to find you; and came back, having found you—for which I was very grateful. Then he went to father and asked leave to speak to me. Then he went to mother. What they said I do not know; but he came straight to me, took my hand, fixed his piercing black eyes on me, and said, 'Hafrydda, I love you.'"

"Was that *all*?" asked Bladud.

"Yes; that was all he *said*; but—but that was not the end of the interview! It would probably have lasted till now, if you had not interrupted us."

"I'm so very sorry, sister, but of course I did not know that—"

They were interrupted at that moment by the servitor, to whom the reader has already been introduced. He entered with a brightly intelligent grin on his expressive face, but, on beholding Bladud, suddenly elongated his countenance into blank stupidity.

"The old woman waits outside, princess."

"Oh, send her here at once." (Then, when the servitor had left.) "This is the person I mentioned who knows about Cormac."

Another moment and the little old woman in the grey shawl was ushered in. She started visibly on beholding Bladud.

"Come in, granny. I did not expect you till to-morrow."

"I thought I was to see you alone," said the old woman, testily, in her hard, metallic voice.

"That is true, granny, but I thought you might like to see my brother Bladud, who has just returned home safe and well."

"No, I *don't* want to see your brother. What do I care for people's brothers? I want to see yourself, alone."

"Let me congratulate you, at all events," interposed the prince, kindly, "on your having recovered your hearing, grannie. This is not the first time we have met, Hafrydda, but I grieve to see that my old friend's nerves are not so strong as they used to be. You tremble a good deal."

"Yes, I tremble more than I like," returned the old woman peevishly, "and, perhaps, when you come to my age, young man, and have got the palsy, you'll tremble more than I do."

"Nay, be not angry with me. I meant not to hurt your feelings; and since you wish to be alone with my sister, I will leave you."

When he was gone Branwen threw back the grey shawl and stood up with flashing, tearful eyes.

"Was it kind—was it wise, Hafrydda, to cause me to run so great a risk of being discovered?"

"Forgive me, dear Branwen, I did not mean to do it, but you arrived unexpectedly, and I let you come in without thinking. Besides, I knew you could easily deceive him. Nobody could guess it was you—not even your own mother."

"There must be some truth in that," returned the maiden, quickly changing her mood, and laughing, "for I deceived my own father yesterday. At the Swamp he found me out at once as Cormac, for I had to speak in my natural voice, and my full face was exposed; but the grey shawl and the metallic voice were too much for him. Dear, good, patient, old man, you have no notion what a fearful amount of abuse he took from me, without losing temper—and I gave him some awful home-thrusts too! I felt almost tempted to kiss him and beg his pardon. But now, Hafrydda, I am beginning to be afraid of what all this deceiving and playing the double-face will come to. And I'm ashamed of it too—I really am. What will Bladud think of me when he finds out? Won't he despise and hate me?"

"Indeed he will not. I know his nature well," returned the princess, kissing, and trying to reassure her friend, whose timid look and tearful eyes seemed to indicate that all her self-confidence and courage were vanishing. "He loves you already, and love is a preventive of hate as well as a sovereign remedy for it."

"Ay, he is fond of Cormac, I know, but that is a very different thing from loving Branwen! However, to-morrow will tell. If he cares only for the boy and does not love the girl, I shall return with my father to the far north, and you will never see Branwen more."

CHAPTER THIRTY FIVE

THE PLOT THICKENS

During the residence of Gadarn at the court of King Hudibras, that wily northern chief had led the king to understand that one of his lieutenants had at last discovered his daughter Branwen in the hands of a band of robbers, from whom he had rescued her, and that he expected her arrival daily.

"But what made the poor child run away?" asked the king at one of his interviews with his friend. "We were all very fond of her, and she of us, I have good reason to believe."

"I have been told," replied the chief, "that it was the fear of Gunrig."

"Gunrig! Why, the man was to wed my daughter. She had no need to fear him."

"That may be so, but I know—though it is not easy to remember how I came to know it—that Gunrig had been insolent enough to make up to her, after he was defeated by Bladud, and she was so afraid of him that she ran away, and thus fell into the hands of robbers."

R. M. Ballantyne

While the chief was speaking, Hudibras clenched his hands and glared fiercely.

"Dared he to think of another girl when he was engaged to my daughter!" he said between his teeth. "It is well that Gunrig is dead, for assuredly I would have killed him."

"It is well indeed," returned Gadarn, "for if your killing had not been sufficient, I would have made it more effectual. But he is out of the way now, so we may dismiss him."

"True—and when may we expect Branwen back again, poor child?" asked the king.

"In a day or two at latest. From what was told me by the runner who was sent on in advance, it is possible that she may be here to-morrow, in time for the sports."

The wily chief had settled it in his own mind that Branwen should arrive exactly at the time when there was to be a presentation of chiefs; which ceremony was to take place just before the commencement of the sports. This arrangement he had come to in concert with a little old woman in a grey shawl, who paid him a private visit daily.

"Do you know, Gadarn, who this youth Cormac is, whom Bladud raves so much about?"

The northern chief was seized at that moment with one of those violent fits of sneezing to which of late he had become unpleasantly subject.

"Oh! ye—ye—y-ha! yes;—excuse me, king, but since I went to that Hot Swamp, something seems to have gone wrong wi'—wi'—ha! my nose."

"Something will go worse wrong with it, chief, if you go on like that. I thought the last one must have split it. Well, what know you about Cormac?"

"That he appears to be a very good fellow. I can say nothing more about him than that, except that your son seems to think he owes his life to his good nursing at a critical point in his illness."

"I know that well enough," returned the king, "for Bladud has impressed it on me at least a dozen times. He seems to be very grateful. Indeed so am I, and it would please me much if I had an opportunity of showing my gratitude to the lad. Think you that there is any chance of finding out where he has disappeared to?"

"Not the least chance in the world."

"Indeed!" exclaimed the king in surprise. "That is strange, for Bladud, who has just left me, says that he has the best of reasons for believing that we shall have certain news of him tomorrow. But go, Gadarn, and consult my doctor about this complaint of yours, which interrupts conversation so awkwardly. We can resume our talk at some other time."

Gadarn obediently went, holding his sides as if in agony, and sneezing in a manner that caused the roof-tree of the palace to vibrate.

Returning to his own room he found the little old woman in grey awaiting him.

"You've been laughing again, father," she said. "I see by the purpleness of your face. You'll burst yourself at last if you go on so."

"Oh! you little old hag—oh! Cormac—oh! Branwen, I hope you won't be the death of me," cried the chief, flinging his huge limbs on a couch and giving way to unrestrained laughter, till the tears ran down his cheeks. "If they did not all look so grave when speaking about you, it wouldn't be so hard to bear. It's the gravity that kills me. But come, Branwen," he added, as he suddenly checked himself and took her hand, "what makes you look so anxious, my child?"

"Because I feel frightened, and ashamed, and miserable," she answered, with no symptom of her sire's hilarity. "I doubt if I should have followed Bladud—but if I had not he would have died—and I don't like to think of all the deceptions I have been practising—though I couldn't very well help it—could I? Then I fear that Bladud will forget Cormac when he learns to despise Branwen—"

"Despise Branwen!" shouted Gadarn, fiercely, as his hand involuntarily grasped the hilt of his sword. "If he did, I would cleave him from his skull to his waist—"

"Quiet you, my sweet father," said Branwen, with a little smile, "you know that two can play at that game, and that you have a skull and a waist as well as Bladud—though your waist is a good deal thicker than his. I'm not so sure about the skull!"

"I accept your reproof, child, for boastfulness is hateful in a warrior. But get up, my love. What would happen if some one came into the room and found a little old hag sitting on my knee with her arm around my neck?"

"Ah, true, father. I did not think of that. I'm rather given to not thinking of some things. Perhaps that inquisitive servitor may be—no, he's not there this time," said Branwen, reclosing the door and sitting down on a stool beside the chief. "Now come, father, and learn your lesson."

Gadarn folded his hands and looked at his child with an air of meek humility.

"Well?"

"Well, first of all, you must tell the king tomorrow, at the right time, that I have just come back, and am very tired and shall not appear till you take me to him while the other people are being presented. Then you will lead me forward and announce me with a loud voice, so that no one shall fail to hear that I am Branwen, your daughter, you understand? Now, mind you speak well out."

"I understand—with a shout, something like my battle-cry!"

"Not exactly so loud as that, but so as Bladud shall be sure to hear you; and he will probably be near to his father at the time."

"Just so. What next?"

"Oh, that's all you will have to do. Just retire among the other courtiers then, and leave the rest to me."

"That's a very short lesson, my little one; would you not like to be introduced to Bladud too? He does not know you, you know."

"Certainly not; that would ruin all—you dear old goose. Just do exactly what I tell you, and you will be sure to go right."

"How like your dear mother you are, my little one, in your modest requirements!"

R. M. Ballantyne

Having finished the lesson, the little old woman retired to a remote part of the palace which, through Hafrydda's influence, had been assigned to her, and the great northern chief, unbuckling his sword-belt, called lustily for his mid-day meal.

Customs at that date, you see, were more free-and-easy than they are now, and less ceremonious. The visitors at the palace of King Hudibras were expected only to appear at the royal board at the evening meal after all the business or pleasure of each day was over. At all other times they were supposed to do as they pleased and shout for food as they happened to require it.

It is perhaps unnecessary to comment on the exceeding convenience of this custom, leaving, as it did, every one to follow the bent of inclination, from earliest morn till dewy eve, with the prospect of an enjoyable *reunion* after dark—during which, of course, the adventures of each were narrated, exaggerated, underrated, or commented on, as the case might be, and the social enjoyments were enhanced by warlike and sentimental song as well as by more or less—usually more than less—thrilling story.

CHAPTER THIRTY SIX

THE DENOUEMENT

It was a sunny, frosty, glorious forenoon when King Hudibras awoke to the consciousness of the important day that was before him, and the importunate vacuum that was within him.

Springing out of bed with a right royal disregard of appearances he summoned his servitor-in-waiting and ordered breakfast.

In the breakfast-room he met the queen, Hafrydda, Bladud, and Dromas—the latter being now considered one of the family—and these five proceeded to discuss and arrange the proceedings of the day during the progress of the meal.

"You will join in the sports, of course, son Dromas," said the king, "and show us how the Olympic victors carry themselves. Ha! I should not wonder if a few of our lads will give you some trouble to beat them."

"You may be right, father," returned the young man, modestly, "for one of your lads has already beaten me at most things."

"You mean Bladud?" returned the king.

"Dromas is only so far right," interposed the prince. "It is true that where mere brute force is required I usually have the advantage, but where grace and speed come into play I am lost."

Of course Dromas would not admit this, and of course Hafrydda's fair cheeks were crimsoned when the youth, accidentally looking up, caught the princess accidentally gazing at him; and, still more of course, the king, who was sharp as a needle in such matters, observed their confusion and went into a loud laugh, which he declared was only the result of merry thoughts that were simmering in his brain.

The reception was to be held in the large hall of the palace. No ladies were to be presented, for it must be remembered that these were barbarous times, and woman had not yet attained to her true position! Indeed, there was to be no ceremony whatever—no throne, no crown, no gold-sticks in waiting or other sticks of any kind. It was to be a sort of free-and-easy conversazione in the presence of the royal family, where, just before the sports began, any one who was moved by that ambition might hold personal intercourse with the king, and converse with him either on the affairs of State, or on private matters, or subjects of a more light and social kind—such as the weather.

At the appointed hour—which was indicated by that rough and ready but most natural of sun-dials, the shadow of a tree falling on a certain spot—the royal family adjourned to the large hall, and the unceremonious ceremony began.

First of all, on the doors being thrown open a crowd of nobles—or warriors—entered, and while one of them went to the king, and began an earnest entreaty that war might be declared without delay against a certain chief who was particularly obnoxious to him, another sauntered up to the princess and began a mild flirtation in the primitive manner, which was characteristic of the sons of Mars in that day—to the unutterable jealousy of Dromas, who instantly marked him down as a fit subject for overwhelming defeat at the approaching games. At the same time the family doctor paid his respects to the queen and began to entertain her with graphic accounts of recent cases—for doctors had no objection to talking "shop" in those days.

We have said that no ladies were admitted to places of public importance, such as grand-stands or large halls, but we have also pointed out that the ladies of the royal family and their female friends formed an exception to the rule. It was, as it were, the dawn of women's freedom—the insertion of the small end of that wedge which Christianity and civilisation were destined to drive home—sometimes too far home!

Gradually the hall began to fill, and the hum of conversation became loud, when there was a slight bustle at the door which caused a modification though not a cessation of the noise.

It was caused by the entrance of Gadarn leading Branwen by the hand. The girl was now dressed in the costume that befitted her age and sex, and it is best described by the word simplicity. Her rich auburn hair fell in short natural curls on her neck—the luxuriant volume of it having, as the reader is aware, been sacrificed some time before. She wore no ornament of any kind save, on one side of her beautiful head, a small bunch of wild-flowers that had survived the frost.

At the time of their entrance, Bladud was stooping to talk with Hafrydda and did not observe them, but when he heard Gadarn's sonorous voice he turned with interest to listen.

"King Hudibras," said the northern chief, in a tone that produced instant silence, "I have found the lost one—my daughter Branwen."

As they moved through the crowd of tall warriors Bladud could not at first catch sight of the girl.

"Ha! Hafrydda," he said, with a pleasant smile, "your young friend and companion found at last. I congratulate you. I'm so glad that—"

He stopped, the colour fled from his cheeks, his chest heaved. He almost gasped for breath. Could he believe his eyes, for there stood a girl with the features, the hair, the eyes of Cormac, but infinitely more beautiful!

For some time the poor prince stood utterly bereft of speech. Fortunately no one observed him, as all were too much taken up with what was going on. The king clasped the girl's hands and kissed her on both cheeks. Then the queen followed, and asked her how she could have been so cruel as to remain so long away. And Branwen said a few words in reply.

It seemed as if an electric shock passed through Bladud, for the voice also was the voice of Cormac!

At this point the prince turned to look at his sister. She was gazing earnestly into his face.

"Hafrydda—is—is that really Branwen?"

"Yes, brother, that is Branwen. I must go to her."

As she spoke, she started off at a run and threw her arms round her friend's neck.

"I cannot—cannot believe it is you," she exclaimed aloud—and then, whispering in Branwen's ear, "oh! you wicked creature, to make such a hypocrite of me. But come," she added aloud, "come to my room. I must have you all to myself alone."

For one moment, as they passed, Branwen raised her eyes, and, as they met those of the prince, a deep blush overspread her face. Another moment and the two friends had left the hall together.

We need not weary the reader by describing the games and festivities that followed. Such matters have probably been much the same, in all important respects, since the beginning of time. There was a vast amount of enthusiasm, and willingness to be contented with little, on the part of the people, and an incredible desire to talk and delay matters, and waste time, on the part of judges, umpires, and starters, but there was nothing particularly noteworthy, except that Bladud consented to run one race with his friend Dromas, and was signally beaten by him, to the secret satisfaction of Hafrydda, and the open amusement of the king.

But Branwen did not appear at the games, nor did she appear again during the remainder of that day, and poor Bladud was obliged to restrain his anxiety, for he felt constrained to remain beside his father, and, somehow, he failed in his various attempts to have a few words of conversation with his mother.

At last, like all sublunary things, the games came to an end, and the prince hastened to his sister's room.

"May I come in?" he asked, knocking.

"Yes, brother."

There was a peculiar tone in her voice, and a curious expression in her eyes, that the prince did not fail to note.

"Hafrydda," he exclaimed, eagerly, "there is *no* Cormac?"

"True, brother, there is no Cormac—there never was. Branwen and Cormac are one!"

"And you knew it—and *she* knew it, all along. Oh, why did you agree to deceive me?"

"Nay, brother, I did not mean to deceive you—at least not at first. Neither did Branwen. I knew nothing about it till she came home, after being with you at the Swamp, and told me that she was impelled by sheer pity to follow you, intending to nurse you; thinking at first that we had let you go to die alone. Then she was caught in the woods by robbers, and she only escaped from them by putting on a boy's dress and running away. They gave chase, however, caught her up, and, had it not been for you, would have recaptured her. The rest you know. But now, brother, I am jealous for my dear friend. She has expressed fear that, in her great pity for you, she may be thought to have acted an unwomanly part, and that you will perhaps despise her."

"Unwomanly! despise!" exclaimed Bladud in amazement. "Hafrydda, do you regard me as a monster of ingratitude?"

"Nay, brother, that do I not. I think that you could never despise one who has felt such genuine pity for you as to risk and endure so much."

"Hafrydda, do you think there is no stronger feeling than pity for me in the heart of Branwen?" asked Bladud in a subdued, earnest voice.

"That you must find out for yourself, brother," answered the princess. "Yet after all, if you are only fond of Cormac, what matters the feeling that may be in the heart of Branwen? Are you in love with her already, Bladud, after so short an acquaintance?"

"In love with her!" exclaimed the prince. "There is no Cormac. There is but one woman in the wide world now—"

"That is not complimentary to your mother and myself, I fear," interrupted his sister.

"But," continued the prince, paying no regard to the interruption, "is there any chance—any hope—of—of—something stronger than pity being in her heart?"

"I say again, ask that of herself, Bladud; but now I think of it," added the princess, leaping up in haste, "I am almost too late to keep an appointment with Dromas!"

She went out hurriedly, and the prince, full of new-born hopes mingled with depressing anxieties, went away into the neighbouring woods to meditate—for, in the haste of her departure, Hafrydda had neglected to tell him where Branwen was to be found, and he shrank from mentioning her name to any one else.

But accident—as we call it—sometimes brings about what the most laboured design fails to accomplish.

Owing to a feeling of anxiety which she could not shake off, Branwen had gone out that evening to cool her fevered brow in the woods, just a few minutes before the prince entered them. It was a strange coincidence; but are not all coincidences strange?

Seating herself on a fallen tree she cast up her eyes towards the sky where a solitary star, like a beacon of hope, was beginning to twinkle. She had not been there more than a few minutes when a rustle in the neighbouring thicket startled her. Almost before she had time to look round the prince stood before her. She trembled, for now she felt that the decisive hour had come—whether for good or evil.

Seating himself beside her, the prince took one of her hands in his and looked steadily into her downcast face.

"Corm—Bran—" he began, and stopped.

She looked up.

"Branwen," he said, in a low, calm voice, "will it pain you very much to know that I am glad—inexpressibly glad—that there is no youth Cormac in all the wide world?"

Whether she was pained or not the girl did not say, but there was a language in her eyes which induced Bladud to slip his disengaged arm round—well, well, there are some things more easily conceived than described. She seemed about to speak, but Bladud stopped her mouth—how, we need not tell—not rudely, you may be sure—suffice to say that when the moon arose an hour later, and looked down into the forest that evening she saw the prince and Branwen still seated, hand in hand, on the fallen tree, gazing in rapt attention at the stars.

CHAPTER THIRTY SEVEN

THE LAST

When Bladud walked out to the Hebrew's hut next day and informed him of what had taken place, that long-suffering man heaved a deep sigh and expressed his intense relief that the whole affair was at last cleared up and had come to an end.

"I cannot view matters in the same light that you do, Beniah," said the prince, "for, in my opinion, things have only now come to a satisfactory beginning. However, I suppose that you are thinking of the strange perplexities in which you have been involved so long."

"I would not style them perplexities, prince, but intrigues—obvious and unjustifiable intrigues—in which innocent persons have been brought frequently to the verge of falsehood—if they have not, indeed, been forced to overstep the boundary."

"Surely, Beniah, circumstances, against which none of us had power to contend, had somewhat to do with it all, as well as intrigue."

"I care not," returned the Hebrew, "whether it was the

R. M. Ballantyne

intrigues of your court or the circumstances of it, which were the cause of all the mess in which I and others have been involved, but I am aweary of it, and have made up my mind to leave the place and retire to a remote part of the wilderness, where I may find in solitude solace to my exhausted spirit, and rest to my old bones."

"That will never do, Beniah," said the prince, laughing. "You take too serious a view of the matter. There is no fear of any more intrigues or circumstances arising to perplex you for some time to come. Besides, I want your services very much—but, before broaching that point, let me ask why you have invited me to come to see you here. Hafrydda gave me your message—"

"My message!" repeated the Hebrew in surprise.

"Yes—to meet you here this forenoon on urgent business. If it is anything secret you have to tell me, I hope you have not got your wonderful old witch in the back cave, for she seems to have discovered as thorough a cure for deafness as I found for leprosy at the Hot Swamp."

"Wonderful old witch!" repeated Beniah, with a dazed look, and a tone of exasperation that the prince could not account for. "Do you, then, not know about that old woman?"

"Oh! yes, I know only too much about her," replied Bladud. "She has been staying at the palace for some time, as you know, and rather a lively time the old hag has given us. She went in to see my mother one day and threw her into convulsions, from which, I think, she has hardly recovered yet. Then she went to my father's room—the chief Gadarn and I were with him at the time—and almost before she had time to speak they went into fits of laughter at her till the tears ran down their cheeks. I must say it seemed to me unnecessarily rude and unkind, for, although the woman is a queer old thing, and has little more of her face visible than her piercing black eyes, I could see nothing to laugh at in her shrivelled-up, bent little body. Besides this, she has kept the domestics in a state of constant agitation, for most of them seem to think her a limb of the evil spirit. But what makes you laugh so?"

"Oh! I see now," returned the Hebrew, controlling himself by a strong effort. "I understand now why the old woman wished to be present at our interview. Come forth, thou unconscionable hag!" added Beniah, in the voice of a stentor, "and do your worst. I am past emotion of any kind whatever now."

As he spoke he gazed, with the resigned air of a martyr, at the inner end of his cavern. Bladud also looked in that direction. A moment later and the little old woman with the grey shawl appeared; thrust out the plank bridge; crossed over, and tottered towards them.

"Dearie me! Beniah, there's no need to yell so loud. You know I've got back my hearing. What want ye with me? I'm sure I have no wish to pry into the secrets of this young man or yourself. What d'ye want?"

But Beniah stood speechless, a strange expression on his face, his lips firmly compressed and his arms folded across his breast.

"Have you become as dumb as I was deaf, old man?" asked the woman, petulantly.

Still the Hebrew refused to speak.

"Have patience with him, old woman," said Bladud, in a

soothing tone. "He is sometimes taken with unaccountable fits—"

"Fits!" interrupted the old woman. "I wish he had the fits that I have sometimes. Perhaps they would cure him of his impudence. They would cure you too, young man, of your stupidity."

"Stupidity!" echoed Bladud, much amused. "I have been credited with pride and haste and many other faults in my day, but never with stupidity."

"Was it not stupid of you to go and ask that silly girl to wed you—that double-faced thing that knows how to cheat and deceive and—"

"Come, come, old woman," said the prince, repressing with difficulty a burst of indignation. "You allow your old tongue to wag too freely. I suppose," he added, turning to Beniah, "that we can conclude our conversation outside?"

But the Hebrew still remained immovable and sternly dumb.

Unable to understand this, Bladud turned again to the old woman, but, lo! the old woman was gone, and in her place stood Branwen, erect, with the grey shawl thrown back, and a half-timid smile on her face.

To say that Bladud was thunderstruck is not sufficient to indicate his condition. He stood as if rooted to the spot with his whole being concentrated in his wide-open blue eyes.

"Is my presumption too great, Bladud?" asked the girl, hesitatingly. "I did but wish to assure you that I have no other deceptions to practise. That I fear—I hope—that—"

The prince, recovering himself, sprang forward and once again stopped her mouth—not with his hand; oh! by no means!—while Beniah, with that refinement of wisdom which is the prerogative of age, stepped out to ascertain whether it happened to be rain or sunshine that ruled at the time. Curiously enough he found that it was the latter.

That evening the doctor of the royal household was summoned by an affrighted servitor to the apartment of Gadarn, who had been overheard choking. The alarmed man of medicine went at once, and, bursting into the room without knocking, found the great northern chief sitting on the edge of his couch purple in the face and with tears in his eyes. The exasperated man leaped up intending to kick the doctor out, but, changing his mind, he kicked the horrified servitor out instead, and, taking the doctor into his confidence, related to him an anecdote which had just been told to him by Bladud.

"It will be the death of the king," said Gadarn. "You had better go to him. He may need your services."

But the king was made of sterner stuff than his friend imagined. He put strong constraint upon himself, and, being not easily overcome by feeling—or anything else under the sun—he lived to relate the same anecdote to his wife and daughter.

The day following, Bladud resumed with the Hebrew the conversation that had been interrupted by Branwen.

"I was going to have said to you, Beniah, that I want your services very much."

"You had said that much, prince, before Bran—I mean Cor—that is, the old woman—interrupted us. How can I serve you?"

"By going back with me to the Hot Swamp and helping to carry out a grand scheme that I have in my brain."

The Hebrew shook his head.

"I love not your grand schemes," he said, somewhat sternly. "The last grand scheme that your father had was one which, if successfully carried out, would have added a large portion of Albion to his dominions, and would have swept several tribes off the face of the earth. As it was, the mere effort to carry it out cost the lives of many of the best young men on both sides, and left hundreds of mothers, wives, sisters, and children to mourn their irreparable losses, and to wonder what all the fighting was about. Indeed, there are not a few grey-bearded men who share that wonder with the women and children, and who cannot, by any effort of their imagination, see what advantage is gained by either party when the fight is over."

"These grey-beards must be thick-skulled, then," replied the prince with a smile, "for does not the victor retain the land which he has conquered?"

"Yea, truly, and he also retains the tombs of the goodly young men who have been slain, and also the widows and sweethearts, and the national loss resulting from the war— for all which the land gained is but a paltry return. Moreover, if the All-seeing One cared only for the victors, there might be some understanding of the matter—though at the cost of justice—but, seeing that He cares for the vanquished quite as much as for the victorious, the gain on one side is counterbalanced by the loss on the other side, while the world at large is all the poorer, first, by the loss of much of its best blood, second, by the creation of a vast amount of unutterable sorrow and bitter hatred, and, third, by a tremendous amount of misdirected energy.

"Look, for instance, at the Hot Swamp. Before the late war it was the abode of a happy and prosperous population. Now, it is a desolation. Hundreds of its youth are in premature graves, and nothing whatever has been gained from it by your father that I can see."

"But surely men must defend themselves and their women and children against foes?" said Bladud.

"Verily, I did not say they should not," replied Beniah. "Self-defence is a duty; aggressive war, in most cases (I do not say in all), is a blunder or a sin."

"I think that my mind runs much on the same line with yours, Beniah, as to these things, but I am pretty sure that a good many years will pass over us before the warriors of the present day will see things in this light."

One is apt to smile at Bladud's prophetic observation, when one reflects that about two thousand seven hundred years have elapsed since that day, and warriors, as well as many civilians, have not managed to see it in this light yet!

"However," continued the prince, "the scheme which runs in my head is not one of war—aggressive or defensive—but one of peace, for the betterment of all mankind. As you know, I have begun to build a city at the Hot Swamp, so that all who are sick may go to that beautiful country and find health, as I did. And I want your help in this scheme."

"That is well, prince, but I see not how I can aid you. I am not an engineer, who could carry out your devices, nor an architect who could plan your dwellings. And I am too old for manual labour—though, of course, it is not for that you want me."

"You are right, Beniah. It is not for that. I have as many strong and willing hands to work as I require, but I want wise heads, full of years and experience, which may aid me in council and guard me from the blunders of youth and inexperience. Besides, man was not, it seems to me, put into this world merely to enjoy himself. If he was, then are the brutes his superiors, for they have no cares, no anxieties about food or raiment, or housing, and they enjoy themselves to the full as long as their little day lasts. There is surely some nobler end for man, and as you have given much study to the works and ways and reputed words of the All-seeing One, I want you to aid me in helping men to look upward—to soar like the eagle above the things of earth, as well as to consider the interests of others, and so, as far as may be, unlearn selfishness. Will you join me for this end?"

"That will I, with joy," answered the Hebrew with kindling eye; "but your ambition soars high, prince. Have you spoken to Branwen on these subjects?"

"Of course I have, and she, like a true woman, enters heartily into my plans. Like myself, she does not think that being wedded and happy is the great end of life, but only the beginning of it. When the wedding is over, our minds will then be set free to devote ourselves to the great work before us."

"And what duties in the work will fall to the lot of Branwen?" asked Beniah, with an amused look.

"The duties of a wife, of course," returned the prince. "She will lend a sympathetic ear to all plans and proposals; her ingenious imagination will suggest ideas that might escape my grosser mind; her brilliant fancy will produce combinations that my duller brain would never think of; her hopeful spirit will encourage me to perseverance where accident or disaster has a tendency to demoralise, and her loving spirit will comfort me should failure, great or small, be permitted to overtake me. All this, I admit, sounds very selfish, but you asked me what part Branwen should play in regard to *my* schemes. If you had asked me what part I am to play in her life and work, the picture might be inverted to some extent—for our lives will be mutual—though, of course, I can never be to her what she will be to me."

With this exalted idea of the married state, Prince Bladud looked forward to his wedding. Whether Dromas was imbued with similar ideas we cannot tell; but of this we are sure, that he was equally devoted to the princess—as far as outward appearance went—and he entered with keenest zest and appreciation into the plans and aspirations of his friend, with regard to the welfare of mankind in general, and the men of Albion in particular.

Not many days after that there was a double wedding at Hudibras town, which created a tremendous sensation throughout all the land. For, although news travelled slowly in those days, the fame of Bladud and his wonderful cure, and his great size and athletic powers, coupled with his Eastern learning, and warlike attainments and peaceful proclivities, not to mention the beauty and romantic adventures of his bride, had made such an impression on what may be styled the whole nation, that noted chiefs came from all parts far and near, to his wedding, bringing as many of their distinguished followers with them as they deemed necessary to safe travelling in an unsettled country. Some even came from the great western island called Erin, and others from the remote isle of the north which lay beyond Gadarn's country, and was at a later period named Ultima Thule.

"I wonder when they're going to stop coming," remarked Gadarn to King Hudibras, as the self-invited guests came pouring in.

"Let them come," replied the jovial king, with the air of a man of unlimited means. "The more the merrier. There's room for all, and the forests are big."

"Some of them, I see," rejoined Gadarn, "are my mortal foes. We shall now have a chance of becoming mortal friends."

It might be supposed that the assemblage of such a host from all points of the compass would, as it is sometimes expressed, eat King Hudibras out of house and home; but this was not so, for it was the custom at that time for visitors at royal courts to hunt for their victuals—to go in, as it were, for a grand picnic on a continuous basis, so that the palace of our king, instead of being depleted, became surfeited with food. As his preserves were extensive, and game of all kinds abundant, the expense attendant on this kind of hospitality was *nil*.

It would have been very much the reverse had it been necessary to supply drink, but the art of producing liquids which fuddle, stupefy, and madden, had not yet been learnt in this country. Consequently there was no fighting or bloodshed at those jovial festivities, though there was a certain amount of quarrelling—as might be expected amongst independent men who held different opinions on many subjects, although politics and theology had not yet been invented.

Great were the rejoicings when it was discovered, by each band as it arrived, that there was to be a double wedding; that the Princess Hafrydda was to be one of the brides, and that the fortunate man who had won her was a famous warrior of the mysterious East, and one of the victors at the great games of that part of the world.

How the ceremony of marriage was performed we have not, after the most painstaking research, been able to ascertain; but that it was performed somehow, and to the satisfaction of all concerned, we are absolutely certain, from the fact that Bladud and Branwen, Dromas and Hafrydda, lived happily together as man and wife for many years afterwards, and brought up large families of stalwart sons and daughters to strengthen the power and increase the prestige of Old Albion.

This, however, by the way. Of course the chief amusement of the guests was games, followed by songs and dancing in the evenings. And one of the favourite amusements at the games was scientific boxing, for that was an entirely new art to the warriors, alike of Albion, Erin, and Ultima Thule.

It first burst upon their senses as a new and grand idea when Bladud and Dromas, at the urgent request of their friends, stepped into the arena and gave a specimen of the manner in which the art was practised in Hellas. Of course they did not use what we call knuckle-dusters, nor did they even double their fists, except when moving round each other, and as "gloves" were unknown, they struck out with the hands half open, for they had no wish to bleed each other's noses or black each other's eyes for mere amusement.

At the beginning it was thought that Dromas was no match at all for the gigantic Bladud, but when the wonderful agility of the former was seen—the ease with which he ducked and turned aside his head to evade blows, and the lightning speed with which he countered, giving a touch on the forehead or a dig in the ribs, smiling all the time as if to say, "How d'ye like it?" men's minds changed with shouts of surprise and satisfaction. And they highly approved of the way in which the champions smilingly shook hands after the bout was over—as they had done before it began.

They did not, however, perceive the full value of the art until an ambitious young chief from Ultima Thule—a man of immense size and rugged mould with red hair—insisted on Dromas giving him a lesson. The man from Hellas declined at first, but the man from Thule was urgent, and there seemed to be a feeling among the warriors that the young Hellene was afraid.

"It is so difficult," he explained, "to hit lightly and swiftly that sometimes an unintentionally hard blow is given, and men are apt to lose their tempers."

This was received with a loud laugh by the Thuler.

"What! *I* lose my temper on account of a friendly buffet! Besides, I shall take care not to hit hard—you need not fear."

"As you will," returned Dromas, with a good-humoured smile.

The Thuler stood up and allowed his instructor to put him in the correct attitude. Then the latter faced him and said, "Now, guard yourself."

Next moment his left hand shot out and gently touched his opponent's nose. The Thuler received the touch with what he deemed an orthodox smile and tried to guard it after it had been delivered.

Then he struck out with his left—being an apt pupil—but Dromas drew back and the blow did not reach him. Then he struck out smartly with his right, but the Hellene put his head to one side and let it pass. Again he struck out rapidly, one hand after the other, without much care whether the blows were light or heavy. Dromas evaded both without guarding, and, in reply, gave the Thuler a smartish touch on his unfortunate nose.

This was received by the assemblage with a wild shout of surprise and delight, and the Thuler became grave; collected himself as if for real business, and suddenly let out a shower of blows which, had they taken effect, would soon have ended the match, but his blows only fell on air, for Dromas evaded them with ease, returning every now and then a tap on the old spot or a touch on the forehead. At last, seeing that the man was losing temper, he gave him a sharp dig in the wind which caused him to gasp, and a sounding buffet on the cheek which caused him to howl with rage and feel for the hilt of his sword. That dangerous weapon, however, had been judiciously removed by his friends. He therefore rushed at his antagonist, resolved to annihilate him, but was received with two genuine blows—one in the wind, the other on the forehead, which stretched him on the sward.

The Thuler rose therefrom with a dazed look, and accepted the Hellene's friendly shake of the hand with an unmeaning smile.

After the sports had continued for several days King Hudibras proposed an excursion—a sort of gigantic picnic—to the Hot Swamp, where Bladud and his friend had made up their mind to spend their honeymoon.

Arrived there, they found that immense progress had been made with the new city—insomuch that Dromas assured Hafrydda that it brought to his mind some very ancient fables of great cities rising spontaneously from the ground to the sound of pipes played by the gods.

R. M. Ballantyne

The baths, too, were in such an advanced stage that they were able to fill them on the arrival of the host and allow the interested and impatient chiefs to bathe.

"Don't let them go in till you give the signal that the baths are ready," said Gadarn to the king in that grave, suppressed manner which indicated that the northern chief was inclined to mischief.

"Why?" asked the king.

"Because, as I understand, you love fair play and no favour. It would not be fair to let some begin before others. They might feel it, you know, and quarrel."

"Very well, so be it," returned the king, and gave orders that no one was to go near the baths until they were quite full, when he would give the signal.

The chiefs and warriors entering into the spirit of the thing, took quite a boyish delight in stripping themselves and preparing for a rush.

"Now, are you ready?" said the king.

"Ay, all ready."

"Away, then!"

The warlike host rushed to the brink of the largest bath and plunged in—some head, others feet, first. But they came out almost as fast as they went in—yelling and spluttering—for the water was much too hot!

"Ah! I see now," growled the king, turning to Gadarn—but Gadarn was gone. He found him, a minute later, behind a bush, in fits!

Pacifying the warriors with some difficulty—for they were a hot-headed generation—the king, being directed by Bladud, ordered the water from the cold lake to be turned on until the bath became bearable. Then the warriors re-entered it again more sedately. The warm water soon restored their equanimity, and ere long the unusual sight was to be seen of bearded men and smooth chins, rugged men and striplings, rolling about like porpoises, shouting, laughing, and indulging in horse-play like veritable boys.

Truly warmth has much to do with the felicity of mankind!

Towards afternoon the warriors were ordered to turn out, and, after the water had been allowed to run till it was clear, King Hudibras descended into it with much gravity and a good deal of what was in those ages considered to be ceremonial effect. This was done by way of taking formal possession of the Hot Springs. He was greatly cheered during the process by the admiring visitors, as well as physically by the hot water, and it is said that while his son Bladud was dutifully rubbing him down in the neighbouring booth, he remarked that it was the best bath he ever had in his life, that he would visit the place periodically as long as he lived, and that a palace must be built there for his accommodation.

From that day the bath was named the "King's Bath," and it is so named at the present day.

Soon after that the queen visited the Swamp and, with her ladies, made use of the bath which had been specially prepared for women; and this one went by the name of the "Queen's Bath" thereafter. Its site, however, is not now certainly known, and it is not to be confounded with the "Queen's Bath" of the present day, which was named after Queen Anne.

Prince Bladud lived to carry out most of his plans. He built a palace for his father in Swamptown. He built a palace for himself and Branwen, with a wing to it for Dromas and Hafrydda, and took up his permanent abode there when he afterwards became king. At the death of his father he added another wing for the queen-mother—with internal doors opening from each wing to the other, in order that they might live, so to speak, as one family. This arrangement worked admirably until the families became large, and the younger members obstreperous, when the internal doors were occasionally, even frequently, shut. He also built a snug house for Konar, and made him Hunter-General to the Royal Household. It is said that, owing to the genial influence of Bladud's kind nature, Konar recovered his reason, and, forgetting the false fair-one who had jilted him, took to himself a helpmate who more than made up for her loss.

Captain Arkal soon found that his passion for hot water cooled. As it did so, his love for salt water revived. He returned to Hellas, and, after paying his respects to his pretty Greek wife, and dandling the solid, square, bluff, and resolute baby, he reloaded his ship and returned to Albion. Thus he went and came for many years.

Little Maikar, however, did not follow his example. True, he accompanied his old captain on his first trip to Hellas, but that was for the purpose of getting possession of a dark-eyed maiden who awaited him there; with whom he returned to Swamptown, and, in that lovely region, spent the remainder of his life.

Even Addedomar was weaned from outlawry to honesty by the irresistible solicitations of Bladud, and as, in modern times, many an incorrigible poacher makes a first-rate gamekeeper, so the robber-chief became an able head-huntsman under the Hunter-General. The irony of Fate decreed, however, that the man who had once contemplated three wives was not to marry at all. He dwelt with his mother Ortrud to the end of her days in a small house not far from the residence of Konar. Gunrig's mother also dwelt with them—not that she had any particular regard for them personally, but in order that she might be near to the beautiful girl who had been beloved by her son.

Gadarn, the great northern chief, ever afterwards paid an annual visit to Swamptown. While that visit lasted there was a general feeling in the palace—especially among the young people—that a jovial hurricane was blowing. During the daytime the gale made itself felt in loud hilarious laughter, song, and story. At night it blew steadily through his nose. After his departure an unaccountable calm seemed to settle down upon the whole region!

Beniah performed with powerful effect the task allotted to him, for, both by precept and example, he so set forth and obeyed the laws of God that the tone of society was imperceptibly elevated. Men came to know, and to act upon the knowledge, that this world was not their rest; that there is a better life beyond, and, in the contemplation of that life, they, somehow, made this life more agreeable to themselves and to each other.

Time, which never intermits the beating of his fateful wings, flew by; the centuries rolled on; the Roman invaders came; the Norsemen and Saxons came, the Norman conquerors came, and each left their mark, deep and lasting, on the people and on the land—but they could not check by one hair's-breadth the perennial flow of the springs in the Hot Swamp, or obliterate the legend on which is founded this Romance of Old Albion.

THE END

Choose from Thousands of 1stWorldLibrary Classics By

A. M. Barnard	Booth Tarkington	Edward Everett Hale
Ada Leverson	Boyd Cable	Edward J. O'Biren
Adolphus William Ward	Bram Stoker	Edward S. Ellis
Aesop	C. Collodi	Edwin L. Arnold
Agatha Christie	C. E. Orr	Eleanor Atkins
Alexander Aaronsohn	C. M. Ingleby	Eleanor Hallowell Abbott
Alexander Kielland	Carolyn Wells	Eliot Gregory
Alexandre Dumas	Catherine Parr Traill	Elizabeth Gaskell
Alfred Gatty	Charles A. Eastman	Elizabeth McCracken
Alfred Ollivant	Charles Amory Beach	Elizabeth Von Arnim
Alice Duer Miller	Charles Dickens	Ellem Key
Alice Turner Curtis	Charles Dudley Warner	Emerson Hough
Alice Dunbar	Charles Farrar Browne	Emilie F. Carlen
Allen Chapman	Charles Ives	Emily Bronte
Alleyne Ireland	Charles Kingsley	Emily Dickinson
Ambrose Bierce	Charles Klein	Enid Bagnold
Amelia E. Barr	Charles Hanson Towne	Enilor Macartney Lane
Amory H. Bradford	Charles Lathrop Pack	Erasmus W. Jones
Andrew Lang	Charles Romyn Dake	Ernie Howard Pie
Andrew McFarland Davis	Charles Whibley	Ethel May Dell
Andy Adams	Charles Willing Beale	Ethel Turner
Angela Brazil	Charlotte M. Braeme	Ethel Watts Mumford
Anna Alice Chapin	Charlotte M. Yonge	Eugene Sue
Anna Sewell	Charlotte Perkins Stetson	Eugenie Foa
Annie Besant	Clair W. Hayes	Eugene Wood
Annie Hamilton Donnell	Clarence Day Jr.	Eustace Hale Ball
Annie Payson Call	Clarence E. Mulford	Evelyn Everett-green
Annie Roe Carr	Clemence Housman	Everard Cotes
Annonaymous	Confucius	F. H. Cheley
Anton Chekhov	Coningsby Dawson	F. J. Cross
Archibald Lee Fletcher	Cornelis DeWitt Wilcox	F. Marion Crawford
Arnold Bennett	Cyril Burleigh	Fannie E. Newberry
Arthur C. Benson	D. H. Lawrence	Federick Austin Ogg
Arthur Conan Doyle	Daniel Defoe	Ferdinand Ossendowski
Arthur M. Winfield	David Garnett	Fergus Hume
Arthur Ransome	Dinah Craik	Florence A. Kilpatrick
Arthur Schnitzler	Don Carlos Janes	Fremont B. Deering
Arthur Train	Donald Keyhoe	Francis Bacon
Atticus	Dorothy Kilner	Francis Darwin
B.H. Baden-Powell	Dougan Clark	Frances Hodgson Burnett
B. M. Bower	Douglas Fairbanks	Frances Parkinson Keyes
B. C. Chatterjee	E. Nesbit	Frank Gee Patchin
Baroness Emmuska Orczy	E. P. Roe	Frank Harris
Baroness Orczy	E. Phillips Oppenheim	Frank Jewett Mather
Basil King	E. S. Brooks	Frank L. Packard
Bayard Taylor	Earl Barnes	Frank V. Webster
Ben Macomber	Edgar Rice Burroughs	Frederic Stewart Isham
Bertha Muzzy Bower	Edith Van Dyne	Frederick Trevor Hill
Bjornstjerne Bjornson	Edith Wharton	Frederick Winslow Taylor

Friedrich Kerst
Friedrich Nietzsche
Fyodor Dostoyevsky
G.A. Henty
G.K. Chesterton
Gabrielle E. Jackson
Garrett P. Serviss
Gaston Leroux
George A. Warren
George Ade
Geroge Bernard Shaw
George Cary Eggleston
George Durston
George Ebers
George Eliot
George Gissing
George MacDonald
George Meredith
George Orwell
George Sylvester Viereck
George Tucker
George W. Cable
George Wharton James
Gertrude Atherton
Gordon Casserly
Grace E. King
Grace Gallatin
Grace Greenwood
Grant Allen
Guillermo A. Sherwell
Gulielma Zollinger
Gustav Flaubert
H. A. Cody
H. B. Irving
H.C. Bailey
H. G. Wells
H. H. Munro
H. Irving Hancock
H. R. Naylor
H. Rider Haggard
H. W. C. Davis
Haldeman Julius
Hall Caine
Hamilton Wright Mabie
Hans Christian Andersen
Harold Avery
Harold McGrath
Harriet Beecher Stowe
Harry Castlemon
Harry Coghill
Harry Houidini

Hayden Carruth
Helent Hunt Jackson
Helen Nicolay
Hendrik Conscience
Hendy David Thoreau
Henri Barbusse
Henrik Ibsen
Henry Adams
Henry Ford
Henry Frost
Henry James
Henry Jones Ford
Henry Seton Merriman
Henry W Longfellow
Herbert A. Giles
Herbert Carter
Herbert N. Casson
Herman Hesse
Hildegard G. Frey
Homer
Honore De Balzac
Horace B. Day
Horace Walpole
Horatio Alger Jr.
Howard Pyle
Howard R. Garis
Hugh Lofting
Hugh Walpole
Humphry Ward
Ian Maclaren
Inez Haynes Gillmore
Irving Bacheller
Isabel Cecilia Williams
Isabel Hornibrook
Israel Abrahams
Ivan Turgenev
J.G.Austin
J. Henri Fabre
J. M. Barrie
J. M. Walsh
J. Macdonald Oxley
J. R. Miller
J. S. Fletcher
J. S. Knowles
J. Storer Clouston
J. W. Duffield
Jack London
Jacob Abbott
James Allen
James Andrews
James Baldwin

James Branch Cabell
James DeMille
James Joyce
James Lane Allen
James Lane Allen
James Oliver Curwood
James Oppenheim
James Otis
James R. Driscoll
Jane Abbott
Jane Austen
Jane L. Stewart
Janet Aldridge
Jens Peter Jacobsen
Jerome K. Jerome
Jessie Graham Flower
John Buchan
John Burroughs
John Cournos
John F. Kennedy
John Gay
John Glasworthy
John Habberton
John Joy Bell
John Kendrick Bangs
John Milton
John Philip Sousa
John Taintor Foote
Jonas Lauritz Idemil Lie
Jonathan Swift
Joseph A. Altsheler
Joseph Carey
Joseph Conrad
Joseph E. Badger Jr
Joseph Hergesheimer
Joseph Jacobs
Jules Vernes
Julian Hawthrone
Julie A Lippmann
Justin Huntly McCarthy
Kakuzo Okakura
Karle Wilson Baker
Kate Chopin
Kenneth Grahame
Kenneth McGaffey
Kate Langley Bosher
Kate Langley Bosher
Katherine Cecil Thurston
Katherine Stokes
L. A. Abbot
L. T. Meade

L. Frank Baum
Latta Griswold
Laura Dent Crane
Laura Lee Hope
Laurence Housman
Lawrence Beasley
Leo Tolstoy
Leonid Andreyev
Lewis Carroll
Lewis Sperry Chafer
Lilian Bell
Lloyd Osbourne
Louis Hughes
Louis Joseph Vance
Louis Tracy
Louisa May Alcott
Lucy Fitch Perkins
Lucy Maud Montgomery
Luther Benson
Lydia Miller Middleton
Lyndon Orr
M. Corvus
M. H. Adams
Margaret E. Sangster
Margret Howth
Margaret Vandercook
Margaret W. Hungerford
Margret Penrose
Maria Edgeworth
Maria Thompson Daviess
Mariano Azuela
Marion Polk Angellotti
Mark Overton
Mark Twain
Mary Austin
Mary Catherine Crowley
Mary Cole
Mary Hastings Bradley
Mary Roberts Rinehart
Mary Rowlandson
M. Wollstonecraft Shelley
Maud Lindsay
Max Beerbohm
Myra Kelly
Nathaniel Hawthrone
Nicolo Machiavelli
O. F. Walton
Oscar Wilde

Owen Johnson
P.G. Wodehouse
Paul and Mabel Thorne
Paul G. Tomlinson
Paul Severing
Percy Brebner
Percy Keese Fitzhugh
Peter B. Kyne
Plato
Quincy Allen
R. Derby Holmes
R. L. Stevenson
R. S. Ball
Rabindranath Tagore
Rahul Alvares
Ralph Bonehill
Ralph Henry Barbour
Ralph Victor
Ralph Waldo Emmerson
Rene Descartes
Ray Cummings
Rex Beach
Rex E. Beach
Richard Harding Davis
Richard Jefferies
Richard Le Gallienne
Robert Barr
Robert Frost
Robert Gordon Anderson
Robert L. Drake
Robert Lansing
Robert Lynd
Robert Michael Ballantyne
Robert W. Chambers
Rosa Nouchette Carey
Rudyard Kipling
Saint Augustine
Samuel B. Allison
Samuel Hopkins Adams
Sarah Bernhardt
Sarah C. Hallowell
Selma Lagerlof
Sherwood Anderson
Sigmund Freud
Standish O'Grady
Stanley Weyman
Stella Benson
Stella M. Francis

Stephen Crane
Stewart Edward White
Stijn Streuvels
Swami Abhedananda
Swami Parmananda
T. S. Ackland
T. S. Arthur
The Princess Der Ling
Thomas A. Janvier
Thomas A Kempis
Thomas Anderton
Thomas Bailey Aldrich
Thomas Bulfinch
Thomas De Quincey
Thomas Dixon
Thomas H. Huxley
Thomas Hardy
Thomas More
Thornton W. Burgess
U. S. Grant
Upton Sinclair
Valentine Williams
Various Authors
Vaughan Kester
Victor Appleton
Victor G. Durham
Victoria Cross
Virginia Woolf
Wadsworth Camp
Walter Camp
Walter Scott
Washington Irving
Wilbur Lawton
Wilkie Collins
Willa Cather
Willard F. Baker
William Dean Howells
William le Queux
W. Makepeace Thackeray
William W. Walter
William Shakespeare
Winston Churchill
Yei Theodora Ozaki
Yogi Ramacharaka
Young E. Allison
Zane Grey